D1636110

THE CHANT OF LIFE

Inculturation and the People of the Land

LITURGICAL STUDIES, FOUR

Mark L. MacDonald, Editor,
for the Standing Commission on Liturgy and Music

 CHURCH

Church Publishing Inc., New York

The chant of life : liturgical inculturation and the people of the land / Mark L.
  MacDonald, editor, for the Standing Commission on Liturgy and Music.
      p. cm—(Liturgical studies ; 4)
   Includes bibliographical references.
   ISBN: 0-89869-299-7 (pbk.)
      1. Episcopal Church—Liturgy. 2. Indians of North America—Religion. 3.
Christianity and culture. I. MacDonald, Mark L. II. Liturgical studies
(Episcopal Church. Standing Commission on Liturgy and Music) ; 4.

Church Publishing Incorporated
445 Fifth Avenue
New York, NY 10016

5 4 3 2 1

Contents

Contributors

Martin Brokenleg is a professor of Native American Studies at Augustana College, Sioux Falls, South Dakota, and Dean of the Black Hills Seminars on youth-at-risk.

Steve Charleston is the President and Dean of the Episcopal Divinity School, Cambridge, Massachusetts.

Ginny Doctor is an Assistant to the Bishop of the Diocese of Alaska.

Marilyn Haskel is Vice President and Marketing Director for Church Publishing Inc.

Mark L. MacDonald is Bishop of Alaska.

Monte Mason is Organist and Musical Director for Saint Martin's By The Lake, Minnetonka Beach, Minnesota.

Leonel L. Mitchell is Professor Emeritus of Liturgics at the Seabury-Western Theological Seminary, Evanston, Illinois.

Clayton L. Morris is Staff Officer for Liturgy and Music for the Episcopal Church, New York, New York.

Malcolm Naea Chun is Secretary General of the Anglican Indigenous Network.

Michael J. Oleksa, Th. D., is Pastor of St. Nicholas Orthodox Church, Juneau, Alaska, and outreach coordinator for Sealaska Heritage Foundation.

Juan M. C. Oliver is Director of The Mercer School of Theology, Garden City, Long Island.

Juan Quevedo-Bosch is Rector of Church of the Redeemer, Astoria, New York.

John E. Robertson is Co-Facilitator of the Success for the Future program serving the indigenous high school students of Bishop Whipple Mission in the Diocese of Minnesota.

William C. Wantland is the retired Bishop of Eau Claire, Wisconsin, and is a member of the Seminole Nation of Oklahoma.

As I landed there, I saw twelve men coming toward me and they stood before me and said: "Our Father, the two-legged chief, you shall see." Then I went to the center of the circle with these men and there again I saw the tree in full bloom. Against the tree, I saw a man standing with outstretched arms. As we stood close to him these twelve men said: "Behold him!" The man with outstretched arms looked at me and I didn't know whether he was a white or an Indian. He did not resemble Christ. He looked like an Indian, but I was not sure of it. He had long hair which was hanging down loose. On the left side of his head was an eagle feather. His body was painted red. (At that time, I had never had anything to do with white man's religion and I had never seen any picture of Christ.) This man said to me: "My life is such that all earthly beings that grow belong to me. My Father has said this. You must say this." I stood there gazing at him and tried to recognize him. I could not make him out. He was a nice-looking man. As I looked at him, his body began to transform. His body changed into all colors and it was very beautiful. All around him, there was light. Then he disappeared all at once. It seemed as though there were wounds in the palms of his hands. Then those twelve men said to me: "Turn around and behold your nation, your nation's life is such."

Black Elk (Lakota)[1]

Introduction

Mark MacDonald

Among the churches of God that are everywhere registered in the dwelling place of Christ, there is nothing distant, nothing is considered foreign.

Pope St. Celestine, +432[2]

Gathering Considerations

Liturgy, in the Christian context, is a language of love. Its horizon is in the gospel joining of human hearts and God's Spirit—not in the domain of technical competence or academic definition. It involves complexities of human nature and culture that defy simple explanation, analysis, or presentation. Therefore, avoiding a solely academic approach, the method of this volume is to provide a number of perspectives in a variety of styles and contexts, aiming at a larger audience. We[3] hope the style of this presentation will help the Church glimpse some of the power and possibilities of inculturation.

Our original intent for this book was to suggest ways "Peoples of the Land"[4] (indigenous or aboriginal nations and peoples)[5] might include elements from their cultures in their Christian worship. We viewed this liturgical inculturation as a missiological priority. Further, we felt that even such localized and specific efforts could benefit the larger Church. Illustrating inculturation in action would suggest ways that others could undertake such a program.

As our work proceeded, however, we realized that some more

basic and broadly considered steps were required. To be effective, we must illustrate what inculturation might mean both for the People of the Land and for a larger Church community. Without a more general illumination of inculturation, we feared the Church could never develop the imagination to encourage or even permit such a project among the People of the Land: the status quo would continue. The cultural expressions that the institutional Church has never been able to allow would continue to exist only in the dreams of the People.

The contributors to this volume represent a number of viewpoints and "cultures" within the larger Church. They all agree that inculturation is a missiological imperative for the whole Church. It is important for all of the diverse "minority" cultures in contemporary society to express the essence of a universal faith in the their own cultural idioms. Inculturation is also a necessity for the dominant culture, including the culture of the dominant ethnic group in the Episcopal Church.[6] The living Word must always present itself in living cultures.

The Standing Liturgical Commission[7] recognized the possibilities of this work and encouraged us to pursue it as Liturgical Studies IV. They generously gave the green light for the work and commended us to the task. Now, after some years of preparation, the materials are gathered and presented in this volume.

The Episcopal Church in the United States is now considering liturgical reform and renewal. Our General Convention has outlined a process that will lead to the production of a new "Prayer Book."[8] Although this is not our focus, our work will highlight some of the important issues to consider in any meaningful liturgical renewal and reform.

As our Church prepares for major new initiatives in evangelism, we believe that inculturation places liturgy high on the agenda of mission, for inculturation describes the place where living cultures encounter the living gospel. We hope this offering of voices, some past and some present, will shed new light on God's future for "every family, language, people, and nation."

What is Inculturation?

This book introduces the idea of inculturation through the variety of voices and perspectives we present. We avoid the more systematic definitions required by a work oriented for liturgical specialists alone. This article provides some preliminary context for our use of the word, especially in regards to the People of the Land. We do hope that readers will refer to some of the helpful introductions to inculturation already available. There are a number of suggestions throughout the footnotes.[9] The work of the 1989 International Anglican Liturgical Consultation in York is especially important for Anglicans.[10]

The first use of the term inculturation in an official church document occurs in the message of the Fourth Synod of Bishops (Roman Catholic) in 1977.[11] Its use signals a profound shift in the Roman Catholic understanding of liturgy, mission, and culture. This change is even more significant in that it has close counterparts in most Western churches, ecumenical and evangelical, including the Anglican Communion.

The term inculturation reflects the use of the "analogy" of incarnation in describing the mission of the church. Father Michael Stogre describes the shift in the Roman Church during Vatican II:

> This analogy with "incarnation" presupposes viable and dynamic cultures with which the Gospel interacts, and will ultimately be incarnated…The implication being that these cultures will not only be enhanced by their encounter with the Gospel, but that the Church itself will be enriched, and, in a sense, become more catholic in its existence.[12]

Many have used the terms "indigenization" or "contextualization" to describe the process of dynamic translation of liturgy into local linguistic and cultural idioms. Inculturation, however, consciously echoes the riches of the Church's teaching on incarnation, showing that the work described reaches beyond the realms of academic analysis or social science. As "Word made flesh," inculturation is a work of God and humanity. The use of the term inculturation also reveals a deeper appreciation in the Christian churches of the "mystery" of human culture and a new awareness of the God given diversity of human culture.

As our understanding of culture and gospel matures in a post-Christendom World, the Church begins to appreciate some new dimensions of the incarnational character of its own mission. After a long period of promoting assimilation into Western culture, the Church is beginning to reaffirm the reality that the Word, made flesh, assimilates into local culture—rather than the other way around. This leads to Anscar Chupungco's definition, helpful to our context:

> For the core of the liturgy is a supracultural reality which the church received through apostolic preaching and preserves intact in every time and place. What inculturation means is that worship assimilates the people's language, ritual, and symbolic patterns. In this way they are able to claim and own the liturgical core they received through the apostolic preaching. Today we have come to regard both the process of inculturation and the claiming of the Christian message by the people as an imperative to evangelization.[13]

Expressing the Essence of Our Tradition

Because of the primal character of culture, it is hard for people to distinguish between the Church's tradition and their own culturally conditioned local expression of it. Chupungco gives the example of the Roman Rite (and, we note, under its influence, many Anglican Rites), which expresses the "sobriety and practicality" of the culture that predominated in the development of the Rite.[14] These values, hidden in the assumptions of one culture, may be passed along as universal and essential features of the its tradition. Other cultures, which may not share the same priority of values, may experience unnecessary barriers to the Good News of God.

Cultural norms and values, hidden in received and promoted liturgical texts of national churches, can often have a chilling effect on the experience of a rite in a different cultural context. The larger American culture's preference for brief and to-the-point liturgies, for example, might have a devastating impact on the funeral practices of a minority culture. A healing gospel message, transmitted in the culturally shaped liturgical vehicle of one group, may not connect with the culturally formed hearts and minds of people in another.

Diversity and flexibility in the reception and expression of cultural values is desirable in the Church's liturgies—both locally and universally. As the first Pentecost demonstrates, the gospel thrives on translation. The Christian gospel is a message truly unique in its capacity to gain clarity in translation to new languages and idioms. Problems in translation only arise when a particular cultural value becomes normative through the domination of one cultural group or constituency. When we attempt to freeze-dry the Word in the experience of one culture, we risk a larger unfaithfulness to the Truth of God. This not only happens in the liturgical translations between the cultures of different people groups, it can also happen between generations.

> Our danger lies in inertia and in failure to recognize, understand, or value our own cultural contexts aright. Provinces[15] should be ready both to treasure their received ways and also to reflect critically on them in the light of their own cultures. They should be wary lest sheer conservatism in liturgy, or an over dependence upon uses from elsewhere, in

fact become a vehicle of culture alienation, making Anglican worship a specialist cult, rather than a people's liturgy. Let us hold fast to the essentials, and follow the cultural adaptability of the incarnation of our Lord Jesus in everything else.[16]

Faithfulness to the Christian tradition demands a willingness to accept diversity in its expression. What may seem a shocking departure from the tradition in one culture, place, and time may be the only way another culture can express the essence of gospel and apostolic truth.

The contemporary Roman Church and, more recently, the Episcopal Church of the Philippines, have reduced the number of barriers to inculturation by producing an *editio typica* of their liturgies.[17] These churches see these basic published liturgies as the place where the Church, and its many cultures, begins the discussion of liturgical appropriateness and expression (in the case of the Philippine Church the *editio typica* is the equivalent of the BCP). There is no attempt at producing a comprehensive liturgy for all of the cultures that exist in a modern pluralistic society and Church. The goal is to establish the principles for movement forward.[18]

The 1979 Book of Common Prayer of the American Church suggests a similar forward moving approach, but its promise for inculturation remains largely unfulfilled. Just as some people saw the computer as nothing more than a fancy typewriter, many people raised on the 1928 Book of Common Prayer could not see the 1979 BCP as anything more than a jazzed up version of the old. The broad horizon of the framers of the 1979 Book was unfortunately constricted to the narrowness of habitual experience and, quite often, the cultural prejudice of its users.

This experience indicates that simply establishing an *editio typica* for the American church will not bring down the barriers that exist between our present situation and inculturation. A different missiology is necessary, especially for the People of the Land.

Missiology and Inculturation

The Classicist Missiology

The Churches of the West have, until recently, operated with what Bernard Lonergan called a "classicist" view of culture.[19] In that view, culture refers to all human activity, assuming that Western Civilization is the pinnacle of human development. This view assumes both the desirability and the inevitability of all peoples becoming "civilized" or "cultured" by following the Western model. Christianity, in this understanding, must also point towards the goal of "culture"—Western Civilization. Western culture is, in this view, the necessary and unquestioned engine of the advance of Christianity.

The effects of the classicist view of culture on the Church's mission were many, most of them devastating to the church and the world. Karl Luckert points out that one causal aspect of this is that Western missionaries carried "the hidden ontology of Western modernity – the impersonal mechanical universe"[20] in their preaching and teaching. Their critique of non-Western religious systems came from the "materialistic scientism" of Western culture rather than strictly religious criteria.[21]

In our modern context, the Church is moving toward an "empirical and pluralistic" view of culture, recognizing a diversity of cultures in the world and in modern urban societies. During the first part of this transition, it is has become common to speak of "accommodations" to local culture in liturgical matters. The underlying assumption here, though softened, still assumes that Western culture and civilization is the pattern for Christian Faith. This neo-colonial view sees "accommodations" as a mission strategy—a "spoonful of sugar," perhaps, until ethnic groups enter the mainstream of Westernized Christianity. Although tempered by greater cultural sensitivity and sophistication, this is still a colonial view. Unfortunately, this appears to be the default position of many modern churches.

During the last quarter of the twentieth century, we see another possibility emerge. Under the influence of an empirical and pluralistic view of culture, missiologists and church leaders began to use terms like "indigenization" and "contextualization" to describe a vital component of mission and evangelization. Among the People of the Land, those same terms describe a process of Church growth and development that is culturally based.

Though the Church has become increasingly comfortable with a diverse view of culture, the classicist view of culture continues to influence the encounters between Western Christianity and many cultures around the world. More than just an embarrassment, classicism cripples the witness of Western Christians in virtually every aspect of its mission. Well hidden in the worldview of many, the equation of Christianity with Western Culture is still, in practice, an unquestioned assumption in the churches of the West. As the dissonance between this assumed worldview and the core values of their faith becomes clearer, Western Churches appear unable to cope with the challenge of a new age. The lack of clarity is a great part of present day uneasy relations with non-Western or non-mainstream cultures. Church institutions careen from timidity at one moment to arrogance in the next.

An additional consequence has emerged in the Western Church's continued identity with Western Civilization: the Church has not been able to adequately differentiate itself from a dominant "post-Christian" globalized Western culture. The Western Church finds itself trapped in its identification with a culture that often celebrates its liberation from the values of the gospel. This association creates a massive obstacle for Christian witness. It obscures the clarity of the gospel among Church members and promotes a form of evangelism that, at times, seems little more than nostalgia for the presumed glory days of Christendom.

Cultural alienation is the consequence for many Christians. They are "children of two worlds"—the dominant "globalized" or "Americanized"[22] culture and a church culture—but not really at home in either.[23] This makes inculturation difficult to imagine for many Christians. Instead of inculturation in their own context, they may borrow from other cultural traditions to achieve a supposed aura of spiritual authenticity. For many, the only alternative seems to be a stale mimic of a romanticized past or a superficial adoption of the symbols of a romanticized foreign culture.

Lamin Sanneh describes our situation forcefully:

> What we have to overcome is the reluctance to admit that English is no longer captured for the gospel, but, on the contrary, that the gospel has been captured by an agnostic, post-Enlightenment culture, a case of sola cultura. What we desperately need is the liberation of the Gospel.[24]

In the not too distant past, Christians clearly believed that the devil lurked in the many local "non-Christian" cultures that the churches encountered during colonial expansion. The dominant cultures of the Western Church reserved the right to make judgments on the suitability of local adaptations to the liturgies of Christendom. This was, presumably, to protect both the local and universal Church from corruption and syncretism. It is now clear, in dramatic contrast, that the most critical place for discernment is in the encounter of Christianity with the overwhelming and pervasive culture of global Americanization. There is a subtle but deep syncretism developing in the Western churches due to a lack of discerning distance from the culture of a globalized modern Western Civilization.

There is also a need for inculturation in this globalized culture. We must temper this need with the recognition that there is a spiritual risk if the church is unable to distinguish itself from a globalizing post-Christendom. Happily, the Early Church provides a model: it aggressively inculturated its message and life in a globalizing Roman culture, even while it took great pains to separate itself from that culture's life-denying elements. The intense formation and discernment of the catechumenate where both inculturation and differentiation occurred, suggests the shape of our modern path to wholeness.

The Doctrine of Discovery

The classicist missiology continues to influence the Western churches relations with all of the many cultures that we recognize in contemporary society. There is, however, a critical additional dimension for the People of the Land.[25] More than in other colonial contexts, a special legal, theological, and philosophical system has oppressed the People of the Land: the Doctrine of Discovery. All efforts at liturgical inculturation will remain inherently thwarted and institutionally unrealizable until the Church abandons this doctrine and its assumptions.

At Canada's General Synod of 2001, the Anglican Council of Indigenous Peoples was given a day to present their program for a new relationship with the Anglican Church of Canada. Some attending the Synod expressed surprise that the Council gave the first half of the day to a repudiation of the Doctrine of Discovery. This doctrine, however, is the pivot of the relationship between the Church and Aboriginal People. The persistence of the Doctrine, in Church and Society, reveals the continuing damage of Colonialism.

"The Doctrine of Discovery" is a useful way of referring to the concept of Terra Nullius. Terra Nullius describes a land uninhabited. Western societies expanded its meaning for the Americas on the basis that the People of the Land displayed no evidence of civilization. The structures of Euro-American culture—buildings, governments, and churches, to name a few—were absent. Because the Americas were "uninhabited," the "Discoverers" received the "right of discovery." They received the "right" to govern, colonize, and exploit this Terra Nullius.

Treaty making, which implies a sovereignty or "peoplehood" for the nations involved, has blunted some of the worst aspects of the

Doctrine of Discovery.[26] Nevertheless, the negative effects of this view have been persistent, pervasive, and deadly, despite official condemnation by virtually every major institution of Western Culture.

The Western Church's history in this matter illustrates the problem. Despite a consistent and laudable support for the treaties and the sovereignty they imply, the churches of the West have continued to ignore those treaties' implications for their own life and governance. The Church among the People of the Land continues to be organized, ruled, and catechized by the intellectual, spiritual, and political boundaries and barriers of colonialism. This is seen most clearly in matters liturgical.

Western mission has not confined the devastation of the Doctrine of Discovery to the People of the Land. Not only did Western Christianity advance with the structures of colonialism, its missional imagination and worldview were, in many respects, defined by it. Many, if not most, models of evangelism view human hearts and minds as a type of terra nullius, uninhabited by any trace of the Divine until the Church brings its teaching and ministry into view.

The environment is also a victim, exploited by those with the right of "discovery." This is a part of the tradition of environmental abuse in the name of economic advantage and technological progress. For their part, the Western churches have shown considerable reluctance to criticize the destructive abuse of the environment and the morally inequitable use of resources by Western societies, particularly in the United States.

There is a notable contrast between the Colonial models of mission of today and those in other ages of the Church.[27] Irenaeus, to give a very ancient example, appears to assume an ongoing incarnational presence of the Logos of God in the life and cultures of people before the singular Good News of Jesus Christ.[28] The Early Church, as demonstrated in Council of Jerusalem (Acts 15) asserted its Universality and Catholicity by *not* insisting "on customs which might actually be neutral in themselves, but which, if they were made binding upon others, would make the worldwide church somehow Old-Testament-Jewish culture-specific."[29]

Recent treatments of Celtic mission indicate another more incarnational model of mission.[30] These examples from other missions and other times suggest new possibilities for a Church open to inculturation. In our present day context, only a missiology that allows the unhindered inculturation of the gospel among the People of the Land is worthy of a Catholic and Apostolic Church.

The liturgical renewal of the Church in Aotearoa (New Zealand), which resulted in the widely used *A New Zealand Prayer Book*, is directly related to the recognition of Maori aboriginal rights and the repudiation of the Doctrine of Discovery. The Church recognized the importance of the treaties and, in the deepening dialogue that followed, recognized the implied peoplehood, nationhood, and sovereignty that is involved. *A New Zealand Prayer Book* is one of the happy by-products.

The existence of the aforementioned treaties, in the Americas as in Aotearoa, implies a different level of engagement and interaction by the Church with aboriginal groups. The respect involved is at a more meaningful level and involves quite different issues than is customary for non-aboriginal ethnic groups within a nation. The Peoples of the Land are, as is often said in American and International Law, dependent sovereigns—they are nations.[31]

Thomas Berger forcefully describes the on-going barriers of colonialism:

> All the things the White man has brought – language, religion, medicine, schools, welfare – when laid side by side constitute a barrier, walling people off from their own past and at the same time from future possibilities. [32]

This barrier has solidified in recent years, despite widespread assumptions to the contrary. Poverty is still everywhere among the

People of the Land (in the US, one third live below the poverty line and over half are unemployed[33]). In the United States, media attention to the profitability of some American Indian Casinos[34] masks the continuing harvest of colonialism—widespread poverty and a rate of death by violence and accident that are the highest of any ethnic group. Ominously, the appetites of "Americanization" are now in a direct line of conflict with the People of the Land. The land and resources of the People of the Land around the world are threatened as never before.

In the context of this great political struggle, the People of the Land are undergoing a cultural renaissance around the world.[35] From the Church's point of view, political liberation and cultural liberation cannot be divorced.[36] As the amazing theology of evangelical Orlando Costas demonstrates, mission and evangelism are one with justice and liberation.[37] In our context this is absolutely clear as a matter of justice and faith: the Church must recognize, within its own structures, the renaissance of the People of the Land by the repudiation of the Doctrine of Discovery. Political liberation and cultural liberation must illuminate each other. For a church that is so intimately based on the "freedom" of nations in matters of liturgy and faith,[38] it is odd that in the Episcopal Church aboriginal nationhood can be so completely ignored. At the barest minimum, repudiation of the Doctrine of Discovery involves the removal of all barriers to inculturation among the People of the Land.

The Power of the Gospel

So far, we have described some of the barriers that inculturation has encountered among the People of the Land. There is another side to the story: God's work of inculturation among the People of the Land, despite the barriers. A new missiology must incorporate the growing body of evidence that inculturation happens, on some level, outside of the approval or intentions of missionary organizations.

As Paul points out in Philippians,[39] the gospel has a power that goes beyond the intent of its human messengers. The vehicle of its presentation does not necessarily have to fully understand or even agree with its goals.[40] A messenger of the gospel cannot see the full impact of its power and reach because of the limitations of cultural bias. This truth was dramatically demonstrated in the history of missions among the People of the Land. Though almost completely unnoticed in the official histories of the missionaries, inculturation did happen, at a number of levels, among the People of the Land.

The earliest translators[41] and catechists for the missionaries were often quite creative in their work. In fact, some, like the great Lakota holy man, Black Elk, appear to have been quite sophisticated and original theologians.[42] These elders were able to craft their Christian message in a way that honored their tribal traditions and values. They attached new meaning to old traditions and old meanings to new traditions, making a transformed expression of the Christian faith and their own tribal identity. Though greatly limited by circumstances, this is an example of transculturation.[43] This was often done without the knowledge or consent of the missionaries, whose spiritual and theological sophistication was rarely on the level of these elders and theologians of the People of the Land. Today, these often unnamed elders stand as unheralded but unequaled examples of faithfulness to the gospel and their relatives. Of particular importance for Anglicanism was the creative work of the Ojibwe Singers of Minnesota, documented in the groundbreaking scholarship of Michael McNally's *Ojibwe Singers*.[44]

In Ojibwe hymn singing, we see a missionary-provided medium expand, adapt, and grow among a people, while the institutional reach of the colonially aligned church remains stunted. The medium's influence grows—and the gospel message with it—beyond the horizon of the missionary organizations that brought it. In fact, during a great part of the past two centuries, church institutions have, most often, merely tolerated the practice, and, in some cases, vigorously opposed[45] the leadership of this creative example of inculturation. Though still vital in Northern Minnesota, Ojibwe singing is rarely recognized for the successful creativity it embodies.[46] Without a worry about institutional validation, it continues as a consolidating, politically energizing, and, ultimately, healing force in Ojibwe life.[47] From the beginning, it has been a rallying point for the large group of Ojibwe people who sought to continue their traditional subsistence lifestyle within a framework that respected the old-ways but incorporated some valued parts of the colonizers' traditions, beliefs, and technology. Most of those involved had only nominal affiliation with church institutions. They were valued neither by the missionaries, who looked for assimilated Americans, nor by the anthropologists, who looked for museum pieces.

A number of other previously unrecognized examples of inculturation are coming to the surface. Translations of long used Indigenous language hymns are now being compared and evaluated.[48] This work reveals a sophisticated and complex process of translation and inculturation on the part of Native communities.[49] These are instances of what McNally describes as "culture in motion." Vital tribal cultures, though under tremendous stress by military occupation, are not trapped in a static tribal traditionalism or in aggressive assimilation. Western scholarship has, for the most part, displayed these as the only options. McNally's work shows the progressive vitality of Ojibwe culture in the face of overwhelming obstacles.

The Gwich'in of the Arctic Regions of Alaska and Canada are another compelling example of unnoticed inculturation. Ojibwe missionary Archdeacon Robert MacDonald, brought the Book of Common Prayer, the Bible, and his own Ojibwe Hymnal to his work among the Gwich'in, beginning in the Ft. Yukon area in 1862. Through a culturally sensitive collaboration with a number of Gwich'in leaders, including his own wife and Chief William Loola, MacDonald's work lead to great success among the people. Its fruit is still strong and clear to this day.

Like the Ojibwe hymn singing, Gwich'in Christianity became a nativist support for a subsistence lifestyle. The great Gwich'in prophet and deacon, the Rev. Albert Tritt, in the early 20th Century, translated his Anglican Christianity into a vibrant, vital, and adaptive culture. The Gwich'in Christian identity became a way of insulating the people from the worst aspects of the invading colonial culture, while, at the same time allowing the people to utilize many of its benefits. It is little wonder that Gwich'in Christian identity is seen as an essential part of their survival in a world that has rarely modulated its hostility to their aboriginal rights and existence.[50] The Gwich'in, along with their other Athabaskan relatives, provide an amazing example of a non-Western Christianity thriving in a Western church culture and broader western colonizing culture. In words that could be applied to the Gwich'in or Ojibwe Singing, Fr. Virgil Elizondo gives a powerful witness to this aspect of inculturation:

> The Word has become flesh in us in the form of our religious practices and traditions. They are the visible expressions of our collective soul through which we affirm ourselves to be who we are in our relationship to each other and to God. Others may take everything else away from us, but they cannot destroy our expressions of the divine. Through these practices we not only affirm ourselves as a people, but we likewise resist ultimate assimilation. Thus they are not only affirmations of faith, but the language of defiance and ultimate resistance. In our collective celebrations, we rise above the forces which oppress us and even seek to destroy us and celebrate publicly our survival. But it is much more than survival; through them, the newborn babies and growing children are initiated into the God-language of our people and thus we are assured that life will continue unto the next generation and generations to come.[51]

In the future it will be valuable to place the history of the gospel among the People of the Land next to other expressions of non-Western Christianity. Virgil Elizondo's work on Mexican-American inculturation, already quoted, is an essential piece of the conversation.[52] Harvey Cox's amazing theological treatment of Pentecostalism in *Fire from Heaven*[53] is another important place to continue. Cox reviews the wide variety of responses to Pentecostalism around the globe and some of the implications for missiology and theology. Though he deals with inculturation only in a tangential way, there is much to be learned from the phenomenon he writes of, which appears to be encouraging a non-Western inculturation in a number of places around the globe. There are other important examples of inculturation to be considered in this conversation, Pentecostal and non-Pentecostal, among non-Western cultures in North America.[54] Africa is also an important place where we will find points of comparison and dialogue.[55]

When examining instances of inculturation in any context outside of the reviewer's own culture, one should expect surprises. Inculturation does not always happen in the way that people outside a culture might desire or predict. It follows the inner and spiritual logic of a given place, people, and culture. What would have potential appeal to an outsider might not be significant or attractive to someone inside a culture. The historical material, as well as more contemporary examples, should keep us grounded in humility. Inculturation will often happen in ways that are quite different from the recommendations or predictions of Western theologians and liturgical specialists.

As non-Western forms of Christianity among the People of the Land and other groups become more familiar, they will undoubtedly reveal much about the power and dynamics of inculturation. The knowledge gained will benefit the Church in many ways. It will demonstrate the irresistible but quiet force of the Incarnation, even in hostile environments. It will also suggest some of the ways that the trajectory and pattern of inculturation manifest in culture.

Most important of all, the history of inculturation among the People of the Land, by demonstrating the pervasive power of God's liberating gospel, points the way towards a church that embraces and embodies a new missiology. From now on, inculturation must be seen as a fundamental element of any gospel based definition of mission. The remarkable genius of God's work among the elders of the People of the Land is a foundation and inspiration for the future of inculturation among the Church and all her many cultures.

A New Missiology for the People of the Land

The connection between incarnation and mission is primary and powerful, revealing in local culture the universal reality that created us and call us to unity with all things, in Christ. This is God's mission and the apostolate of the Church.[56] Archbishop Anastasios Vannoulatos describes it this way:

> The goal of Christian mission is the incarnation of the Logos of God into the language and customs of a country and the growth of an indigenous Church, which will sanctify and endorse the people's personality.[57]

For the People of the Land this has a special relevance. Though ancient to the Church, an incarnational missiology is new, when contrasted with the approach of colonialism. An incarnational missiology, the heart of inculturation, suggests a greater compatibility with the basic theological insights that create the spiritual and political reality of the People of the Land.

Vine Deloria, Jr., in his critique of Western theology, has been quite influential among the People of the Land, despite the diversity of contexts among them. His book *God is Red* is familiar to many.[58] Particularly important is his criticism of Western theology's preoccupation with the temporal aspect of Jesus' proclamation of the

Kingdom of God.[59] North American Indians, Alaska Natives and, it appears, other Peoples of the Land, think of the work and presence of God primarily in terms of place, though not ignoring the significance of time. In comparison with Western thought, some of the difference in worldview can be illustrated by the Inuit/Inupiat word "vik," used to signify both place and time.

"Place" and its capacity for the Sacred, has always been central to Indigenous identity and survival.[60] The connection of Land, People, and Spirit gives birth to all life. Yet, in the encounter with the West, the theological importance of this connection for indigenous peoples is a problem. It is the heart of the conflict between the "First, Second, and Third Worlds" of modern "development" and the "Fourth World" of the People of the Land.[61] This schism is a major part of the dissonance between the People of the Land and the colonial churches of Western Christianity.

Viewed positively, however, Deloria's critique underlines, from a Christian perspective, the importance of Incarnation to the People of the Land. The Word "made flesh" in the Incarnation is the sanctification of both time and place. If John's declaration of the universal relevance of the Incarnation has any truth at all (John 1:1-14), then the spirituality of the People of the Land has a home, if not in the institutional life of the Western Churches, then in God's own Mission in the Universe—becoming flesh in time and place.

The Way Forward

Inculturation, though successfully completed in other generations of the Church, is "still to be accomplished in the new technological and globalized world we live in."[62] As such, inculturation is an essential missiological frontier for the whole Church. It will challenge the Church to deeper engagement in human culture, on one side, and in the mystery of Christ's Incarnation, on the other.

Our times challenge us to be true to the gospel in ways that will immeasurably broaden our horizon. One must strain to find precedents for this moment in the Church's history. It is a call to conversion and transformation that rivals the mission horizon of the Early Church.

So far, the Church has rarely ventured beyond neo-colonialism,[63] supposing that modern Western liturgical reforms and texts will lead to effective liturgy among the People of the Land and other ethnic minorities. Further, simply adding flavor to Western liturgies by permitting exotic ethnic props or non-western music is not inculturation. To allow this transformation institutionally, the Church must welcome dynamic encounters with vital cultures. With these encounters, the risk of transformation is embraced. A transformation that is anticipated in the missionary instructions of Jesus:[64] announce the nearness of God to the people and place, invite the people to "turn around" their lives, and eat and drink whatever they provide. This was extraordinarily difficult prospect for a pious Jew of the First Century. They were being asked to stretch their horizons beyond what they ever imagined possible. They were the first to be called to inculturation.

The missionary instructions of Jesus are difficult for us, too. We are apt to think of ourselves as the already converted. Jesus points us to a different reality and a deeper conversion. The most important part of the conversion and transformation happens in the hearts of the messengers. Jesus asks us to encounter strangers in settings that promise a frightening intimacy. He calls us to recognize the presence and power of God in people and places—an act that surprises us into a new world.[65] The implication is very important to consider: the greatest boundaries to success in the mission are in the hearts of the missioners.

This Book

In the early stages of work on this volume, Malcolm Naea Chun (see Malcolm's essay later in this volume) focused our attention on the importance of accommodating the pastoral needs of the People of the Land. Malcolm notes that most of the liturgies of the Book of Common Prayer happen within Church buildings. Among the

Peoples of the Land, however, there is an urgent need for home and family related liturgies as demonstrated, for example, in the popularity of the "Home Blessing" in *A New Zealand Prayer Book*. Malcolm helped us to maintain a local and pastoral flavor to all of our work.

Michael Oleksa and Bill Wantland provide some local theological context for our work. We believe that this will be valuable to the People of the Land and to others, as it connects the local to the universal context of all theology. Though inculturation is, by definition, local, the catholicity of the Church demands a conversation that is both local and universal. Juan Quevedo-Bosch expands this consideration in a different direction by giving us insight into the global context of liturgical matters at the present time.

Continuing this universal and local dialogue, we include an important contribution to this discussion from the Church in Taiwan. It illustrates the possibilities and potential of inculturation from a completely different local perspective. I am grateful to Taiwan's former Bishop, the Rt. Rev. John Chien, and its present Bishop, the Rt. Rev. David Lai, for their insightful help in our discussions of inculturation.

For the People of the Land, one example of the possibilities for a local community can be seen in the work of Martin Brokenleg and others (see the sections on the development of a Lakota Liturgy). Ginny Doctor's contribution portrays another local context. John Robertson's approaches this concern for the local from a broader perspective. He emphasizes that inculturation, especially among the People of the Land, must be from the local community. Steve Charleston extends this, reminding us that we must be careful and respectful in using materials from outside our own local context.

Throughout, we implicitly acknowledge that liturgical inculturation involves much more than the production of liturgical texts. For many cultures, space, movement, and music are the most vital elements of worship. Juan Oliver's work on the inculturation of liturgical space reveals some important aspects of this concern.

Musically, we have a piece from Marilyn Haskel that helps us to begin this all-important conversation.

Along with the Introduction, the essays by Lee Mitchell and Clay Morris engage some of the questions of identity and accountability that will accompany inculturation within Anglicanism. Lee asks us to consider the essential aspects of Anglican liturgy. He addresses one of the most vital questions concerning our future and our ability to adapt to it. Clay's reflections on liturgical leadership help us to approach another complementary matter: what kind of community, what kinds of leaders can mid-wife inculturation both in a local community and the broader community of communities which is the Church?

A final thought: This work introduces inculturation for the whole Church with a special focus on the People of the Land. We are reminded that the Modern Age of Mission, now ending, began with the Church's mission to Native North America five centuries ago. Those who bring these words to the larger Church hope that a new age of hope for all people will begin in the context of justice and reconciliation for the People of the Land.

Notes

[1] From *The Sixth Grandfather: Black Elk's Teachings Given to John G. Neihardt*, edited by R. J. DeMallie, University of Nebraska Press, Lincoln and London.

[2] Ep 14 (PL 50, 485). I am grateful to Mark R. Francis for this quote in his "Liturgical Inculturation: The State of the Question" (*Liturgical Ministry*, vol. 6, Summer 1997).

[3] The "We" of this volume are the various contributors and the many people who participated in developing the community of this work. The greatest share of the work for this volume occurred in a series of meetings and liturgies in the 1990's. Two meetings in particular, one in Minnesota—attended by The Rev. Michael

Merriman (representing The Standing Liturgical Commission), Malcolm Naea Chun, the Rev. John Robertson, and the Rev. Mark MacDonald - and one in California – attended by The Rev. Dr. Clay Morris, The Rev. John Robertson, The Rev. Hone Kaa, Malcolm Naea Chun, the Rev. Mark MacDonald, and the Rev. Dr. George Armstrong - are noteworthy for this volume. At these meetings in particular, a group of people participated in the "spiritual awakening" that shaped the production of this book. Two liturgies, one at the General Convention of 1991 in Phoenix, and the other, held by Indigenous Peoples in 1992 at the Washington National Cathedral and coordinated by The Rev. Carol Gallagher (now the Suffragan Bishop of Virginia), inspired the imaginations of many.

[4] For a discussion of the use of this phrase to describe Indigenous or Aboriginal Peoples or Nations see "The Church and The Peoples of the Land," by M. MacDonald, *First Peoples Theology Journal*, Vol.1, No. 1, July 2000, pp. 11ff.

[5] Dr. Owanah Anderson subsequently published *An Anthology of Native American Services of Worship* (Office of Native American Ministries, Episcopal Church Center, New York, NY). This is the best collection of resources presently available for Episcopalian congregations. It contains the fruit of a number of years of liturgical experience.

[6] See M. MacDonald, *Strategy for Growth: Multiculturalism in the Episcopal Church* (published as a joint effort of Inter-Cultural Ministry Development of Province VIII of the Episcopal Church, The Episcopal Diocese of Minnesota, and the Office of American Indian/ Alaska Native/ Native Hawaiian Ministries of The Episcopal Church). The Episcopal Church's historic ethnic constituency is often unrecognized as an ethnic constituency. This is a fundamental problem in developing an adequate missiology for the Church in North America.

[7] The change to The Standing Commission on Liturgy and Music had not yet taken place.

[8] There is some question as to what medium is most appropriate for the "Prayer Book "(see Clay Morris' article in this book). How much will we be using a "Book" after the revision? Already, many congregations use leaflets or other forms made possible by new technologies. Where will technology take us after the process of revision mandated by General Convention is completed?

[9] Anscar Chupungco, OSB, is must reading on Inculturation. His influential books on the topic are *Liturgies of the Future* (New York: Paulist Press, 1989); *Liturgical Inculturation: Sacramentals, Religiosity, and Catechesis* (Collegeville, MN: The Liturgical Press, 1992); and *Tradition and Progress* (Washington, DC: The Pastoral Press, 1994). Mark Francis provides a very helpful and concise update in "Liturgical Inculturation: The State of the Question" (*Liturgical Ministry*, vol. 6, Summer 1997).

[10] See *Liturgical Inculturation in the Anglican Communion* edited by David R. Holeton (Bramcote: Grove, 1990). Also helpful from an Anglican perspective are *Inculturation: The Eucharist in Africa* by Phillip Tovey (Bramcote: Grove, 1988) and *Anglican Liturgical Inculturation in Africa* edited by David Gitari (Bramcote: Grove, 1994).

[11] W.B. Fraizier, MM, "Nine Breakthroughs in Catholic Missiology, 1965-2000," *International Bulletin of Missionary Research*, Vol. 25, No. 1, January 2001, p. 12.

[12] Michael Stogre, S.J. *That the World May Believe: The Development of Papal Social Thought on Aboriginal Rights*, Sherbrooke, QC: Editions Paulines, QC, 1992, p. 155.

[13] A. Chupungco, *Progress and Tradition*, op. cit., p. 2.

[14] A. Chupungco, *Progress and Tradition*, op. cit., pp. 28ff.

[15] Here, we are referring to Provinces of the Anglican Communion, like ECUSA for example.

[16] Sec. 8, "Down to Earth Worship," The York Statement of the Third International Anglican Liturgical Consultation, York, 1989; *Liturgical Inculturation in the Anglican Communion*, edited by

David R. Holeton, Grove, Bramcote, 1990, p. 13.

[17]See especially A. Chupungco, *Liturgies of the Future*, op. cit., pp. 34 ff.

[18] Chupungco's discussion of methodology is very helpful at this point. See *Liturgical Inculturation: Sacramentals, Religiosity, and Catechesis*, pp. 37ff.

[19]B. Lonergan, *Method in Theology*, (London, Darton, Longman, and Todd, 1973, pp. 326-327:

> On classicist assumptions there is just one culture. That one culture is not attained by the simple faithful, the people, the natives, the barbarians. Nonetheless, career is always open to talent. One enters upon such a career by the diligent study of the ancient Latin and Greek authors.

See, also, Stogre, SJ, op. cit. pp. 131ff.

[20] Karl W. Luckert, *The Navajo Hunter* Tradition, p. 5 (The University of Arizona Press, Tucson, 1975).

[21] Ibid. p. 4ff.

[22] Lamin Sanneh, "The Gospel and the Globe: A Profile of Professor Lamin Sanneh," *Berkeley at Yale*, Winter 2002, No. 20, pp. 14-15.

[23] Holeton, op. cit., p. 15.

[24] Lamin Sanneh, op. cit., p. 15.

[25] The best introduction to the history of the American Indian/Alaska Native Missions through the Episcopal Church is *400 Years: Anglican/Episcopal Mission Among American Indians*, by Dr. Owanah Anderson (Forward Movement Publications, Cincinnati, 1997.).

[26] It is important to note that the "Aboriginal" People of the Land in Australia were not involved in treaty making due to "Terra Nullius." The colonizers considered the land uninhabited. This is, today, a major issue for the Aborigines of Australia.

[27] Orthodoxy, in general, has had a different stance towards other

cultures encountered in Mission, for example:

> We affirm that all cultures are capable of communicating the grace and love of God. Reception of the good News of Christ does not destroy culture. Rather, it enables culture to be transformed. By taking on our human nature and entering in to our history, Christ enables our ways of life to be purified so that they become a means of communion with Himself. We have felt emboldened to use the symbolism of "transfiguration" (metamorphosis) to describe this process, for it is the inner content and meaning of culture that must necessarily undergo this transformation and not its outward forms. (Report of the Pan-African Orthodox Consultation, 2-7 December 1997, Kampala, Uganda, *Orthodox Mission*, published by the Orthodox Patriarchate of Kenya and Irinoupolis.)

See also *St. Symeon the New Theologian On the Mystical Life: The Ethical Discourses, vol. 1: The Church and the Last Things*, translated and introduced by Alexander Golitzen, St. Vladimir's Press, Crestwood, 1995, pp. 33f.

[28] Mary Ann Donovan, *One Right Reading: A Guide to Irenaeus*, The Liturgical Press, Collegeville, 1997, p. 174.

[29] Gitari, op. cit., p. 11.

[30] John Finney, *Recovering the Past: Celtic and Roman Mission*, Darton, Longman, Todd Ltd, London, 1996.

[31] See Thomas Berger's excellent summary in *Village Journey: The Report of the Native Alaska Native Review Commission*, Hill and Wang, New York, 1985, Chapter Five, pp. 117ff.

[32] Thomas Berger, op. cit. p. 13.

[33] Compare this to the unemployment during the "Great Depression" where unemployment was roughly one fifth of the population.

[34] The majority of American Indian Casinos are not sufficiently profitable. They are, in so many cases, merely an opportunity to

provide employment or to modify the effects of the chronic under funding of the US Government's treaty mandated obligations to the People of the Land.

[35] See Achiel Peelman, *Christ is a Native American*, Orbis, Toronto, 1995.

[36] Holeton, op. cit., p. 39.

[37] Orlando Costas, Christ *Outside the Gate*, Maryknoll: Orbis, 1982. *Liberating News: A Theology of Contextual Evangelization*, Grand Rapids: Eerdmans, 1989.

[38] Such foundational documents as the Preface of The First Book of Common Prayer (1549), the Preface of the American Book of Common Prayer (1789), and Article XXXIV (Of the Traditions of the Church) of the Articles of Religion underline the importance of this to Anglicanism. It is enticing to speculate that this core respect for sovereignty and peoplehood is related to the attraction of Anglicanism for the People of the Land.

[39] Philippians 1:15-18.

[40] See Lamin Sanneh, *Christian Missions and the Western Guilt Complex*, http://www.asu.edu/clas/religious_studies/home/cmg.html.

[41] See Sam Gill, "Native Americans and Their Religions," in *World Religions in America* edited by Jacob Neusner, John Knox Press, Louisville, 1994.

[42] See Clyde Holler, *Black Elk's Religion: The Sun Dance and Lakota Catholicism*, Syracuse UP, 1995. John Neihardt, <u>Black Elk Speaks</u>, U of Nebraska Press, 1961. Michael Steltenkamp, *Black Elk: Holy Man of the Oglala*, U of Ok Press, Norman, 1993.

[43] See Chupungco, *Liturgies of the Future*, op. cit. p. 31. Transculturation is the mutual reciprocity between culture and liturgy whereby through insertion and absorption neither lose their identity.

[44] Michael McNally, *Ojibwe Singers: Hymns, Grief, and a Culture in Motion*, Oxford, 2000.

[45] McNally, ibid. pp. 96ff.

[46] An exception was the recognition given by *The Witness* magazine at their awards banquet at the 1997 General Convention in Philadelphia.

[47] McNally, op. cit. especially in the Conclusion.

[48] See Gill, op. cit. While working with Navajo elders on the translation of Psalm 141, we discovered that the Navajo translator had creatively used Navajo culture to express the Psalmist words. "The evening sacrifice" was translated by referring to Navajo practice of offering of yellow cornmeal as the sun sets. An Ojibwe elder told me that she was trained in her Ojibwe culture and Christianity by using the Ojibwe Hymnal.

[49] Lamin Sanneh, *Translating the Message: The Missionary Impact on Culture*, Orbis Books, 1989, 1996; "Christian Mission and the Western Guilt Complex: A Proposal," *Christian Century*, April 8, 1987.

[50] See Murray Carpenter, "The Gwich'in and ANWR – The most Anglican group of people in the world fight for the right to protect a way of life," *The Witness*, Vol. 84, No. 1-2, Jan/Feb 2001.

[51] "Popular Religion and Cultural Identity: Mexican Experience in the USA," Virgil Elizondo, *http://www.religion-online*.

[52] See also by Elizondo: *Galilean Journey: The Mexican American Promise*, (in its eighth edition, Maryknoll, Vermont, Orbis Press, 2000), *The Future Is Mestizo: Life Where Cultures Meet*, (in its sixth edition, Colorado Press, 2000).

[53] Harvey Cox, *Fire from Heaven*, Addison Wesley, Reading, 1995.

[54] See Kirk Dombrowski's Dissertation: *Against Culture: Contemporary Pentecostalism in Native American Villages Along Alaska's Southeast Coast*, 1998. Although this is an anthropological and social analysis, it does describe some of the dynamics of Pentecostalism in an aboriginal setting.

[55] See, especially, Gitari, op. cit.

[56] See Ephesians 1 and Colossians 1.

[57] Anastasios Vannoulatos, "Discovering the Orthodox Missionary Ethos," *St. Vladimir's Theological Quarterly*, Vol. 3, 1964, pp. 144-145. Please see the stunning introduction to Fr. Michael Oleksa's *Orthodox Alaska*, St. Vladimir's Press, Crestwood, 1992

[58] Vine Deloria, *God is Red*, Jr., Fulcrum, Golden CO, 1994.

[59] Ibid. especially, Chapter Four.

[60] See the outstanding introduction to North American Native Spirituality, *The Sacred*, by Peggy Beck and Anna Walters, (Navajo Nation Community College Press, Tsaile, 1977). This book gives one of the best available introductions to the "family" resemblance of the very diverse expressions of spirituality among The People of the Land of North America.

[61] See Michael Stogre, op. cit., p. 23ff.

[62] John Zizioulas quoted by Dean Robert George Stephanopoulos in the Sixth Annual Stolberg Lecture, available through The Cathedral Foundation, Inc., 1140 Madison Ave., Covington, KY, 41011, p. 23.

[63] Phillip Tovey, *Inculturation: The Eucharist in Africa*, Grove, Bramcote, 1988, p. 30.

[64] Luke 10:1-12.

[65] See examples of this in the Women at the Well (John 4) or The Ethiopian Eunuch (Acts 8:26ff).

Acknowledgments

A number of people should be acknowledged in the production of this book. Malcolm Naea Chun deserves the greatest portion of credit, as his vision and commitment was essential throughout. Phoebe Pettingell has also given so much to this project, as an editor and inspiration. Finally, each of the contributors to this volume deserves special note for his or her participation in the on-going conversation on inculturation.

I am personally indebted, in terms of my own involvement in this project, to the people of Good Shepherd Mission in Ft. Defiance, Navajo Nation and the people of St. John-in-the-Wilderness Church, Red Lake Nation. Their wisdom and insights are so very important to my thinking. Along with all of the trail-blazing elders, thinkers, and healers who are mentioned in this volume, they have been doorways to a new world for me.

The Standing Commission on Liturgy and Music, along with Church Publishing Inc., has been both helpful and patient. I am very grateful. The advice and help of Malcolm Naea Chun, John Robertson, Cynthia Faust, Ginny Doctor, and Virginia MacDonald has been essential to this work. Thank you.

In any list of acknowledgements associated with the People of the Land in the Episcopal Church, Owanah Anderson and Helen Peterson deserve special honor and mention. Without their work, dedication, and vision this book would barely be a dream.

Mark L. MacDonald, Editor

We are one race, Mankind. We must view all people as assets having purposes to be challenged, developed, fulfilled, and deployed. Our noblest visions and highest ideals must take form and become substance in our lives as we share this earth with one another. Let no one be denied this hope. Let us commit our wills, collectively, to making this so.

Ted George[1]

Ritual and Inculturation: Reclaiming Native Tradition in Christian Liturgy

Malcolm Naea Chun

Every Sunday, some thirty years ago, just before the collection was taken, the Bishop or Dean at our cathedral would move to the step where the altar rails would soon be placed so he could greet and bless any children who came forward to give a special offering in honor of their own birthday. The money they held in their hands, a set sum of coins, fell into what looked like a little plastic bank. The Bishop or Dean would lay his hands on their heads and invoke a blessing. I remember this well because I had a good view from the choir seat in the front row in the days when I sang soprano.

I also remember the one time I was finally given money to offer for a blessing for my birthday. It was not all that much fun, for you had what seemed like the entire cathedral congregation looking at you. I remember when one kid, who didn't have enough money, cried and apologized to the bishop, who laughed and proclaimed aloud to everyone saying that it was okay. Boy, was that kid embarrassed. I think we all felt that way. I never did it again.

Bishops and Deans have come and gone at our cathedral and it has been a long time since this was done. I don't know if I miss it at all and no one else seems to remember it. We hardly ever do anything so public nowadays, especially if it takes so much time. I don't yearn for its return, for in hindsight it was not an experience of any significant change or recognition, but what I do miss is that

nothing better has ever replaced it, nothing at all. The only ceremonies and rituals we have now that touch our personal lives are
baptism, usually as an infant, which we would scarcely remember;
weddings, which are often more memorable for the family and
friends gathered than the bride and groom; and funerals, in which,
if it is our own, we are certainly not active participants!

Are ceremonies and rituals that important? For people today it
appears they are not. Yet they should be, according to what
anthropologists and the like have been saying about the importance of rituals for any society, from so-called "primitive" or tribal
to modern. Cultural anthropologist Clifford Geertz writes, "in a
ritual, the world as lived and the world as imagined fuse under the
agency of a single set of symbolic forms, turn out to be the same
world..."[2] And that worldview of the people is not "as subjective
human preferences but as the imposed conditions for life implicit
in a world with a particular structure."[3] Hence, "elaborate initiation rites, as among the Australians; complex philosophical tales, as
among the Maori; dramatic shamanistic exhibitions, as among the
Eskimos; cruel human sacrifices, as among the Aztecs; obsessive
curing ceremonies, as among the Navajo; large communal feasts, as
among the Polynesian groups—all these patterns and many more
seem to one people or another to sum up most powerfully what it
knows about living."[4]

There is an absence of ritual and ceremony in modern life. This
was certainly noted by Joseph Campbell when he complained to
Bill Moyers in the interviews for *The Power of Myth*. He said,
"There's been a reduction of ritual. Even in the Roman Catholic
Church, my God...they've forgotten that the function of ritual is
to pitch you out, not to wrap you back in where you have been all
the time. ... The rituals that once conveyed an inner reality are
now merely form. That's true in the rituals of society as well as the
personal rituals of marriage."

Campbell thought the irrelevance of rituals in modern society
has much to do with the waning of religious instruction and

responsibility. The people, he believed, who have been keeping ceremonies and rituals alive are priests and ministers; but the modern day storytellers are the filmmakers and fiction writers. Campbell said, "What is unfortunate for us is that a lot of the people who write these stories do not have the sense of their responsibility. These stories are making and breaking lives. But the movies are made simply to make money. The kind of responsibility that goes into a priesthood with ritual is not there. That is one of our problems today. … So the youngsters invent themselves, and you have these raiding gangs, and so forth—that is self-rendered initiation."[5]

Ceremonies and rituals continue to remain important for native peoples through the world in one form or another. I was reminded of this by the Rev. Canon Hone Kaa of Pihopatanga (Maori Bishopric) in Aotearoa (New Zealand) as we talked about theological education from an indigenous perspective. He said that if he had the chance he would like to teach a theology course based on native peoples' understanding of the life to death cycle. In that moment, I realized that he was on to something.

In the earliest descriptions of native traditions it is stated how so many activities from birth to death, such as farming, fishing, carving canoes, healing, building a house, and many others, were religious activities, or, in our language, "ho omana." Literally this word is "an act that imbues something with mana or spiritual power," and today that is equated with the word "religion." An example of this concept is our highly misunderstood tradition of carved images as the "worshiping of idols," but again, in our earliest native commentary, it was recognized that a carved wooden image is only a carved wooden image, and that God/gods were in the heavens. This is why it is stated that offerings were invoked to the sky and not to the images.[6] So the purpose and practice of rituals related to the everyday tasks of living are for "protecting from evil, blessing with good things, prestige, well-being [health] and happiness …"[7]

In teaching others how to use our method of reconciling family difficulties and problems I have found it somewhat humorous when some, who have gone through catechism in their younger days, find it so difficult to lead the family through prayers. It is explained that prayers are crucial to this process because we need help and guidance ourselves in order to help and guide the family through its crisis, and we need to pray for our own protection. By beginning the process with prayer, we also create a sacred time, and remind the family that the discussions to take place are very different from everyday conversation. When this is understood, such enabled persons in turn can help our families who may not be so "religious" to recognize the importance of prayer in our traditions and for their own family life. If we find it so difficult to pray in public with our own people, how is it even possible for us to share our prayers with each other in corporate worship together? This is why the Church must become involved in our lives.

The closure of most of these rites was feasting because "… the feast was a sharing of dedicated foods; and the giving and taking of presents was actually a general exchange in which the prestige and pleasure of giving and receiving was enjoyed by all concerned."[8] We feasted at the beginning of the life cycle, at birth, and for remembrance of passage of time or anniversaries, for adulthood, for children, for welcoming guests, and finally in celebration of the end of the life cycle and for the memorial of that life. It is through the act (and expression) of feasting that we publicly and physically demonstrate "*aloha*" (affection), prestige, hospitality, and a good time; social, economic, and psychic security; and the solidarity of living '*ohana* [extended family], the *kupuna* (ancestors), and '*aumakua* (guardian spirits), [which] were the considerations affecting all family ceremonials."[9] The practice of such behavior would ensure the continuation of relationships by sharing resources, underscoring friendships and relationships through honoring members, and creating an atmosphere that eases potential tensions, thereby binding a community together. As these rituals, ceremonies, and feasts touch so many and go so deep into the vitality of our people, it is imperative that the Church be involved. How much richer the experience when the Eucharist is understood as such a feast.

Then there were many traditional occasions, rituals and ceremonies that required the help of a specialist or a priest. They were highly trained professionals like the many imported, seminary-educated, priests we have, but with one difference—in our local traditions they were people recognized by the community for the gifts they practiced and how they behaved, not as self-appointed individuals who felt "called." Their use of their gifts became the vehicle in which the "ho'o," that is the process of imbuing in "ho'o mana" could be done. In our traditions there is a very real and recognized role for the priesthood that is central to maintaining our religious expression and this is why the Church should, and needs to be, involved.

When I was still working for our native affairs office a colleague, the economic development officer, came to me asking for a favor. He had a family that was having a special kind of problem that he thought was more cultural in origin and thought that I could help them.

I called the family and talked with them. It turned out that the father of this family had just inherited from his grandfather some special carved stones. He loved his grandfather and so he accepted the gift, although being a Christian he was not comfortable with his grandfather's request that he wash and feed the carved stones. He left them in the house and for several days since had been bothered by dreams. He'd kept silent about this situation until the day before I called. He had gone down to the local general store and while buying some groceries, he overheard a Chinese woman talking to the cashier about a dream that she was having. It was the very same dream he had been having for the past several days. He became agitated and his wife finally persuaded him to call someone for help.

He called my fellow worker right away, as they had been meeting to conclude an economic loan, and besides, we were the native affairs office. I told my co-worker that I wished I could help him but I was leaving for Europe to attend a World Council of Churches meeting. However, I could recommend two things. I would call a friend, a native minister in the United Church of Christ, to see if he could help out. The second thing I suggested was that he take the carved stones to the ocean and wash them. He was to place them in a well protected place in his house and then speak to them as if he was speaking to his beloved grandfather. He was to say that he wanted to keep the stones because they were his grandfather's and to tell of his profound love for that man. But he could not do what he had promised his grandfather because he lived in a different time and place.

I rang my friend up and explained the whole story to him, but he said that he, too, was going to be busy the next day. I asked if the new native minister just back from seminary could help out, and my friend laughed and said, "Oh, no, no. He doesn't believe in such things." What good is a minister for these people if due to his "beliefs" he cannot help a distressed family of his own people? Who else will help them? What are we teaching in those schools that our people come back with a useless education and we have to re-train them to be effective with their people? Maybe in time, my friend replied, they will be okay. In the end, he went to the family and blessed them and their house and the carved stones. And everything was all right.

If there is to be a deep experience and understanding of the Gospels, they need to become part of our experience, our understanding, and way of life; then Christian theology must be part of our world as much as our world would have to be part of the Church's. But all one needs to do is to look in the Book of Common Prayer, in the hymnal, or any other forms of Christian practice of life, and the majority of what we know about living as native peoples is not there. Even in translated Bibles, prayer books, hymnals, and other religious literary and educational publications in Native languages the essence of native rituals and ceremonies is still lacking.

Yet, the Bible was the first literary publication of our language and has contributed a distinctive legacy in our language between common, everyday words and usage to that of sacred occasions, prayers, and other religious uses. Without the continuance of this part of our language in our daily lives we may lose much of the sense of the sacredness of rituals and ceremonies that are so central to our life cycle, because we will no longer know how to appreciate the language. In a way, the English language, that is the King James/Shakespearian English of "Thee and Thou," has been the closest to a form of a sacred, ritualistic, language. True, writes biblical translator Stephen Mitchell, "English-speaking readers usually think of biblical language as Elizabethan: magniloquent, orotund, liturgical, archaic, full of *thees and thous and untos and therofs and prays.*"[10]

This is why Joseph Campbell commented, "they've translated the Mass out of ritual language and into a language that has a lot of domestic associations. The Latin of the Mass was language that threw you [the English speaker] out of the field of domesticity."[11] If not in the Church, where else will this part of our traditions be kept alive? In a modern world, surrounded by the dominance of English and American ways, native people have few opportunities to use their own language in their own land. At least a service in our own language would provide a refuge and possibility for one of the seeds for the language to flourish again. This is why the Church should and needs to be involved. And yet,

> In a really renewed liturgy we shall not be content with texts translated from another language. New creations will be needed. It remains true that the translation of texts from the Church's tradition is an invaluable exercise and necessary training for

the drawing up of our own texts, with the results that the new forms adopted should in some ways grow organically from forms already existing.[12]

Several years ago I bought a small out-of-print book of our folk stories in our language and translation. The last entry was a Christian prayer attributed to the last great traditional priest who became a Christian convert. It is a great prayer that is chanted. In time, I discovered that this attribution was not completely accurate. It appears, through other early printed sources, that this prayer was composed by a former warrior who had become a Christian. His name was Ka'eleoWaipi'o. He was the son of a man renowned for his skill in debate and in the traditional martial arts. Ka'eleoWaipi'o was part of the defeated army when the islands were united under one chief, but his life was saved by the wife of the victorious chief. As part of that court, he learned how to read and write and became a Christian, following the example of the woman who saved his life. It was said that he was "a man of learning ... who composed the dirges to Jesus." Furthermore, "Ka'eleoWaipi'o replaced the words of an 'ana'ana [sorcery] prayer with that of a Christian prayer. This prayer is called 'Kuaikulani.' It is a prayer of salvation and a prayer used on a day of trouble or distress."

It is evident that this prayer was well known. In an early printed account the native author wrote that when he was asked to lead a prayer he used "the prayer of Ka'eleoWaipi'o" when no words would come to him to lead in a spontaneous prayer. In translation:

Arise, stand up, stand,
fill up the ranks, stand, lest we be in darkness, in night,
You who are harsh, gather, stand.
A great God, an almighty God,
is Jehovah the one from the heavens.
A God dwelling in the heights, on the tips of the winds,
within the floating clouds, a rising fog upon the earth,

a rising rainbow on the ocean,
Jesus, our Redeemer from the far away lands to here,
from the zenith to the horizon, the rain from heaven falls,
Supreme Jehovah, our desire.
Sing praises to the moving heavens, the earth rejoices,
the Word has been received: knowledge, power, life.
Gathered at the Council of the chiefs, pray devoutly to Jehovah,
powerful priest for the islands, like a torch that knows our wrongs.
We all shall live, saved through Jesus. Amen.

Until recently this early, and possibly the first, prayer composed by a native Christian was forgotten from use. Today, its use in our services demonstrates the possibilities and potential that native insight has for new liturgies to further the "preaching of the gospel" for all peoples and communities, as did the transformation of the Church from Jewish to Greek in the early Christian tradition and history.

This can be accomplished when the opportunity for expression is received not as a threat to the prevailing culture of the Church, but as one of God's gifts, a gift that enlarges the Church's vision to the world. This process has existed since the first contact with missionaries, when native peoples reacted to the words and behavior of those missionaries. As first encounters led to deeper exploration and understanding, people like Ka'eleo Waipi'o began to express the Christian experience from their own insight. Some theologians have used different terms to describe this new phenomena, such as "contextualization," "indigenization," and/or "inculturation."

> Inculturation at the grass-roots means, among other things, stimulating liturgical and catechetical creativity in the community. In either case, a framework is needed at the outset, within which members of the community can exercise their gifts. Christian sacraments and celebration have their

own character and purpose which cannot be altered. This character and purpose must speak to the community through the forms and expressions of their own culture.[13]

So what might a native Book of Common Prayer look like? A recent example can be found in the New Zealand Prayer Book (1989). In it one can find some initial and tentative attempts at what Shorter is describing. Included are two special Maori rituals, the blessing of a home and the unveiling of a memorial (head-stone), that are central to contemporary Maori life, and now they add a possible new dimension to the life of all New Zealanders. In particular, there is a Song of Praise where the two languages lie side by side, and one can see in the Maori the invocation of the tradi-tional ancestral names of Ranginui (commonly known as "Sky Father") and Papa-Tuanuku ("Earth Mother") and in the English its equivalent "for the beauty of these islands."

This is not the de-emphasizing of what already exists. Without exception, central to our common faith is the Eucharist; however, validating the centrality of the Eucharist are the special prayers and rituals of our life cycle which serve as supplements to the unity of our communion of faith. For us they enhance, intensify, direct and give a deeper experience to, "Christian sacraments and celebration that have their own character and purpose which cannot be altered." Among these life cycle rituals must be the rites and prayers for the giving of names in a person's life; the recognition of the first birthday; the blessing of homes and places of work, the land that they are built on, the vehicles that transport us; the bless-ing of traditional objects of social value such as quilts and other prized items of prestige; the process and ritual in which we are able to reconcile personal or familial grievances; and especially the ritu-als, ceremonies, and prayers that we use to heal ourselves, literally called "prayers of thanksgiving and prayers of remembrance;" and the cleansing of the home and mourners during and after a death.

These rites and prayers remain in keeping with the ideals that their presence continues, namely, "protecting from evil, blessing with good things, prestige, well-being [health] and happiness..."

I do not think we should be afraid to share this material with other peoples, especially if it can help others. "There are no secrets. There's no mystery. There's only common sense," said Oren Lyons, Onondaga Faithkeeper.[14] These are the things that give us our identity and their wide use by our people may guarantee that they will not be lost or forgotten. We know God exists and when people exploit and abuse God's gifts ultimately they will destroy themselves. We should not be afraid. Now, in another time this would naturally have become a real prayer book, that is, something you and I could hold in our hands. In our communities it would probably be found in many households, even among those who are not in communion with us. I wonder if this prayer book would be welcomed in the homes and churches of other people. Probably not, and I would suspect in some circles it would be looked upon as a waste of time and funds.

We know what it feels like when people talk about wasting funds in this context. There was a time that the publisher of our native Hawaiian language Bible stopped printing so they could use the savings to print and smuggle Bibles into China. They stopped printing our Bible on the premise that since we all knew English there was no purpose in having a Bible in our language. It was a waste, they thought, so for nearly a generation our children were baptized and confirmed without receiving a Hawaiian Bible. Many families had none in their homes and, in fact, the last edition of this Bible could only be found in rare bookstores at a horrendous cost.

This situation, which was becoming quite desperate, was finally reversed because two elderly native women at a care home for native elders embarked on a project to hand type the entire Bible in large print so they would be able to read it. Their determination led people like myself to finally speak up, and argue that our language was not dead or useless and that the Bible, being the first printed expression of our language, was primary to our cultural survival. The publishing house recanted and, although the price has dramatically increased, we have a promise from them that our Bible will always be available.

This is why we should support the idea that such gifts, as culturally relevant services, should be received as supplements and made readily available to all through the ability to store them on computer, whether on the Internet or on file disks, ready to download when needed. We can print them as books in the communities that will use them intimately or they can be adopted or adapted by communities that would like to experience them once or more in their lives as gifts, if they so choose. The texts, rubrics, explanations, and even the sounds can be shared so that people can not only study them, but become intimate with them. Preventing another situation like the one with the Bible publishing house, we will no longer become so dependent upon others to control our worship and spiritual growth, and we will be able to determine the cost of production and expenses for our community needs, hopefully saving funds and trees, too.

This use of modern technology may help the sacredness of small communities and groups of people, like ours, to flourish, instead of deteriorating under the unity of conformity. But, it also will challenge us and other similar communities, as well as the dominant culture of our Church, to explore, practice and experience true diversity by providing a world full of alternative forms to the structure of the Eucharist and other rites of our common faith, without the excuse that such forms do not exist or are not available.

The storage and sharing of "new" liturgies and rites is only a tool that has the potential, as all tools have, to make our work and creation easier and more refined. For us it will help to restore and to heal a people from the damage of cultural destruction. This may well serve as a test as to how well we know our own people when we become more engaged in the life of our communities than ever before as a Church that truly proclaims itself to be among the people.

This is a tool that could compel all of us to consider what being "in communion" really is and means to be. The use or non-use of "new" ways of worship may be a true test of that communion, that true relationship of partnership with each other, beyond the nominal means that we have been attempting and struggling with.

Bibliography

Campbell, Joseph with Bill Moyers, *The Power of Myth,* DoubleDay, New York, 1988.

Geertz, Clifford, *The Interpretation of Cultures,* Basic Books, Inc., New York, 1973.

Mitchell, Stephen, *Genesis: A New Translation of the Classic Biblical Stories,* HarperCollins, New York, 1996.

Shorter, Aylward, *Toward a Theology of Inculturation,* Orbis Books, New York, 1988.

Wall, Steve and Harvey Arden, *Wisdomkeepers: Meetings with Native American Spiritual Elders,* Beyond Words Publishing, Inc., Oregon, 1990.

Notes

[1] Chair, Native American Committee, Diocese of Olympia, 1994.
[2] Geertz, 1973, 112
[3] Geertz, 1973, 128
[4] Geertz, 1973, 132
[5] Campbell, 1988, 82
[6] Malo, 1997
[7] Handy et. al., 75
[8] Handy et. al
[9] Handy et. al., 75
[10] Mitchell, 1996, xiv
[11] Campbell, 1988, 82
[12] Shorter, 1988,192
[13] Shorter, 1988, 263
[14] Wall, 1990, 64

Great Spirit!

You did reveal Your loving concern to our ancestors so that they called You the Great, Holy, and Mysterious One—Wakantanka, the Creator and Sustainer of all.

In Your love, You gave us Mother Earth; The Wonders of Heaven; and the Beauty of Nature for our enjoyment, where all could live in peace as sisters and brothers of Your creation.

For centuries our people walked in beauty before You! For this rich heritage, help us to be eternally grateful!

Because You are ever a Great, Eternal and Living Spirit, in due time, You chose to send Your Son among us that all peoples might know Your continued love and concern.

Guide us in our days; help each of us as Your children to be proud of our great heritage, to know and to be who we are, and to share with others becoming one humanity within Your everlasting love, as the many colors come together to form the rainbow in the sky.

Finally, gracious Father, give us New Visions of Your Will and help each one of us to have a share in each other's accomplishments. Amen.

The Rt. Rev. Harold S. Jones[1]

Incarnation into Culture: Becoming the Church in a new millennium

Clayton L. Morris

When Christians gather in communities populated by people of different races and cultures, they discover that it is difficult for people from one culture to participate in the value structure of another. In its ongoing dialogue about the complementary issues of prejudice and inclusivity, the church has found a new patch of ground on which to stage conversation. Whether the distinction between cultures is a matter of race, culture or gender, as it strives to eradicate prejudice and promote inclusivity, the church is beginning to focus on a question that moves beyond the primary topics. Is it possible for a dominant culture to see value beyond its own cultural habits and assumptions?

Conversation about prejudice and inclusivity must note that the habits, values, and assumptions of one culture do not automatically apply to other cultural contexts. All too often the two sets of habits, values, and assumptions are not recognized by either group as roughly analogous.

For example, people who live in rural communities value the act of greeting one another as they pass on the street. It is almost impossible to imagine passing someone without, at least, a simple nod. City folk, on the other hand, who encounter hundreds, or even thousands of people between home and work on the subway, wouldn't consider noticing anyone but a close friend in that chance encounter. People from each of these perspectives find the opposing habit difficult to understand and engage.

The development of inclusivity demands interactivity. Inclusivity is not automatically accomplished when the established group lets down its cultural barriers and welcomes the stranger. It is, rather, a process of the stranger and host getting to know one another and developing a relationship that makes it possible for host and stranger to belong to the same community. Inclusivity turns the process of welcoming into an occasion of renewal for the whole community. It is not the one being invited in who must be changed and "educated" in order to fit into the existing culture. The newcomer changes and educates the community every bit as much as the community changes and educates the newcomer.

The essays in this volume speak to issues of inclusivity that are specific to Native American communities in the Episcopal Church. The Christian era in America includes an embarrassing history of governmental and ecclesial manipulation of the lives of our native sisters and brothers. But as our native brothers and sisters find a Christian witness and a Christian way of being, they represent a perspective the entire church needs to know.

Inculturation of Anglicanism in North America

When the Episcopal Church gets dressed for an important occasion—the Sunday Eucharist, for example—it wears mostly English clothes. The language is English. The musical repertoire and artistic representations are mostly English. The assumptions guiding worshipers as they interact with the liturgy are consistent with English custom. Until the Episcopal Church discovered that its constituency was not mostly comprised of persons of British lineage transplanted to the American continent, Episcopal liturgists assumed that their task as educators was to raise the worshiper's level of liturgical, aesthetic and social sophistication. Converts to the Episcopal Church from other denominational bodies were often seen as folks anxious to elevate their social standing in the community. Worshiping in the English style contributed to that goal.

From the cultural and historical perspective of the casual American observer, the process of inculturation that facilitated the transfer of British religious habit and style from one side of the Atlantic to the other was a natural and unremarkable one. For the most part, the transplanting of Anglicanism to America seemed a simple matter of Anglicans moving to a new home and bringing their religious baggage with them. Over time, the Anglican Church in the United States found its niche in American society, where it thrived without much need for self-critical analysis until the race riots of the 1950s and the crisis of the Vietnam War in the following decade. To the extent that this process of inculturation was accomplished easily, it is because the newcomers to the American continent were not usually interested in dialogue with the cultural life of the resident Native population.

From the same perspective, the nineteenth-century transplanting of Anglicanism amidst cultures around the world seemed more complicated. Christian theology and British custom collided with foreign cultural, religious, and philosophical patterns and assumptions. From the British missionary's point of view, the appropriate resolution was obvious. Christianity *and* British civilization seen in combination, as the superior system, had to replace the inferior, indigenous civilization, along with its religious heritage.

Thus, until the last decades of the twentieth century, the inculturative energy in the Anglican Communion has been a process of supplanting supposedly inferior levels of religious, social, and political traditions with supposedly superior English versions. Anglicans have sought to *improve* the lot of the people they evangelized, working to better the world through the application of their theological, ecclesial and religious perspective.

Looking To The Future

As the church enters the new millennium, everything is different. The 1979 Book of Common Prayer put baptism in a central focus of the liturgical life of the Episcopal Church. And in placing the initiatory rite in a central focus, the prayer book also rearticulated the meaning of baptism and of participation within the life of the church. The 1979 baptismal rite makes explicit what is, at best, implicit in the earlier rite. When the community prepares to baptize an adult, the formative process is focused on the church's ministry of reconciliation, and it becomes clear that the primary ministers in the Christian community are its baptized members.

This is a shift in the way the church understands participation in the life of the church. In the older, more established model, new Episcopalians were added to the church's membership by birth, not baptism. The baptismal rite was observed as a pleasant formality, but it didn't bear the burden of articulating the church's mission. In that older vision of church within culture, the clergy were seen as the ministers, and the church's members were recipients of the church's ministry. In the newly articulated vision of a renewed baptismal theology, the church—the baptized—are the ministers. The world is the mission field.

All this is a process of inculturation; a process of articulating the Gospel of Jesus Christ in a changing cultural setting. For the Episcopal Church in the United States, the new cultural setting is one in which Christians realize that their sisters and brothers in Christ are not the Episcopalians in their neighborhood with whom they attend church. Rather, the brothers and sisters with whom Christ calls them to be reconciled are all the human beings on the planet.

This new realization demands a re-inculturation of Christianity for Anglo-American Episcopalians. For twenty years, the baptismal and Eucharistic rites of the 1979 Book of Common Prayer have quietly urged the church into a renewed vision of the connections between ministry and worship. The church has resisted, sometimes not so quietly, the establishment of that new vision. Congregations have consciously, or perhaps unconsciously, wrapped the celebration of these rites in 1928 prayer book clothing, so as to obscure the prophetic voice of the incarnate One among us.

And so, the church struggles today to face the truth proclaimed by the prayer book. God created a world of wholeness and beauty.

That wholeness has been shattered by greed. God's children are scattered in hunger, homelessness, poverty, disease, and despair. The disciples of Christ are called to realize God's creative vision of wholeness and beauty. It is easy for Episcopalians to talk about inculturating third world people into a normative *Anglican* understanding of church. The more difficult task for Episcopalians is to understand that for the church to become what it needs to be, it must understand itself, and be understood, as a body of people working to restore the wholeness of Creation.

Christianity and Native America

Christianity came to Native Americans violently. Government agents swept into healthy communities forcing people to abandon their traditional worldview in favor of European religious and cultural sensibilities. The witness of Black Elk, a Lakota who lived on the Pine Ridge Reservation in South Dakota, chronicles that history.[2]

The life of Black Elk, who was born in 1866, is a useful example in a study of the inculturation of Christianity because his experience represents a unique combining of two cultures into an integrated whole. He struggled to reconcile two sets of contrasting elements. He was a Native American forced to live in the context of a culture which was applying European cultural sensibilities to the American scene. Within the boundaries of his own worldview, he struggled to make sense of two religious systems; his native tradition and that of the Roman Catholic Church.

In the course of his career, Black Elk functioned both as a medicine man and catechist, providing a confusion for those who have studied his life. Was he a native healer who used the Catholic Church to his political advantage? Was he a Christian who played on his native culture in order to further his Catholic zeal? Or, was he an well-integrated human being who found a commonality in his traditional culture and new-found religion which could be synthesized in order to provide for the welfare of his people? Is it possible that he was years ahead of his time, inculturating Christianity into Native culture?

Religious behavior, for the traditional Native American, is bound up with everyday life. Spirituality is an aspect of one's approach to the exigencies of day-to-day survival. Religion, as a distinct segment of life to be practiced in isolation from the ongoing daily round, is unknown.

In the old Lakota system, ceremony and spirituality were woven into the fabric of culture, scarcely existing as a separate entity. "Traditional religion," as one religious position among others, is a product of the reservation period (1865-1890), during which the Sun Dance, once the central Lakota religious ritual, became the central ritual of traditional Lakota religion. There is a world of difference between the two.

The distinction between Native ritual practice and Native American religion is roughly analogous to the distinction between the religious experience of the Amish community and the practice of Christians belonging to mainstream American denominations. The Amish incorporate their religious convictions into their daily routine while most Christians observe their convictions as one aspect of life.

The scope of this short essay doesn't allow a description of the complex ritual system of a native community. But the place of the Sun Dance in the experience of the Lakota people and its impact on the development of a Christian consciousness in that community cannot be ignored.

The Sun Dance, in the pre-reservation life of the Lakota people, was the ritual that bound the community together and expressed its worldview and way of being. It was an event in the experience of the people that gave cosmic meaning to life and maintained economic and political stability in the tribe. One sees, in Holler's description of the Sun Dance, a community event that gathered the people in the presence of the Holy One, rehearsed the hopes, sorrows, dreams and needs of the people and through the witness of a leader called the community to the task at hand, and in the process, considered and responded to the needs of the poor.

After the Civil War, westward expansion caught the attention of the country, and that drive put the U.S. Army in direct contact with native communities. The complicated result of this meeting—military slaughter countered the government's response of confinement on reservations—is not the subject of this essay. But it is important to note that the ritual life of the Lakota people was banned by the government agents because their cultural prejudice could not see beyond the surface of the Sun Dance experience to appreciate the integrity out of which it emerged. For those agents, the Lakota's piercing and potlatch, which represented courage and commonality, could only be read as brutality and waste.

The response of church and state to the ritual life of the native community was brutal. The government sought to eradicate Native languages and ritual practice. As a result, it simultaneously criminalized the community's ritual life and economic system. History has recorded the sad legacy of these tragic events. While church and state were sufficiently committed to their *enlightened* worldview to force it on the tribal communities in their charge, they were either unable or unwilling to support native communities in the process of transition to a way of life acceptable to church and state.

What happened in the brutal nineteenth-century encounter between these two American cultures? Why did it seem necessary for the dominant Anglo culture to destroy, or at least contain the powerless native community? Does the experience of the Lakota community, in its development, use, and loss of the Sun Dance, have something to add to the church's quest for a renewed sense of mission? Is it possible that the threatening feature of Native culture and ritual practice was its integration with nature and the whole of life? Could it be that the new Americans, as they came into contact with the Native population, encountered images that were so engaging that they had to be repulsed?

Native American members of the Episcopal Church are often Christians with experience of their tribal ceremonial tradition. Thus, they have the luxury of crafting Christian ceremonial and a congregational lifestyle evocative of their traditional spirituality. Perhaps, as they explore the relationship of ethnic roots to Christian practice, the church in general will find the possibility of recovering a sense of groundedness that tribal culture affords.

An Ecclesiology for the new millennium

The difference between good and evil in Christian thought can be seen in the contrast between communal sharing and personal greed. The New Testament is filled with contrasting images of the community's acts of mercy in response to human need, and the foolishness of private hoarding of the world's goods. The baptismal covenant is, itself, grounded in the notion that the task of the church is restoring the unity of creation—that is—gathering ALL God's creatures into the circle. The giant flaw in human consciousness is the nagging fear that the communal approach doesn't work. So, all people are tempted to keep something aside against that failure. Some become obsessed with the private acquisition of wealth, and eventually, this increasingly voracious greed tests the limits of Earth's ability to support life, and the human population is split into two groups; some who live in luxury, and others who starve.

One way to find protection from the human responsibility to live in community is to create distance from images likely to conjure up the urging of conscience. Congregations tend to gather people of similar ethnic, social and economic identity. Thus, *all God's children* are seen to be all the people in the neighborhood. In affluent communities, talk of hunger simply doesn't compute. Everyone within view is healthy and well fed. Even the Eucharistic celebration, intended to remind worshipers of the centrality of abundant feasting among all who come to the table, is denigrated by the habit of celebrating it without anything identifiable as food.

Without the voice of prophecy to keep the church on task, it is inevitable that commitment to inclusivity and community slowly degenerates into the defense of tradition and stability. The project of maintaining a culture in which everyone is honored and protected as a member of the community is eventually lost in the private, personal, acquisition of spiritual well being and religious security.

Over the course of the twentieth century, the prophetic voice within the church has called its members to accountability. The restoration of baptism and Eucharist at the center of the church's worship life began a process which has continued with calls to restore an abundant use of image, symbol, and gesture in the context of renewed commitment to preaching aimed at converting the church to its ministry of reconciliation. The church is currently in a pitched battle over style in liturgical celebration. Should the *traditions* of the late nineteenth and early twentieth centuries be protected and reinforced for the future, or should the church re-examine its ritual life in the context of its call to mission, in order to find new (or perhaps the transformation of old) ways of leading God's people into lives devoted to peace, justice, and the celebration of radical inclusive community?

The choice to re-examine the church's experience of the nineteenth and twentieth centuries is the process of re-inculturation described at the beginning of this essay. The church's task is one of restoring the ritual integrity of its corporate life, in order to reassert its task of ministry in and to the world.

The Native Christians of North America are engaged in a courageous exploration of how Eucharistic rites, that are expressive of their traditional worldview, might be crafted. From a northern European cultural perspective, this exploration is threatening. It seems that our native sisters and brothers are exchanging Anglican ritual patterns and theological assumptions for something else. But from a vantage point outside both perspectives, the view is more like one of two cultural perspectives in search of patterns which will make sense in this new millennium. To some degree, both cultures have realized that the ecclesial patterns of the late nineteenth and early twentieth centuries are no longer sufficient to support Christ's ministry to the world.

Our native brothers and sisters bring to the table a unique gift that must not be squandered. As a people still in possession of their traditional, native, ritual forms, they provide all of us with a glimpse of a pre-enlightenment approach to life and spirituality. If the larger community can see that these people once thrived in a cultural circumstance that promoted respect for the earth which feeds and sustains life, and understood the need to provide for all creatures, perhaps their witness can lead the church forward into a renewed sense of its own identity. And even more to the point, if Christians in the new millennium can find the courage to investigate a culture in which life and religion are one, not two realities, a new sense of what the church must and might be will be free to emerge.

Notes

[1] First American Indian bishop of the Episcopal Church.
[2] see Clyde Holler in *Black Elk's Religion: the Sun Dance and Lakota Catholicism,* Syracuse University Press, 1995.

The belief that life forces are present within the land, and emerge at the impulse of the Creator Spirit, is consistent with the picture presented in Genesis 1. According to the imagery in the chapter of Genesis, all vegetation and animal life emerge from the land at the summons of God.

The Rainbow Spirit Elders[1]

Frigid Cold Can't Stop
the Holy Spirit

Ginny Doctor

*"We use to sing old Indian hymns up at the Mission. Everybody could
sing. That church would roar . . . I can still hear that singing . . ."*
The late Art Matthew, Tanana Elder.

I have been in Alaska since September of 1993 serving as an
Episcopal missionary. Most of the time I have been based in
Tanana, an Athabascan village about 130 miles west of Fairbanks.
Tanana has a rich Anglican history as its geographic location, the
confluence of the mighty Yukon and the Tanana Rivers, made it a
focal point for trade, commerce and Christian formation. I have
heard many stories of the "Mission" days when people came from
all around, mostly by dog team, in winter, and boat, during the
summer, to attend services at the Church of Our Savior Mission.
But there came a time when all of that activity slowed down and
things changed along the Yukon. These changes affected the religious and spiritual life of the people.

• • •

When I first moved to Tanana I heard folks talk about "White
Alice." I had no idea what they were referring to, but thought that
if I listened I would find out. That didn't happen. One day, while
with some friends, I finally asked about "White Alice." My friends
said they would take me to meet her. We traveled on a gravel road
about 12 miles into the hills behind Tanana. At the top of a hill

were four structures that looked like the old drive-in movie screens. My friend said, "Meet White Alice."

White Alice, I discovered, was a military installation; part of the Distant Early Warning System. The drive-in screens were actually radar screens. This installation was abandoned in the early 1980s in favor of satellite communication. The U.S. government just deserted this site after spending millions of dollars to build it. After meeting White Alice, I saw a parallel between her and Tanana church history. Both White Alice and St. James Mission (successor of the Church of the Savior) had been abandoned. I took to calling Tanana the "Diocese of White Alice." Some saw the humor, others didn't.

I went to Tanana not to do ministry "to" the people but to do ministry with the people. I understood quickly that the people liked to sing. I spent hours practicing the guitar, chording songs, and learning new ones. This would become an important aspect of my ministry. At my first service, there to be just a helper, the lay reader wanted me to do everything. I was reluctant. I told him to just do as he always did and that I would help with the singing. When it came time for the sermon, he looked at me and said, "Now we will have some words from Ginny." Being totally unprepared to give a sermon, I saw it as a good opportunity to tell the congregation who I was and what I was doing in Tanana. We struggled through some hymns and gospel type songs. I hadn't yet learned enough to be effective. The elders in the congregation like the hymns from the 1940 Hymnal, while the younger people like the gospel type songs. I spent several hours with an elder who went through the Hymnal and told me the songs that were the "good ones." Hymns like "Nearer My God to Thee," "What a Friend We Have in Jesus," "I Need Thee Every Hour," and "Jesus Calls Us O'er the Tumult," were some of the favorites. Happily, I grew up singing in a choir where those kinds of hymns were sung every Sunday.

• • •

This past Christmas was a time when we all had to use the gifts that God gave us to use.

A couple of days before Christmas one of the Tanana "Uncles" died. We would have to do a funeral during the Christmas season. The weather forecast was for extreme cold. The village leaders had planned a Christmas celebration at the community hall. We were asked to bring an ornament to put on the sparsely decorated tree. This ornament was to be a memorial for a loved one. One by one people came forth, put their ornament on the tree and named the loved one who was being remembered. Athabascans are good about remembering those who have gone before and many tears were given that night. In that cold community hall, where outside the temperature had dropped to -45 degrees, those tears glistened from strings of lights. There was warmth. The Holy Spirit was present and breathing warm air into the hearts of the people.

From the hall we moved to St. James' Mission, a log church that sits prominently in the center of town on the north bank of the Yukon. Our two deacons, the Rev. Helen Peters (perpetual deacon) and the recently ordained the Rev. John Starr (transitional deacon) were busy getting things ready when I arrived. John always rings the bell twice, about fifteen minutes apart. He rings it for a long time so folks know it is time for church. When I left my cabin that night it was so cold and clear that the ringing bell sounded as if it were next door. Loud and strong, clear and sweet, calling the people to come and worship.

We were all vested and ready to begin. Helen said, "Let's pray now." The three of us formed a circle holding hands while Helen prayed that the Holy Spirit be present with us and for God's guidance and direction. It was time to begin. We opened with "Angels We Have Heard On High." As I lead the hymns there comes a point where I stop singing (but not playing the guitar) so that I can listen to the voices. That night, it was a wondrous sound with all those voices, indeed a choir of angels. We moved through the service and at the "Peace" everyone smiled and was greeted with warm hugs or hearty handshakes. There is nothing brighter than the smile of an elder at Christmas. Finally, the cup was put away, the leftover bread stored for the next day. With dimmed lights and coldness outside, we closed with "Silent Night, Holy Night." The people were warm, the Holy Spirit was present, and as the doors opened we saw the night and above the frozen Yukon we saw Christmas Eve's stars of wonder.

On Christmas day, it was still cold. After the Christmas day service we walked up to the Tanana Elder's residence to take Holy Communion to those who could not make it to the church. Mary Starr served her husband, Paul, and me a tasty Christmas dinner of moose steak and hand picked low bush cranberries from the wilderness.

The next day, it warmed up to -20 degrees. I traveled to the village of Hughes to perform Christmas service for the villagers. Hughes is 120 miles northwest on the Koyukuk River. I was flown there by Dan Treakle, lay pastor/pilot for the Lutheran Association of Missionaries and Pilots with Bishop Mark MacDonald also along for the trip. Upon landing, we saw there was a fire warming the newly constructed church. We walked through newly fallen snow over to the church. One of the villagers soon came out and welcomed us. The people began to gather and Bishop Mark led some Christmas songs with the guitar. He gave a short sermon and blessed the people. The bishop and the pilot then left to fly to Rampart, another village on the Yukon River. The people of Hughes rarely get the opportunity to receive the sacrament and Bishop Mark gave me special permission to bring Holy Communion to them. The moment was awesome for me as I looked into the glistening eyes of the elders and placed the holy body of Jesus in their hands. After the service, I suggested that we return later for singing and praise. This is what we did. We sang every song that I knew and some that I didn't. And then I began to hear that "roar."

• • •

I return to Tanana in time to help with the funeral for the "Uncle" that died. It is cold again, -50 degrees, but a clear beautiful day. All three of us—the deacons Helen and John and I—conduct the service at the school gymnasium. Our little log church is too small for everyone who has come to pay their respects and comfort the family. The service concludes and, as is the custom, we open the casket for people to say goodbye. I lead several songs that the people know well. We didn't think to bring our songbooks. The body is taken to the mission for burial in the mission cemetery. Many men worked for two days to dig the grave in the frigid weather. My friend Paul has obtained special permission from the school board to use the school bus to transport people to the Old Mission, about three miles outside of town. As I exit the bus, Uncle's sister, Hannah, says to me, "Aren't you going to take your instrument?" I reply, "Of course, just forgot." After the committal, following tradition, the men fill in the grave while the women sing. Hannah wants me to play. Some say it's too cold but I am willing to try.

A big bonfire has been lit. I get as close to the fire as I can stand. I play the songs that I have learned since being in Tanana. I can see the Old Mission Church. I can feel the presence of the Holy Spirit. It doesn't matter that I can't feel my fingers because I began to hear that "roar." Everybody is singing, that church is roaring.

I can still hear that singing.

Notes

[1] *From Rainbow Spirit Theology: Towards an Australian Aboriginal Theology*, (Harper Collins, Australia, 1997).

This also goes for the churches. They say, "God is looking at you; he is not happy with the things you do, and for not believing him." And also, "On this earth there is no Holy Being," is often heard by others. If the second is true, then what is it you are standing upon? What makes you strong? It is the Holy One who makes you strong; so why say there is no Holy Being on earth – for it is not true! I believe in the Holy One, for I am sure of his existence. A person is born upon this earth. His or her mother's and father's veins and blood were put together to create that boy or girl. There is a Holy One – he is not gone. The white people depend upon the earth the same as we depend upon it; it is the everyday part of their lives, but they are doing all sorts of bad things to it – the very earth that is the living part of us.

Ch'ahadiniini' Binali (Navajo)[1]

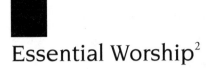

Essential Worship[2]

Leonel L. Mitchell

When I was a parish priest, I noted that there were three things that tended to get deeply confused by the parishioners:

- The faith once delivered to the saints
- The Anglican Tradition
- The way the Rector Emeritus liked to do things

Unfortunately this confusion is not confined to one parish or to the Episcopal Church. By and large, we are not very good either at helping others to sort these out, or sorting them out ourselves. We tend to confuse things that we find appealing with the core of Christian worship.

The problem becomes particularly acute when we are dealing, not with one eccentric parish, but with the entire problem of cultural relationships. The late Leo Melania, coordinator of prayer book revision during the preparation of the Book of Common Prayer 1979, told me that, although he had encountered the Anglican Church of Canada in his youth, he had never seriously considered becoming an Anglican, since he was of Syrian, not English, ethnicity.

This may be an extreme example, but it is difficult for those of us who do worship in English even to imagine what it means to be an Anglican who speaks French, Spanish, or Korean. How much of what we associate with the worship of the Episcopal Church must a Navajo adopt to be an Episcopalian?

The Core of Christian Worship

Vatican Council II, in its seminal "Constitution on the Sacred Liturgy"[3] offered these directives, which are sage advice worth listening to:

> The liturgy is made up of unchangeable elements divinely instituted, and of elements subject to change. These latter not only may be changed but ought to be changed with the passage of time, if they have suffered from the intrusion of anything out of harmony with the inner nature of the liturgy or have become less suitable.[4]

The document went on to speak of "legitimate variations and adaptations to different groups, regions, and peoples,"[5] and recognized that, "In some places and circumstances...an even more radical adaptation of the liturgy is needed."[6]

In this context we should note two resolutions of the 1988 Lambeth Conference. Resolution 22: Christ and Culture reads:

> This Conference...urges the Church everywhere to work at expressing the unchanging Gospel of Christ in words, actions, names, customs, liturgies, which communicate relevantly in each contemporary culture.

Resolution 47: Liturgical Freedom reads:

> This Conference resolves that each Province should be free, subject to essential universal norms of worship and to a valuing of traditional liturgical materials to seek that expression of worship which is appropriate to its Christian people in their cultural context.

We might then begin by asking ourselves just what in our liturgical tradition is *of the essence* of Christian worship. What is the core of Christian liturgy? If our standard is the same as Vatican II, then our list will be very short indeed. Divinely instituted elements in the liturgy include:

- proclamation of the gospel;
- assembling for worship;
- celebration of baptism with water;
- celebration of the Eucharist with bread and wine;
- ministry of reconciliation (in some form); and
- praying of the Lord's Prayer.

You may be able to think of something else, but it is a very lean core. I would personally wish to add to that core those elements that have been a part of the Christian tradition of worship since patristic times:

- offering of daily prayer;
- weekly celebration of the Lord's Day;
- observance of at least the major festivals of the church year; and
- an ordered ministry of Word and Sacrament.

Daily Prayer

The daily offices, in their current form, are heavily dependent on Benedictine monasticism, but the idea of daily services of prayer did not begin with the monastics. Cathedrals and large city churches had public services of psalm singing and prayer from the end of the persecutions, and much earlier Christian writers spoke of daily prayers, morning and evening, as a part of Christian life. Presumably this was a part of the church's inheritance from the synagogue, where the eighteen benedictions were said twice daily, and individuals were obligated to recite the *shema* three times. Presumably this was the context in which the disciples asked Jesus to teach them to pray, and the Lord's Prayer in addition to, or instead of, the *shema* became the prayer of Christians.

The Lord's Day

The celebration of the Lord's Day, the day of resurrection, on the first day of the week, with the celebration of the Lord's Supper probably goes back to New Testament times. The expressions "Lord's Day" and "Lord's Supper" are related. From at least the time of Justin Martyr in the second century, Christians have kept the Lord's Day with a service of Word and Sacrament including the reading and preaching of the gospel, the offering of prayers, and the celebration of the Eucharist.

The Church Year

By contrast, the liturgical year was rather slow in developing. Easter and Pentecost began to be observed in the second century, and Epiphany shortly thereafter. Lent was in place by the time of the Council of Nicea. Christmas, which began in Rome in the third century, spread to the rest of the church in the fourth. Since then the Church of Scotland in the sixteenth century has been unique among major Christian churches in abandoning it—and they have brought it back. It is certainly possible to be a Christian without observing Christmas (or there were no Christians in the apostolic church), but it has become a stable part of Christian observance.

The liturgical calendar is shaped largely by the seasons: Christian observance of Easter has always been tied to the first full moon of spring (with Lent and the long season of Pentecost falling into place accordingly); Christmas became fixed on the calendar in relation to the winter solstice. Interesting questions arise, therefore, when these seasonal feasts are celebrated in the Southern Hemisphere. Should Christians in that hemisphere continue to keep the traditional feast dates, or should they reschedule them to conform to their own seasonal calendar? As far as I know, no church has done this.

Christian Initiation

The liturgical seasons have also been integrated, since at least the fourth century, into the celebration of Christian Initiation, with preparation of candidates for baptism during Lent, baptism at the Great Vigil of Easter, and the fifty days of Eastertide as the time of *mystagogia*, during which the neophytes were incorporated into the sacramental life of the church.

The World Council of Church's ecumenical statement, *Baptism, Eucharist, and Ministry* (a.k.a. "The Lima Document") makes a valuable distinction between those things which are necessary for baptism and those which should find a place in a comprehensive service of Christian Initiation. In the first category we place baptism with water, and the confession of faith in the triune God. In the second category are such actions as making specific promises, blessing the water, anointing with chrism, and laying on of hands—actions that make clear the meaning of what we are doing but are not strictly necessary for "full initiation by water and the Holy Spirit."

The Ministry of Word and Sacrament

We no longer claim, as Cranmer did in his preface to the Ordinal of 1550, that:

> It is evident unto all men, diligently reading Holy Scripture and ancient Authors, that from the Apostles' time there have been these Orders of Ministers in Christ's Church—Bishops, Priests, and Deacons."[7]

We do however continue to assert the following:

> The Holy Scriptures and ancient Christian writers make it clear that from the apostles' time, there have been different ministries within the Church. In particular, since the time of the New Testament, three distinct orders of ordained ministers have been characteristic of Christ's holy catholic Church.[8]

Christians have traditionally been ordained to the Ministry of Word and Sacrament by the laying on of hands with prayer. This ministry has traditionally, but not universally, been called the priesthood or presbyterate. This ministry has included presiding at the community's liturgy and preaching the gospel. It has also included the ministry of reconciliation. (According to Frederick Dennison Maurice, even those churches that consider the preaching of the gospel to be the only function of the minister hold in some way to the ministry of reconciliation, given that preaching is understood by them to be the *way* to absolve sinners.)

The ministry of *episkope* or episcopal oversight always has been exercised in some way within the church, although not always by people we would call bishops. Men and women always have been ordained to a ministry of *diakonia*. (I would like to say more about the diaconate, but, unfortunately, our theology and practice of *diakonia* is sufficiently confused to make it difficult to say exactly what the Christian tradition of the diaconate is, or ought to be. Certainly, it is an area in which all of our churches today have fallen short of our theological standard.)

A Minimum Standard
A church ordering its liturgical life in this way would, without doubt, be Christian—and worshiping in accordance with Christian tradition. In fact, one of the truly remarkable ecumenical breakthroughs of the twentieth century has been the recognition, exemplified by the Lima Document, of these principles by a wide spectrum of Christian theologians and churches.

The Anglican Tradition
If we consider the Chicago-Lambeth Quadrilateral as a defining statement for Anglicanism, then the only necessary addition to the above minimum standards is the insistence that *episkope* be exercised by bishops and ordinations be under their presidency. Of course, we should not be surprised to find that we have added so

little to the basic core of Christian worship. The Quadrilateral itself describes its four points as:

> the principles of unity exemplified by the undivided Catholic Church during the first ages of its existence; which principles we believe to be the substantial deposit of Christian Faith and Order committed by Christ and his Apostles to the Church unto the end of the world.[9]

Anglicanism has often described itself as having no distinctive doctrines or practices, but holding the faith of the undivided Catholic Church. If it is true that Anglicanism is simply a particular expression of the Catholic Church, then we shall be hard pressed to find things that are distinctively and essentially Anglican.

What then is the Anglican tradition in worship? If there is a single thing that might be termed characteristic of Anglican worship it is that it be in the language of the people. Unfortunately, this principle has been stated more frequently than it has been implemented. A few years ago, for example, only one parish in a diocese in Argentina had any services in Spanish. Of course the American Prayer Book, or portions of it, does exist in Spanish, French, Korean, Lakota, Navajo, and Chinese, but they are translations of the English into those languages. The "language of the people" is more than words that are comprehensible. It must use the thought forms of the people. It must be compatible with the culture. As the preface to the Canadian Book of Alternative Services says:

> Liturgy is not the gospel but it is a principal process by which the Church and the gospel are brought together for the sake of the life of the world. It is consequently vital that its form wear the idiom, the cadence, the worldview, the imagery of the people who are engaged in that process in every generation.[10]

I would add, "in every place," for we offer our thanks and praise, in the words of the Rite I Eucharistic preface, "at all times, and in all places."

In his book, *The Identity of Anglican Worship*, David Stancliffe, the Bishop of Salisbury, came up with three ingredients he felt could be labeled "Anglican":

> First, there is an integrated feel about Anglican liturgy that has its origins in the union of heart and mind, of word and sacrament, of text and ceremonial. Our worship is earthed in a theology, which is incarnational, and a sacramentality, which is organic and affirmative.... Our liturgy is ordered, not regimented, and it is related to how we think and how we live.
>
> Second, and closely related, we are people of the book, or rather, of a family of books. In spite of cultural differences, the revised books for worship produced by the Churches in the family of the Anglican Communion still show a remarkable family likeness. This is also true of ceremonial.... Our tradition does not exist in the abstract: it needs to find its own climate and memory in order to embody its dignity.
>
> And third, there is an elusive but very distinctive Anglican style, which has a lot to do with the acceptance and integration of a number of different layers, which create a sense of unity by inclusion, rather than of uniformity.[11]

These ingredients seem to me archetypically Anglican. When you hear them you say, "Oh, yes! Quite so!" but you find them difficult to exegete and apply. This does not mean that they are not true.

Perhaps Stancliffe's most important statement is, "Our tradition does not exist in the abstract: it needs to find its own climate and memory in order to embody its dignity." Anglicanism only exists in actual congregations in the member churches of the Anglican Communion, which means that it must be different from time to time and place to place.

Cultural Diversity

Over the last century, Anglicans have become used to a great deal of diversity in liturgical celebration. Initially it was diversity from parish to parish, or diocese to diocese, but now it is diversity within the same congregation. I remember one parish bulletin that included both Morning Prayer and Sermon at 11 a.m. on Sundays, and Rosary and Benediction in the evening, sponsored by the parish chapter of the Society of the Living Rosary of Our Lady and St. Dominic. And this was before the 1979 Prayer Book appeared! Today charismatic folk Masses, stately choral Eucharists, and family celebrations with children's hymns and multimedia sermons may all coexist in one parish.

This same diversity is possible among cultures, both within the multicultural context of the United States and internationally. We recognize that Chinese Anglicans may not choose to sing Anglican chant, and we readily make allowance for cultural diversity in music and art. We need also to make allowances for it in prayer forms and ritual gestures. In spite of its great beauty, the Roman collect form as rendered into Cranmerian English is not the only possible prayer form for Anglicans. Some Native Americans, for example, choose to pass a pipe during the exchange of the peace. The pipe is a sacred symbol in their culture, and its use at the peace is important to some congregations. For others it is a part of the "old way" they left behind when they accepted Christianity. If Anglicanism is Catholic Christianity, then it must be possible to be genuinely Anglican and authentically Lakota, or Syrian, or African American, or Japanese. We all understand this, and, I am sure, subscribe to it in theory, but in practice we are often uncertain whether congregations that do not use "traditional" Anglican church music or wear "traditional" Anglican vestments are genuinely Episcopalian. But if we take our theology seriously and believe in the Incarnation of the Word of God and in the catholicity of the Church, then not only Christianity, but also Anglicanism is set free from its bondage to any one cultural expression. In fact, an Anglican liturgy rooted and grounded in the gospel and in the indigenous culture is more Anglican than an imitation of Canterbury Cathedral in Ghana or of King's College, Cambridge, in Fiji.

Perhaps the question we really need to ask is what should American Anglican liturgy look like? In 1790, the answer was clear. It was supposed to look like English Anglicanism without the prayers for the king, just as American society was English society without the king. Today the United States is no longer an extension of England, nor is the Episcopal Church simply the Church of England in America. The Book of Common Prayer 1979 has moved us in new and different directions, directions which the other Anglican Churches appear to wish to follow or to parallel. But our culture is not homogenous. We are a polyglot, multicultural nation, and the Episcopal Church can be truly an American church only if it is prepared to be multicultural.

The Prayer Book

The Book of Common Prayer in its multiple national, regional, and linguistic identities, along with the various alternative service books of those churches which have not revised their prayer books, are distinctively Anglican. But simply having a service book does not make a church Anglican. The Orthodox, Roman Catholics, and Lutherans have service books, but their service books are tools to be used in the celebration of the liturgy, not objects of quasi-reverence. To an extent unparalleled in other churches, Anglican identity is formed by the Prayer Book—a book of common prayer for the people of God, not an altar book for the minister.

The Anglican Prayer Books do have a family resemblance, but they are not clones. Some of the resemblance comes from our sharing of the common Christian core of worship, but it is more than that. The New Zealand Prayer Book, even when the overtones of Cranmer's mellifluous English are replaced by Maori or Tongan, remains undeniably Anglican, as do Zanzibar's Swahili Mass and the Eastern Orthodox-like liturgy for India. It has been said many times, but it is the use of the Prayer Book as a primary theological source that makes it distinctive.

Anglican Style

There is also "an elusive but very distinctive Anglican style." It is, in fact, so elusive, that it is almost impossible to talk about. For example, in 1972 the Lutheran Liturgical Conference at Valparaiso University in Indiana celebrated the then brand-new Rite II liturgy of the Episcopal Church from *Prayer Book Studies 19* as a part of their conference. As good Missouri Synod Lutherans, they did not invite any Episcopalians to participate in the celebration except as members of the congregation, but they followed the rubrics carefully. The planners even telephoned me and asked for advice whenever they were uncertain about what was intended by a given rubric. It was in many ways a most interesting service (they sang better than most Episcopalians!), but none of the Episcopalians present experienced it as anything but a Lutheran service. When all was said and done, "The voice was the voice of Jacob, but the hands were the hands of Esau." The elusive "style" was Lutheran.

It is precisely at this point that we tend to get into trouble, because what we often mean when we say that something is not authentically Anglican is that it isn't "our kind" of Anglican. It doesn't fit our cultural expectations. We aren't expecting a mariachi band for lessons and carols!

We confuse our picture of an ideal Anglican liturgy with the essence of Anglican worship, but our picture is hopelessly culturally conditioned, whether it be English cathedral liturgy, solemn Mass at St. Mary the Virgin's, or the family Eucharist at a suburban parish. The examples of cultural imperialism masquerading as Christian missionary activity are too numerous and well known to need repetition, but the offense is seldom deliberate. Often the cultural components are an integral part of our vision of the church, and, just as frequently, the cultural elements are quite attractive to the potential converts. One common aspect of this experience was expressed this way by an Asian Christian:

> Fascinated by the new Christian faith and associating it with the "advanced" Western culture (technology, in particular), Asian converts have probably idealized and absolutized [Western] Christian values.... Unfortunately, it led to a denial of native culture and values; Christians became alienated from their own people. They were eager to learn and adapt the new Christian expression, including liturgies and music. Eventually, they became so attached to these forms that they regarded them as the absolutely authentic way of Christian expression.[12]

The conversion of the barbarian tribes of Europe to Christianity in late antiquity was in one sense as much their initiation into Roman culture as it was into Christianity. The Roman church did not impose a Latin liturgy on unwilling barbarians. They adopted it gladly as evidence that they had become a part of "the mainstream" of Roman culture. There was little market for Mass in Gothic. It was only when missionaries encountered the ancient civilizations of China and India that the question of adapting Christianity to non-Western cultures was seriously raised. Today "inculturation" is an important concept for global Christianity. The Indian theologian D.S. Amalorpavadass, has reminded us:

> The church cannot be truly catholic or universal until it is truly incarnated in a people and inculturated according to various cultures. The task and

responsibility of realizing inculturation in all aspects and areas of its life and society and evolving a theology of inculturation belongs to the local church whose task is preaching the gospel.[13]

This is a crucial principle. It is not the job of white middle-class liturgists in the Episcopal Church to attempt to decide what kind of liturgy is appropriate for a convent in Tanzania or a country church in Haiti. The local church celebrating liturgy ultimately determines what its liturgy will be. Our task is much more modest, but not unimportant. We need to bear witness to the Tradition that has been passed on to us, so that inculturation does not become the distortion of the liturgy and also of the gospel that it celebrates. How a local church incarnates that Tradition is not something that can be dictated from outside. Our task is to educate and to set guidelines, so that the local church may know that its liturgy is indeed Christian and Anglican. More than this we cannot accomplish and should not attempt.

Notes

[1] *Stories of Traditional Navajo Life and Culture*, (Navajo Community College Press, Tsaile, 1977).

[2] Originally presented as an address to the Association of Diocesan Liturgy and Music Commissions meeting in Chicago, November 1994.

[3] *Sacrosanctum Concilium.* December 4, 1963.

[4] Op.cit. 21.

[5] Op.cit. 38.

[5] Op.cit. 40.

[7] The Book of Common Prayer 1928, 529.

[8] The Book of Common Prayer 1979, 510.

[9] The Book of Common Prayer 1979, 877.

[10] *The Book of Alternative Services of the Anglican Church of Canada* (Toronto: Anglican Book Centre, 1985), 10.

[11] *The Identity of Anglican Worship*, edited by Kenneth Stevenson and Bryan Spinks (Harrisburg: Morehouse, 1991), 132f.

[12] I-to Loh, "Contemporary Issues in Inculturation: Arts and Liturgy: Music," address to 12th International Congress, Societas Liturgica, York, 1989.

[13] D.S. Amalorpavadass, "Theological Reflections on Inculturation," address to 12th International Congress, Societas Liturgica, York, 1989

Those people will wander this way.... they will be looking for a certain stone.... They will be people who do not get tired, but who will keep pushing forward, going all the time. They will keep coming, coming.... They will travel everywhere, looking for this stone which our great-grandfather put on the earth in many places.... These people will not listen to what you say: what they are going to do they will do. You people will change: in the end of your life in those days you will not get up early in the morning, you will not know when day comes.... They will try to change you from your way of living to theirs.... They will tear up the earth, and at last you will do it with them. When you do, you will become crazy, and will forget all that I am teaching you.

Sweet Medicine (Cheyenne)[1]

Where Will the Native American Liturgy Come From?

John E. Robertson

Liturgy is one rationale for the acceptance of the changes that a Native American presence and voice would create in the Episcopal Church. I have modified this presumption to an exploration of some of the realities, personal and global, of using liturgy to hide rather than engage the pluralism, and the fear of it, in the whole of God's People. This exploration will not provide answers but will raise questions. This exploration may become part of the ongoing discussion to shape the questions and the potential answers concerning liturgy in the modern world and the Church. We as human beings can only ask the questions, the answers belong to God. We cannot hear the answers but can feel them in the unifying and freeing of God's People and Creation from alienation, oppression, and destruction. Liturgy has to be a part of the answers for the Church because, "For us, as much as for primitive societies, it is a good ritual system which will enable us to find meaning in the universe and in our own lives."[2]

These feelings of alienation and oppression arise from the question of, "Why is the Church not able to recognize and respond to the pluralism in Western Society?" This exploration would have given me a forum to challenge and confront the theologies and liturgies of the Western world. I would have been able to show my rational, reasoning capabilities and knowledge of the Western Christian tradition, thought, and practice. This question and pursuit of an answer would have allowed me to say that I was as valid and important as everyone else because I had all this knowledge. I still felt empty and lost as I tried to develop this point. The literature I was exploring finally began to create a journey, a journey that I will try to articulate in a manner that will allow others to join in the dialogue to shape the questions in such a way that God's will and redemption will be the answer.

The journey started with a look at inculturation theology, "the on-going dialogue between faith and culture or cultures." More fully, it is the creative and dynamic relationship between the Christian message and culture or cultures.[3] This home base seemed to be ideal because it talked about the relevance "to the countries of Europe and North America. For example, which have been Christianized and now de-Christianized, as it is to the cultures of the Third World in which the gospel has only recently been proclaimed for the first time."[4] This seemed like the ticket to assessing and criticizing the Church for not addressing the pluralism in its own backyard. It almost seemed that the answer was there and the Third World could help define the answer. As I tried to find the Episcopal response to inculturation theology, I was pulled to the responses contained in the Vatican II statements and practices for theological and liturgical discussions of inculturation.

The statement of Fr. Pedro Arrupe, SJ, in response to the 32nd Congregation of the Society for Jesus defined inculturation as:

> The incarnation of Christian life and of the Christian message in a particular cultural context, in such a way that experience not only finds expression through elements proper to the culture in question (this alone would be no more than a superficial adaptation) but becomes a principle that animates, directs and unifies the culture, transforming it and remaking it so as to bring about a "new creation."[5]

This seemed to provide a sound basis for the creation of liturgy that would speak to the pluralism of Western society and give freedom to the indigenous people to speak to their own needs and cultures. Somehow, I stumbled across a debate between Miika Ruokanen and Paul Knitter, with comments by William R. Burrows, in the international Bulletin of Missionary Research, April 1990, over the implications of Vatican II concerning the status of non-Christian religions and the role of these religions in salvation.

This discussion reframed the other materials that I had been contemplating using in my confrontation. I had been intent on raising the issues of why in the North American religious literature was there little recognition of the process of inculturation, the recognition of the impact of 1492 on the development of the Christian religious mission, or anything else I felt were the inculturation issues confronting the American Church and the Episcopal denomination. Burrows' statement on the discussion opened the doors of my perception:

> Rather than in the terms set out in the clash between Knitter and Roukanen, it seems that a development of the Catholic magisterium ought to articulate both "Christian" and "extra-visible-Christian" salvation as one and the same process of gaining a divine center for life, and dialoguing with other traditions to see if they have potential for helping achieve deeper understanding of justification-as-conscientization.
>
> This may seem far removed from missiology [or liturgical process]. It is not. It involves gaining clarity about the salvation Christians believe mission-as-evangelization must make manifest. And interreligious dialogue can be the very important task not asserting that a vague form of salvation is offered in other traditions, but the urgent effort to clarify what light can be cast and resources offered by other traditions to overcome human misery. We are only at

the beginning of such a dialogue. Both Roukanen's
caution on overstating what the council has said and
Knitter's urgency about getting into the business of
overcoming the barriers to human liberation caused
by religious division are important aspects of a mul-
tifaceted effort to clarify Christian mission.[6]

The statement moved once again to the role of liturgy. How was
this so? The importance of a center for life, and a deeper meaning
for life, allude to symbols that speak to those people moving into
contact with the reality of modernity in their world, which means
Western Christian society. This means a reciprocal presence of non-
Christian religions in the modern world, Western society. The challenge is for all people to understand and describe the presence and
reality of God in their midst. I realized this could be called theology.

The journey has proceeded down the road to theology. Theology
needs to be understood and a part of any liturgy. This is in evidence
in the literature where there is the theology of liturgy, liturgical theology, and the theology of specific liturgies. The idea of being in the
realm of theology put me in a panic. Now what do I do? Because
home base had become uncomfortable but the journey was interesting, I decided to continue on to find a place where I was comfortable and supported by the literature that I had at my disposal. The
journey was enhanced in an article by Diana L. Eck on the World
Council of Churches unit on Dialogue with People of Living Faiths
January, 1990 consultation in Baar, Switzerland. The consultation
produced a document, which she summarizes as stating:

> "We are clear, therefore," the statement goes on to
> say, "that a positive answer must be given to the
> question raised in the Guidelines on Dialogue
> (1979), 'is it right and helpful to understand the
> work of God outside the Church in terms of the
> Holy Spirit?' We affirm unequivocally that God

the Holy Spirit has been at work in the life and traditions of peoples of living faiths."

The final brief section of the document, "Interreligious Dialogue: A Theological Perspective," suggests that "our recognition of the mystery of salvation in men and women of other religious traditions shapes the concrete attitudes with which we Christians must approach them in interreligious dialogue." It insists, as well, that interreligious dialogue must "transform the way in which we do theology." "We need to move toward a dialogical theology in which the praxis of dialogue together with that of human liberation will constitute a true locus theologicus, i.e., both a source and basis for theological work."

Such theological thinking will be grounded firmly in a Christian context and the language of commitment particular to the Christian community. Yet, such theological thinking must be undertaken in full awareness that theologians and thinkers of other traditions not only "listen in" on our conversations, but are engaged in interpreting religious plurality in the context of their own traditions of faith. A new era of theological thinking has surely begun.[7]

This statement caused a reflection on how "we change and the world changes, and we approach God with new problems and new questions. The language of theology must be able to hear and respond to these new experiences without changing its age-old witness to the Eternal and Unchanging God."[8]

I was pulled back to inculturation by an article by D.S. Amalorpavadass, "Theological Reflections on Inculturation."[9] This article was an expansion of the statement of the World Council of Churches consultation concerning theology and culture. The idea that "the type of thinking we have on religions will determine our theologizing and practice of inculturation as well as our theological understanding and practice of dialogue in relation to evangelization, the mission of the Church, and the whole Christ-mystery."[10] This was beginning to move toward an understanding of inculturation in Native America. The criticism that is present in Indian country of Western, Christian, inculturation is articulated:

> Let us make no mistake about it. Nor gloss over matters. A missionary from any country, whether from Europe or America goes from a particular church and is a child of his own national culture. He is not culturally free and cannot be considered to be culturally neutral. A missionary who imposes western culture in the name of orthodoxy, as the pure form of Christianity, who asks the new converts to make a clean break with their ancestral culture and religious tradition or who forbids some prevalent practices within that church because they are derived from local culture and other religions, is acting with the cultural bias of the sending church or nation. This applies to the western missionary of yesterday and to the Asian missionary of today who goes to Africa and Latin America. Even in the name of Christianity or the gospel and even for the sake of orthodoxy and authenticity, the one culture embodied in a church cannot and should not judge another culture within which another church has to live and emerge. If one were to do so, one would be reducing another culture with its church to the state of the judged.[11]

This discussion of theology and inculturation continued to speak to the contemporary Native American situation by discussing the discernment and evaluation of inculturation in a culture. Who is qualified based on the previous statement for the task? Is it local leaders or those that judge or outsiders?

> Here by outsiders is meant those who do not iden-
> tify with a people, who are foreign to their culture,
> who look at inculturation experiment as observers,
> whose knowledge of culture is mere intellectual
> knowledge based on data or information. Instead, a
> culture can be understood only from within, out of
> a lived experience, when one is in solidarity and
> empathy with a people or church.

> However, every evaluation done from within need
> not be correct either. As a matter of fact today, the
> resistance to change or inculturation or dissociation
> of Christianity from western culture and expression
> of the gospel through local cultures and religions
> comes not from outsiders or from missionaries but
> from so-called insiders, from local people, and from
> the leaders of the local Christian communities.[12]

This is not only a challenge to the Native American culture and church but to the pluralism confronting the American church in general. Some of the other articles in these two volumes of *Studia Liturgia* speak to the needs for liturgical inculturation of the western culture itself. The article continues with a description of why some local cultural inculturations alienate and hinder further evangelization:

> For owing to several centuries of westernization, the
> people have become so alienated from their culture,
> have acquired such a colonial mentality, and reflex as
> to stick on to foreign culture as the only guarantee of
> the authenticity and purity of Christian faith. Every
> alienation calls for conscientization and liberation.[13]

This means that we have to continue to look for a common approach to inculturation. How can the church speak to all cultures? What is the common denominator that all cultures and religions have? The stepping-stone is faith. "Let us also add for sake of clarity that faith transcends nature and cultures, and calls every person, people, and culture to self-transcendence."[14] This transcendence becomes manifest in spirituality. This spirituality leads to discernment of the process of inculturation and the development of the contextual theology present in the culture. The importance of this "process and guidelines for inculturation suggested for the Third World could be considered by those involved in the inculturation of liturgy in Europe, North America, Australia, New Zealand, etc."[15]

The search for a Native American understanding of an inculturated liturgy is directed by the addition of the spirituality approach to the theological reflection on inculturation.

> Therefore a third approach, called 'spirituality approach' as integrating factor, may be added to the 'theological' and the 'anthropological.' Christianity with its spirituality as its dynamic core, meeting religions and cultures in the depths of their being, can arrive at basic unity and an experiential synthesis, as for example, (Native American) Christian Spirituality Experience. This is the deepest form of inculturation in a two-way approach merging at the core level in the heart of each other in peak experience. This spiritual experience is one of the sources of theology (*loci theologic*i) as well. Hence, spirituality experience approach is an equally valid theological reflection on inculturation.[16]

The above discussion focused back onto the Native American theology or absence thereof in the Western Christian hallowed halls of academia. Spirituality becomes the focus of most of the material on Native Americans. This focus has left us out of the theological supermarket. The Rt. Rev. Steve Charleston says:

> The Native spirituality craze, therefore, may account for the neglect of a Native People's Christian theology. Well-intentioned shoppers (at the theological supermarket) may have simply thought that this talk about spirituality was the voice of Native America in the religious dialogue. In addition, up to a point, they are right. Traditional Native spirituality does represent a major and crucial voice for Native People. It is a voice that has frequently been misquoted, distorted, or co-opted, but it's a voice nonetheless. I am certainly not prepared to argue against a legitimate role for that spirituality. In fact, I am going to argue that this spirituality is something extremely central to Native America and to the Christ, and faith. Still, the spirituality section alone does not complete the supermarket. It still is not an expression of a Native Christian viewpoint. As good (or bad) as these works may be at articulating Native tradition, they do not offer a clear voice for Native American Christianity. They are not a Native People's Christian theology. Instead they are the source for materials for that theology—they are reference points, or commentaries.[17]

The idea behind what Steve Charleston is proposing is that any people, but specifically Native Americans in this instance, cannot have a New Testament, with Christ at the center to fulfill the covenant of God, without an Old Testament. This can be a challenge for the once tribal people of Europe to consider in their attempt to re-Christianize their own people. Is their covenant with God through the tribes of Israel or through their own "lost" tribes of Europe? What is the "old" testament of the Native American Christian? Why is it important? Let us journey back to the theological supermarket to find out what could happen:

> Well, first of all, it would give us a new vocabulary in dealing with what we've been describing as Native spirituality. For example, a great many of those books in the supermarket would become Old Testament commentaries. They would be books about source materials of Native America's Old Testament. Books about the traditions of Old Testament times, about the culture of Old Testament times, about the personalities of Old Testament times, and the theology of Old Testament times. We might start treating them more seriously and critically, since they would be describing the foundational theology for a contemporary Christian theology...
>
> ...Instead of Western writers hacking away at Native spirituality, we would begin to see the emergence of more theologians from within the Native community itself. Native American women and men could finally speak for themselves not as gurus for Western theological science fiction, but as reputable scholars for an Old Testament tradition. Their voices would be clear and distinct. They would be listened to seriously. These speakers would not necessarily be Christian, but would be treated with respect by the Christian community, just as Jewish scholars are respected. Their contribution to the larger interfaith dialogue would be profound. It would change us. It would open us up to a whole new dimension in theological exploration.[18]

This is a radical challenge to the hallowed halls of Western academia. The challenge of inculturation takes on the mantle of liberation theology. A liberation theology that speaks to all that live in this time and place in history here on the North American continent. It is a Christ centered theology, in the words of the Native American theologian, Steve Charleston:

> I am not glossing over the Old Testament of Native America with the Western whitewash of a theology that gives out a few quick platitudes about the "Christ of all Cultures." When I speak of a fulfillment of Native America's Old Testament, I mean just that: a Christ that emerges from within the native tradition itself: that speaks of, by, and for that tradition; that participates in that tradition: that lives in that tradition. Grounded in the old testament of Native America, it is the right of Native People to claim fulfillment of Christ in their own way and in their own language. I am not looking simply to paint the statues brown and keep Western cultural prejudices intact. I am announcing the privilege of my own people to interpret the Christian canon in the light of Israel's experience. Whether this interpretation is compatible with western opinions is open for discussion.[19]

These are strong words that reflect the realities of the twenty-first century. People around the world are seeking a reformation of the Christian church. This reformation will be just that, a reformation of theology to:

> An "earthly" affair in the best sense of that word: it helps people to live rightly, appropriately, on the earth, in our home. It is, as the Jewish and Christian traditions have always insisted, concerned with "right relations," relations with God, neighbor and self, but now the context has broadened to include

> what has dropped out of the picture in the past few hundred years: the oppressed neighbor, the other creators and the earth that supports us all. This shift can be seen as a return to the roots of a tradition that has insisted on the creator, redeemer God as the source and salvation of all that is.[20]

The idea that change is occurring in the cultures and people is exciting. The Episcopal Church is poised, in my mind, to ride the theological wave into the twenty-first century. The basis of the Episcopal liturgy is beyond the roman rite that is bound up in the Vatican II debate over inculturation. The Episcopal Book of Common Prayer has the potential to respond to the emerging theologies based on spirituality. The Book of Common Prayer has the open forms of worship that can meet the needs of communities and cultures coming together to pray. Since the basic principle of Episcopalians is the way we pray is the way we believe, the liturgy of the denomination is alive.

I was drawn to Episcopal Church based on the liturgy contained in the Book of Common Prayer. I think that with an open heart, body, mind, and soul, the emerging theologies can fit into the Book of Common Prayer, hence, the Episcopal Church.

The example I'll use to demonstrate this, from a Native theological perspective, is the Easter Vigil. The Native communities have a tradition of ceremonial fires. These fires burn throughout the fast, sun dance, or ceremony. The fire can be kindled at sunset on Holy Saturday. The people would feed each other with food, prayer, and fellowship. Most could or would go home for the evening while fire keepers would be at the fire. This is a time of teaching and renewal around the fire. In the morning, people return to complete the ceremony, in this case, the Easter Vigil. The whole service would not be difficult to match up with what Steve Charleston called the "Old" Testament of the Native People. This is the role of liturgy, to be the primary theology of the people in symbols that can communicate to God and themselves that they are a community in the New

Testament fulfillment of their "Old" testament.

Liturgy defines the community of believers as they define the liturgy that they believe. Ritual acts may be spontaneous, but they are taken from a great tradition of symbolic acts. We understand their meaning, because we are a part of the same tradition.

This may seem a strange place for a study of the meaning of ritual to wind up. But ultimately the meaning of ritual is festivity, the celebration of redeemed creation and ourselves as a part of it. It is a participation in the Divine life, and a sharing in its love. For Christians this means union and communion with Jesus Christ in the paschal mystery of his death and rising again, with its promise of abundant life and fullness of joy. If ritual worship offers us less than that, we have been cheated.[21]

I do not feel cheated, as my journey has brought me to a new horizon. This horizon is beginning to show the full panorama of the potential in the use of the Episcopal liturgy. I realize that here in the hallowed halls of academia, it may feel like the sunset of Native American theology, but from where I am now and where I will be, in native America, it is the Easter sunrise.

Notes

[1] Quoted in *In the Spirit of Crazy Horse*, by Peter Matthiessen (Viking, New York, 1983).

[2] Leonel L. Mitchell, *The Meaning of Ritual* (Wilton, CT: Morehouse-Barlow, 1988), 14.

[3] Aylward Shorter, *Toward a Theology of Inculturation* (Maryknoll, NY: Orbis, 1988), 11.

[4] Ibid., 12.

[5] Pedro Arrupe, "Letter to the Whole Society on Inculturation," in *Other Apostolates Today: Selected Letters and Addresses of Pedro Arrupe SJ* ed. J. Aixala (St. Louis, 1981), 172-181.

[6] William R. Burrows, "Comments on the Articles by Ruokanen

and Knitter," *International Bulletin of Missionary Research* 14, no. 2 (1990): 63-64.

[7] Diana L. Eck, "On Seeking and Finding in the World's Religions," *The Christian CENTURY* 108, no. 15 (1990): 454-456.

[8] Leonel L. Mitchell, *Praying Shapes Believing: A Theological Commentary on the Book of Common Prayer* (Minneapolis, MN: Winston Press, 1985), 3.

[9] D.S. Amalorpavadass, "Theological Reflections on Inculturation," *Studia Liturgica* 20, no. 1 (1990) 36-54 and no. 2 (1990) 116-136.

[10] Ibid., no. 2: 119.

[11] Ibid., no. 2:122.

[12] Ibid., no. 2:123.

[13] Ibid., no. 2:123.

[14] Ibid., no. 2:124.

[15] Ibid., no. 2:127.

[16] Ibid., no. 2:129.

[17] Steve Charleston, "The Old Testament of Native America," in *Lift Every Voice: Constructing Christian Theologies from the Underside*, eds. Susan Brooks Thistlewaite and Mary Potter Engel (New York: HarperCollins, 1990), 52.

[18] Ibid., 53.

[19] Ibid., 59.

[20] Sallie McFague, "An Earthly Theological Agenda," *The Christian CENTURY* 108, no. 1 (1991): 15.

[21] Mitchell, *The Meaning of Ritual*, 133.

They read print, they went to prayers, to meeting, to testimony services, to preaching services, and when they sang, they sang their songs as they had their old chants to the tunes of the `ala`apapa hula of Kukuehi and others, and quavered like the `alala hula of Kawaikuapu`u and his School. So sang Kelou Kamakau, Ka`ele-owaipi`o, Ku`oko`a, and the rest. They sang their songs with the belief that the kingdom of God would not be displeased with their way of singing so long as it was sung with a humble heart by a penitent, one whose prayers were uttered in faith.

Samuel Manaiakalani Kamakau[1]

Singing for Life and Music in the Small Parish

Marilyn Haskel

What is your earliest recollection of a religious song? Which was more meaningful: the music, the words, or the act of singing? What effect did it have on you then? What is its effect on you now?

I once attended a workshop where participants were asked that first question.. Thinking backwards from an initial recollection, I pushed myself to remember earlier and earlier church events and their musical connection. Since my family attended church twice every Sunday when I was very young, once in the morning and again in the evening, I had much to remember. But it was a song from Sunday School that is the earliest music in church that I remember from about age three. It was a favorite song of all of us children, and we would ask for it again and again. It was called "Blue-eyed Violet." I tried to recall the words, but couldn't get past the first line "Blue-eyed violet with your pretty head . . ." What had not faded was the complete tune, and the delicious joy I had felt over forty years earlier when our teacher said we could sing our favorite song.

The next time I went to my parent's house, I located the little navy blue book that was, as best I could determine, the only source of "Blue-eyed Violet." I was astounded to find that it was the only song in that collection that I could remember. What truly shocked me was to discover that the text made no mention of anything obviously religious, yet—even at that young age—I had known that God made the blue-eyed violet and that's why we were singing about it in church.

By the time I was four, the family church was using *Hymns for Primary Worship*, and my parents gave one to me and my sister to keep at home on the piano. My favorite song in that book was the Negro spiritual "Lord, I want to be a Christian." Of course, we sang all the standard hymns in church, but the musical milestones that mark my earliest spiritual experiences are not the great hymns that I have come to love today, but these lesser songs that are neither great music nor deep theological statements.

The anamnesis of our earliest memorable religious music creates a powerful criterion for our individual expectations of what church music should be—either by encouraging us to seek to imitate that music or to antagonize the experience. What we seek to recreate or destroy is perhaps not so much the music itself as the feelings that were evoked.

In my experience parishes also have communal criteria for what constitutes church music, a collective vision of what music in a viable parish should look like. This may or may not be in agreement with the individual criteria of members. The telling point, however, is the extent to which a community has had dialogue about its expectations for music. Where no dialogue has occurred, there often exists an imposed expectation enforced by a priest/musician. This may be helpful, but it may result in confusing signals given by the community to those who plan the liturgy. These confusing signals will permeate the process when a church calls a musician or priest to employment.

Many small churches have an expectation of matching their music to the style and structure of a much larger parish with far more resources. The result is something akin to decorating a Cape Cod cottage in the style of a baronial castle. The correct components necessary for living are there, but in stunning disproportion. People keep bumping into the oversized musical furniture trying to negotiate movement throughout the liturgical house. I call this the Faux Large Parish Model.

Another model that has been used or aspired to by many small parishes is this: one parish, one resident-expert church musician—a person who knows "good" music from "bad" and who imparts that "knowledge" to others. I call this the Resident Expert Model. When it becomes impossible to find or pay for such a person, small parishes despair of having any music at all, and some even cease singing. It often does not occur to parishioners that a Sunday liturgy without any singing is barely liturgy. When music is considered an add-on to the so-called *real* liturgy—the spoken word—not having any is merely an inconvenience of circumstance. On the contrary, the musical part of liturgy is a sign that points to that which we need and revere as true and necessary in our ritual acts of worship. As such, music must embrace a vitality, a liveliness, and a commitment that will strengthen weak hearts and feeble knees.

God is revealed through music and we must realize that peoples' preference for hymns and songs that help them discern and express God's will is going to be quite varied. By condemning people when they do theology through music and which a resident-expert musician does not consider "good," we are hindering the primary order of ministers, the laity, from doing what they are entitled to do. This does not negate the need for teaching and leadership, nor is it an attempt to rid the church of those "temperamental" musicians. Rather, it is a call to acknowledge that an imposed form of music is neither teaching or leadership.

> Artists deserve respect and support, for the genius with which they have been gifted opens avenues to the transcendent as an eschatological sign. Simple folk must also be encouraged to share the song of the heart, for if good can come out of Nazareth and God can inhabit human flesh, then grace can choose its song.[2]

To begin discussing music in the small parish, I want to introduce the concept of Singing for Life. I believe that singing is a basic need within the quality of life inherent in the Gospel. We are urged to seek wholeness, to care for each other deeply, and to seek a spirituality that will nurture our faith. Singing for Life means both "to sing forever" and "to sing for one's very existence." Less a fanciful play on words than a compact simplicity that I use to show the gravity of what I believe to be true, Singing for Life means doing one's best to sing the right notes, to understand the words and mean them, and to join with others enthusiastically to be an embodiment of the truth contained in what is being sung. To sing the right notes because that is what the composer wrote is less the point than to sing the right notes because it initiates an interaction with others who also sing the right notes. This interaction empowers a credo by two or three singing together as with one voice. Singing the right notes is the mechanical necessity for the greater goal of participating in a communal act of faith.

In this essay I want to first consider that Singing for Life encompasses the song, the singer, *and* the singing which we shall see are not mutually exclusive. Although I use the terms of vocal music, I believe that the concept of Singing for Life ultimately embraces all music making. Second I will address considerations specific to the small parish when Singing for Life is the goal. Finally, I will briefly explore how Singing for Life is ministry.

Singing For Life

When I was in the Master's program at Hartford Seminary, my advisor was Sr. Miriam Therese Winter, a Medical Mission Sister who, some years earlier, had embraced the spirit of Vatican II by writing and recording many contemporary religious folk songs for solo voice, guitar, and the close harmonies sung with sisters from her community. Perhaps their most popular selection was "Joy Is Like the Rain," a period piece marking the incredibly fast-moving and pervasive changes in church music during the early 1970s. Sr. Miriam also had a degree in organ and Gregorian chant. This juxtaposition of classical training and contemporary folk style marked the journey of many of us working in churches at that time.

During the course of my studies, Sr. Miriam completed her Ph.D. in liturgy studies at Princeton University. The published book of her dissertation, *Why Sing? Toward a Theology of Catholic Church Music*, The Pastoral Press, 1984, contains an extensive discussion of the Roman Catholic documents on church music and explores her perspective on that history. She raises questions about late twentieth-century issues in church music that have yet to be addressed in a systematic way. I have found her questions engaging, and I am convinced that her discussion, which manages to avoid fruitless debates about musical style and issues of taste, opens a pathway through the continuing dialogue about music in the church.

Articulating the theological themes that underlie music in the church's liturgy, Dr. Winter makes significant observations about music around the time of the Vatican Council. Even though some may argue that these observations are indigenous to Roman Catholics, they, nevertheless, parallel much thought about music in Protestant circles as well.

The Perfect Offering

The pre-Conciliar Church as the *societas perfecta,* divinely instituted, hierarchically ordered, is theologically described as the *mysticum corpus,* with all of its members functioning in perfect coordination. Jesus, as Head of the Body, is High Priest of the eternal covenant, ordained by God to "perfect and lead to perfection as many as were to be sanctified," who presents at the heavenly altar the *offertorium* of his Church: the Mass, the sacrifice of Calvary, offered "in an unbloody manner . . . . the same now offering by the ministry of priests who then offered Himself on the cross." The silent laity attend the Mass and join themselves to this perfect offering, so that along with the Divine Victim, their prayers will arise like incense as a sacrifice of praise. Song is part of this offering, "a foretaste of the heavenly liturgy" in which the Church "is united with the never-ending procession of the Blessed in heaven, who sing hymns in praise of the Spotless Lamb." Song is an act of consecration. It is for God, not for people. Sacred chant, perfectly rendered, the Divine Office, sung precisely as prescribed by those duly appointed, is the Church's perfect prayer of praise. Among Church musicians, concern is for the song. Nothing must mar its flawless perfection, nothing profane, nothing banal. The song is the perfect offering. The song praises God.

Pastoral Experience

The Conciliar Church is a Church on the move. The *populus Dei* joins with Jesus, *Pascha nostrum,* in his journey through death to life. The *ecclesia* is made manifest when, assembled at the sacrificial banquet, all actively participate in a communal experience, a personal experience, of Jesus as Redeemer and Lord. Liturgy is the source and summit of the activities of the Church, its celebration a pastoral experience of the priesthood of all believers. Singing creates the experience, for song is celebration. Singing serves the assembly, enabling *communitas,* uniting minds and hearts. Among liturgists, particularly, concern is for the singing. The goal is a singing assembly. Singing is a pastoral experience because it reaches out to people, connects them with each other, mediates the Word of

Life to an assembly of believers, puts the power of the liturgical event in touch with human need. The singing praises God.

Sign and Symbol

The post-Conciliar Church is the *sacramentum mundi*, an eschatological sign, a symbol of hope and healing in the midst of a suffering world. Jesus, Lord of human history, love incarnate, chose to make this world the primary arena of grace in order to prepare the way for the world that is to come. Salvation is the kingdom of justice and the kingdom is in our midst. Prayer is a shared responsibility, the cultic expression of culture, where the signs and symbols of a commitment in faith are lifted up in praise. "People in love make signs of love, not only to express their love but also to deepen it. Love never expressed dies. Christians' love for Christ and for one another and Christians' faith in Christ and in one another must be expressed in the signs and symbols of celebration or they will die." And "among the many signs and symbols used by the Church to celebrate its faith, music is of preeminent importance." Song is important, not for itself, but for what it can accomplish. It is a tool of transformation, capable of effecting a conversion of the heart. Song is for the singer, The singer praises God.[3]

Dr. Winter goes on to point out that these themes are not mutually exclusive and cannot be so. There are elements of truth and value in each, and that has been part of the problem. At this time in history, we are caught in a transition that leads many to agonize that we are losing our beloved musical traditions which are being replaced with music of dubious quality and limited value in the name of full participation. Can it not be said that the liturgy that church music is wedded to, also in transition, maintains its roots in long traditions, yet embraces the now and reaches toward the future? The church has yet to establish a theology of music that pulls together the valuable legacies of the perfect offering, the pastoral experience, and sign and symbol as aspects of a single theme that culminates in describing the church in praise of God. Dr. Winter says, "Such a theology must address with equal care the singer and the singing and the song. . ."[4]

For the purpose of this essay, I will use these simple definitions for The Song, The Singer, and The Singing:

> **The Song:** A musical composition, created either formally or informally, which serves as an expression of faith.
> **The Singer:** One who makes the created song audible.
> **The Singing:** A communal act of the interaction between The Song and The Singer.

The Song

Thirty years ago, when I was a new teacher, it was quite easy to identify church music. If I played a recording of organ music and asked junior high students what it was, they would invariably reply, "church music!" Today, many students would have no context for identifying church music, and those who did might be hard-pressed to describe exactly how church music sounds compared to other kinds of music. Is this a problem?

In the era of "The Perfect Offering" The Song was heavily prescribed. It had to be constructed a certain way and performed a certain way by certain people with certain things in mind. Of course, the prescription changed periodically. At one time, music with interweaving multiple melodic lines sung by the choir (polyphonic music) was outlawed because the text couldn't be understood by the people. Scriptural psalms sung to tonal formulas gave way to metrical tunes and text paraphrases because they were well-liked by the people. The prescription designated that certain melodic intervals and particular harmonic progressions were easier for the people to sing than others. Because of this, the rules for hymn writing are exacting and rather narrow, making the composing of hymns a strenuous discipline. (Always considered a good thing where religion is concerned.) Recently, however, we find that people can hear and imitate many melodic intervals once considered taboo, especially when the music resembles what they hear in popular music. Is this a problem?

Is it possible to make a "Perfect Offering" with an imperfect song? I submit that even a song of poor quality can express the faith and be redeemed by The Singer or The Singing, just as it is possible to hear the Word of God within a bad sermon. The key is the fertile soul and the hungry spirit of the seeker which is open to surprise and the unpredictability of the Holy Spirit. Humankind must have songs that feed, but a soul's fertile readiness is the ground upon which the seeds of faithfulness grow into a mature spirituality.

The definition I have given for The Song allows the possibility that a broader spectrum of song may exist for church music. Informally created music may be defined as what we call folk music or even spontaneously improvised tunes. Past generations were taught to believe that there was a dichotomy between the secular and the sacred. It would seem in some contexts today there is a blurring of that division. Texts considered sacred are set to music that might have been considered secular in past times. If we substitute the word *profane* for secular—with *profane* meaning "marked by contempt or irreverence for the sacred"[5]—it is easier to place some texts into this category; however, contemporary times have little to say about profane music apart from texts.

Historically some great musical works with religious texts were created by composers who, while not exactly antagonistic toward faith, were not necessarily seeking to support it. Should one examine the heart and mind of the composer before the song is deemed worthy of expressing the faith, or can one believe that the Holy Spirit is at work in the hearts and minds of those who hear?

I once had a theology professor who found it impossible to support my writing about theological themes in hymns. As I studied contemporary theology and the new texts then proposed for *The Hymnal 1982*, I became excited by the parallels between the contemporary theology I was reading and how hymn writers were addressing the same theological themes in the newest texts. My professor felt that, unless I could show that the hymn writer credited a text as adhering to the views of a certain theologian, I had no academic right to make a connection. And furthermore, he had wondered, how was my work of interest, as most people don't pay attention to the words of hymns anyway!

Besides learning something about my theology professor, I relearned what I knew as an artist: we synthesize and integrate ideas into our creations which reflect, as if in a beautifying mirror, the truths of the age. The writing of hymn or song texts may be an inexact science for some academicians, but the artist's expression allows creative space for the ordinary person to discern great truths and "do theology" for themselves.

A characteristic of The Song has long been its ability to teach the faith—to put into artistic form those words that we believe to be the foundation of Christianity. The Song is prayer and, as such, follows the principal kinds of prayer outlined in the Catechism (BCP p. 856-857)—adoration, praise, thanksgiving, penitence, oblation, intercession, and petition. These words could also describe a range of parallel emotions, but Episcopalians are often embarrassed by strong emotion, preferring highly intellectualized texts that appeal predominately to the rational mind. And yet, in times of deep personal grief or loss, we may have been surprised by the power of a song that remains outside our normal repertoire. We are wary of admitting that this may be a legitimate function of The Song because we have been so conditioned to expect that The Song must stand alone on its integrity as an intellectualized combination of good music and good poetry. This expectation is a remnant of "The Perfect Offering," and, certainly, it is one truth of The Song, but if we are Singing for Life, we must keep the pristine image of "The Perfect Offering" in relationship to The Singer and The Singing.

For ages The Song has borne the weight of being the primary vehicle of the musical expression of faith. We often speak of church music as though it is nearly synonymous with The Song. The Book of Common Prayer indicates that instrumental music may be used from time to time, but we have always been a bit distrustful of the uncontrollable venue of non-texted music. We are conditioned by our experience of "program" music (that which was composed to describe a story or scene) and thus, need to know just what the composer intended before we can be sure if it is an acceptable vehicle for revelation.

When musicians speak about The Song, we tend to speak about either its technical aspects or its properties, usually in an objective or even academic way. By "technical aspects" I mean the details of the construction, such as how one musical phrase leads to the next one; how the highest note is also the textual climax; how the tune or harmonies progress in a fitting manner with the text; or how one should sing The Song—its speed or mood, the performance style, where one should breathe, etc. By "properties" I mean that ability of music to transcend the spoken word, to heighten poetic text, to reach deeply into human experience and longing, and to give meaning even while leaping beyond the perimeter of the rational mind. The technical aspects are easily defined, but the properties are amorphous and difficult to speak of. Rarely do we say how one might make use of music's properties for prayer, or why the mastery of the technical aspects of music are an important factor in the process of discernment or meditation. Perhaps we fear that we will be accused of committing the sin of worshiping the beauty of the music. When we hear someone remark about the beauty of nature or a spectacular sunset, Christians rarely attribute that statement to anything other than an indirect acknowledgement of God's goodness.

I believe that musicians can intuitively understand how prayer, meditation, or discernment through music is accomplished and as a result, sing, play, conduct, and teach knowing something that we expect others to perceive when they hear the music also. Some people will readily understand as we do and be able to share experiences with us without needing to articulate them. We will know immediately that they "get it" because of the *way* they sing, the look on their faces, the body language that communicates what they feel. But when someone attempts to "tell their story" about what they experience when they sing certain music, we dismiss the story (and often the person telling it) as an emotional response, especially if we believe the music to be inferior. We have not learned to value the early journey of the growing Christian. Nor have we learned how to teach people having basic emotional responses to music to carry that response into a spiritual discipline of praying, discerning, and meditating through music.

During times of stress in a parish, The Song may become a source of contention because it no longer speaks with authenticity to the gathered community. Perhaps songs that are true for part of the community do not engage the rest of the people. These growth pains may erupt into name calling and evaluative statements about differences in taste. One group may complain that some like music of inferior quality and shallow meaning while another group finds fault with wordiness and lack of feeling they believe is preferred by others. What is being called taste is, in reality, a difference in the expression of faith and its meaning for life. Until people are able to share their stories and are guided to engage each other on the level playing field of intent to live the Gospel, fights grounded in the trivia of taste, economic differences, and ethnic backgrounds will keep the real issues of living as Christians at bay. In such cases The Song cannot be a reconciling vehicle because it is the issue of contention. But often at these very times of conflict the church asks musicians to find music that everyone will like. Today, that is becoming less and less a possibility and is probably the wrong goal anyway. Do we *like* the scripture that is read? Do we *dislike* a creed?

The Song is an important component of church music, but it does not stand alone. When the other two components, The Singer and The Singing, are considered, The Song can be put into realistic balance and freed of the tyrannical myth of needing to be of inerrant good taste.

The Singer

I don't remember a time when I didn't sing; it's as natural to me as breathing, drinking water, or sleeping. Since I've never had to explain why I breathe, sleep, or drink water, I'm not sure how possible it is for me to say why I sing. If I were forbidden to sing, I would still sing in my mind, which happens spontaneously anyway. I often wake with a song in my mind—one that I haven't thought of in years. I don't know what prompts these diurnal themes.

Singing is something one must do to learn to value it. If one has been conditioned to believe that their ability to sing is sorely hampered by a lack of skill, then any pleasure derived from singing will be jeopardized. That is what has happened in American society. There is very little singing "just for fun." People have been discouraged from singing either by styles of music that are more for listening than for joining in, or they have self-selected not to sing because someone told them they couldn't sing. Singing isn't necessarily for someone else to hear. Singing is for feeling—for being—an aerobic exercise that initiates breathing in and out in a kind of controlled way to give vent to acclamation, to mourning, to affirmation, to distress, to prayer.

Why is it that singing at gatherings such as diocesan conventions, ordinations, or services of new ministry is so invigorated? Is it just the sheer numbers of people singing a hymn that may have sounded feeble in the parish just a few days before? Or is it that the singers rejoice in being together on this occasion that inspires The Song? Recall here two quotes from Sr. Miriam: "Christians' love for Christ and for one another and Christians' faith in Christ and in one another must be expressed in the signs and symbols of celebration or they will die." And " . . . among the many signs and symbols used by the Church to celebrate its faith, music is of preeminent importance."[6] The Song must be brought to active life by The Singer.

In the Episcopal Church we have perfected The Song but neglected The Singer. We have by action, if not rhetoric, promoted the belief that a well-crafted, theologically sound body of music will, in and of itself, create a singing church. For the white, Eurocentric, educated person in the pew, perhaps that is true. However, as the ethnicity and experiential inventory of the Episcopal Church changes, The Song is sorely challenged and The Singer is ever more in need of remedial work.

Does one have a Christian responsibility as The Singer? Doing one's best is a characteristic of being a Christian. To sit in the pew refusing to sing is at a minimum to ignore God's gift of a voice and to stifle one's ability to praise and worship. God has also given us the gift of prayer. Some are better at praying than others, but we tend not to evaluate that gift. Praying is simply something Christians do. So is using the voice to sing. Scripture verifies this with numerous accounts of gatherings where singing was a natural part of the events in our salvation history: Miriam leading the people in song at the Red Sea; the prophet Isaiah predicting the flowering of the desert accompanied by singing; the admonishing letter to the Ephesians to turn from drunkenness to be filled with the Spirit and to sing psalms; and the account of the great celebration of thousands as they sang in full voice in the Revelation.

The Catechism teaches us that one of our duties is to grow: ". . . to set aside regular times for worship, prayer, and the study of God's ways."[7] The study of God's ways presumes that one will learn, perceiving and discerning God's will. It is fairly commonplace, however, that many refuse to grow beyond The Song they learned as Christians in infancy. The Song, itself, includes the full spectrum of tune and text, easy to hard, for each step along one's faith journey. As The Singer's faith grows, so too must the choice of The Song that serves as one's expression of that faith. The responsibility of the parish musical leadership is to provide access to the full spectrum of choices of The Song.

It is Paul who adds to this discussion when he says in I Corinthians 14:15, "I will pray with the spirit, and I will pray with the mind also. I will sing with the spirit, and I will sing with the mind also." The Singer whose only criterion for church music is the desire for intellectual stimulation in the words and music of The Song must balance singing with the mind with singing with the spirit where our hearts are engaged and we allow ourselves to be moved to be the people of God. So, too, those who limit themselves to the spirit song must grow to sing with the mind.

Our parishes are communities of people who are in differing places in their growing faith. In the debates over what music a parish will use, the leadership must acknowledge this reality and offer the full spectrum of The Song. We are being called to more than tolerance for differing preferences of music. We are being given a challenge to "seek and serve Christ in all persons . . ." and ". . . respect the dignity of every human being."[8] Parish leadership may need to teach and lead music that is not their personal preference, but which is food for the journey of The Singer who is a new Christian. This is servant ministry.

If The Song is, at times, less important for what it is than for what it can accomplish, there may need to be more opportunity for The Singer to be engaged by The Song. The parish music leadership has a responsibility to assess and initiate, if necessary, opportunities for singing not only in liturgy, but throughout the life of the parish nurturing The Singer wherever possible. Singing is something one must do to learn to value it.

Singing a cross section of popular songs from different eras for fun at parish suppers is one way to help a congregation find its voice. Alternatively, simple rounds or new acclamations could be taught briefly at vestry or altar guild meetings. The annual retreat could include singing short songs as a way to focus the group after break-out sessions. Instead of singing Happy Birthday at coffee hour, why not teach "God grant them many years" in *Wonder, Love, and Praise*[9] which can be used for birthdays, anniversaries, farewells, and other life passages.

For parishes that are musically challenged both in leadership and singers, one might want to pick a few short selections to teach and repeat often. It is possible to learn something besides the Doxology to use on numerous occasions. All of Church Publishing's hymnals offer many possibilities. One could plan a hymn or song refrain as a response repeated throughout the opening prayer of a parish meeting. In Advent, for example, use the refrain to "O come, O come, Emmanuel"; in Epiphany: "This little light of mine" or the refrain to "We three kings"; in Lent: the refrain to "Lead me to Calvary" in *Lift Every Voice and Sing*;[10] during the Easter season use the refrain to "Alleluia, alleluia! Give thanks to the risen Lord"; during the long "green" season use "Jesus Christ, Son of God" in *Wonder, Love, and Praise*;[11] and so on using refrains people may know from memory or new ones that are short enough to learn by rote. Use a resource such as *The Rite Song*[12] to locate appropriate selections. One person can listen to the melody playback on the CD-ROM and then teach everyone. The easiest way for people to learn to sing something is to hear someone they know demonstrate it by singing. This is far superior to hearing the melody played alone, and it provides a ministry opportunity for someone to be a song leader.

In most parishes The Singer is in need of much nourishment,

but is also under the pressure of much greater expectation. Dialogue about how we use music in our spiritual lives and telling each other our stories will help initiate the nurturing and begin to build a trust level. Expanding the use of music in the parish, both in frequency and style, will also help. And finally, addressing the responsibilities of The Singer for growth as one's faith grows will begin to establish a church that is Singing for Life.

The Singing

Where have you joined in such exuberant singing that you were overwhelmed with the joy of it? When have you been moved deeply by the apparent sincerity of those singing? Have you ever been surprised by a new understanding of God's will as you sang with others? When did you last join others in singing a song that everyone knew all or most of by heart?

Singing with a group of people, especially if it is a group that shares a life together, has a strong impact on the individual singer that singing alone does not. The sense of togetherness, of shared intent, increases the strength of the single person's voice. One is not alone in this world; others believe these words you are singing and have these same hopes and dreams. This reassurance creates a subtle, but strong tie between the people who participate in corporate singing. Is it any wonder that social movements often develop a theme song?

A number of years ago, a friend joined me at a national conference of Episcopal musicians. After the opening service, he said, "Oh, I wish my parishioners could hear this singing. Then they would understand what I'm trying to get them to do." This musician knew that a transforming experience helps create a vision one will seek to recreate. Once someone has heard and participated in enthusiastic congregational singing, (s)he will remember the sound, the feeling, and the heightened awareness that it brings.

Attending a Sunday service at The Upper Room Bible Church in New Orleans, I witnessed another purpose of corporate singing.

The church sanctuary occupied the top floor of a spacious house. It was furnished with pews facing a dais where five singers with hand-held microphones functioned as song leaders. There was a professional pre-recorded accompaniment tape, another musician at an electronic keyboard, and a parishioner stationed at an over-head projector to keep the appropriate transparency for the music projected on the wall. The pastor's role was to speak during the instrumental interludes about the themes of the day, to quote from scripture, to exhort parishioners to increasingly enthusiastic participation, and to give well-rehearsed verbal cues for the next selection to be sung.

From a purely mechanical standpoint, the seamless hour-long mixture of corporate and solo singing with verbal exhortations was exceptionally well-coordinated between singers, pastor, keyboard, tape, and projection. The point of this extended opening rite was to call down the Holy Spirit who would then be present throughout worship. Most of the congregation didn't seem to need to look at the projected music since they knew it from memory and sang it with energy and accuracy. As newcomers, the seven of us Episcopalians were grateful for the aid and joined in easily.

The learning for me was not about the ease with which a room of a hundred or so people could be engaged by the latest of electronic wizardry and professional leadership, but the clear understanding by everyone in the room that it was the *congregation* that called forth the Holy Spirit—not the pastor or the musicians alone, but the congregation. The look on their faces, the sound of their singing, the level of engagement in the room all contributed to a sense that this was corporate prayer. When I hear anemic singing in some of our churches, I wonder that any visitor would be inspired to come back, let alone the Holy Spirit! The missing ingredient is people who are mentally and emotionally present, engaged, and enthusiastic. Singing together is a catalyst that can help people be present, engaged, and enthusiastic, but it is not the panacea. The desire for God must be present in the hearts and minds of people who can then learn how to express that desire outwardly in such ways as singing strongly with conviction. The power of this outward expression is a valuable tool for evangelizing newcomers and visitors. Enthusiasm and sincerity are infectious. For those who come seeking what they can often characterize only as "something more," it will be apparent that "it" is here.

Another aspect of The Singing can be illustrated by describing the way psalms are sung in monasteries and convents. When women or men in religious community sing together, particularly as they chant the psalms, they engage in a kind of corporate singing that is marked by the calm, but powerful, intensity of complete togetherness. It is achieved by each person relinquishing the need to assert leadership and, instead, listening to the breathing, inflection, and speed of everyone chanting, fitting one's own voice quietly into the corporate sound. Besides a heightened awareness of others in the community, one becomes aware of The Presence in a most powerful way. The relaxed monastic sense of time and the *now* of prayer creates a calm focus that is certainly possible in the small parish, or in a mid-week service attended regularly by a small group of people.

I have defined The Singing as "A communal act of the interaction between The Song and The Singer." I have been using the word *communal* to mean that the entire assembly is actively engaged. I also believe that communal can mean being actively engaged in *listening* to a rehearsed person or group. In this case, all listeners are mentally present and interactive intellectually and spiritually with those who are singing.

For many, the communal act of interactive listening will be foreign since we often use music as background sound. We may be aware it is there, and it may contribute to our emotions somewhat peripherally, but we are not deeply engaged with it. Interactive listening requires an aural perception of musical lines and phrases, of the subtle shading and nuances of expression, of the overall form of the music, the heightened awareness of the text as it matches the artistry of the music, and finally, the relationship of the music to the rest of the ritual act. It may be a musically sophisticated person who can do such listening, and it is what is expected that people do when choirs or soloists sing. It is the same kind of listening required for sermons. Also, it can be prayer by the individual, or by a group, on behalf of the larger gathered community. Some congregations misunderstand this form of The Singing as being so individualized that it should not be included in a communal service.

A Singer can transform The Song from a mediocre composition to a meaningful vehicle for the Word on some occasions and The Singing can do the same. When this happens, it is a coincidence of skill, belief, commitment, and grace. This is not to say that the quality of The Song doesn't matter, but rather to point out the matching importance of The Singer and The Singing in the three-way interplay that constitutes what we call church music. C. S. Lewis tells a brief story that illustrates what I mean.

> When I first became a Christian, about fourteen years ago, I thought that I could do it on my own, by retiring to my rooms and reading theology, and wouldn't go to the churches and Gospel Halls; . . . I disliked very much their hymns which I considered to be fifth-rate poems set to sixth-rate music. But as I went on I saw the merit of it. I came up against different people of quite different outlooks and different education, and then gradually my conceit just began peeling off. I realized that the hymns (which *were* just sixth-rate music) were, nevertheless, being sung with devotion and benefit by an old saint in elastic-side boots in the opposite pew, and then you realize that you aren't fit to clean those boots. It gets you out of your solitary conceit.[13]

Considerations Specific to the Small Parish

W hy should the small parish be singled out for special consideration in this discussion? In some parishes there seems to be the belief that everyone can sing and most do when in church. However, in many small parishes there is frequently a real or perceived dearth of musical talent, skill, or ability that keeps whole groups of people silent in church. Perhaps these small parishes are in areas of economic distress or other hardship. At this time, in the early twenty-first century, the relief provided by the local creative folk musician who historically helped make cultural or economic deprivation more tolerable by providing music that addressed these difficulties is largely non-existent. Many schools in such areas have deleted basic music training from their curricula. Personal creativity may have been replaced by the escapism of television.

Whatever the reasons for the lack of music in these churches, there are ways to begin to address this absence. People need to sing. A starting point toward developing a parish that is Singing for Life is to understand the small parish in its context and local culture.

The Importance of Demographics
Small communities vary according to their unique demographics which include geographic location, prevailing culture, community religious history, means of livelihood, and the generational legacy.

The demographics of a parish are an important consideration when deciding what music would be successful in the liturgy. Two hypothetical examples will help to illustrate this.

St. Mark's is a very small parish located in a small community within commuting distance of a major metropolitan area on the Pacific Rim. St. Aidan's, which is the same size as St. Mark's, is located in southeastern West Virginia and is nearly eighty miles over mountainous roads from the closest "city" of 22,000 which is in another state.

St. Mark's has a significant Asian-American population and is shaped by the international business experiences of many of its parishioners. St. Mark's was established ten years ago by three young families who had moved into town from the city as they began to rear children. St. Aidan's was established at the beginning of the twentieth century and is attended by people who have always lived in that community. Those who are employed work in small, local businesses that provide goods and services or they make a hundred-mile round trip daily to work in the power plant.

The only other churches in the area of St. Mark's are a Presbyterian megachurch, a small Baptist church, a Buddhist temple, and two non-denominational churches. St. Aidan's is surrounded by four other churches: Methodist, Baptist, Catholic, and Pentecostal. All of these are larger than St. Aidan's except the Catholic church.

Comparing these two parish contexts, it is easy to see how the choice of music in each parish might be different. St. Mark's may grow by appealing to young families who may not be Episcopalians or who may be unchurched. A known body of congregational music may be quite limited or even non-existent. On the other hand, St. Aidan's has few newcomers and has been singing out of Episcopal hymnals since it was established. However, even though they have *The Hymnal 1982*, they sing few of the newer selections, preferring those they knew in *The Hymnal 1940*.

The challenges to Singing for Life may be greater in those parishes which cannot be as clearly defined by their circumstances as the examples of St. Mark's and St. Aidan's. Some parishes may have a stronger influence than another in, say, its generational legacy. For example, I recently returned to my childhood parish and observed that little had changed in nearly forty years. My high school classmates who still attend that church are worshiping in the same way they had as children. The music had not changed at all. The generational legacy there is very strong and resists change.

The Parish Mindset

A congregation's mindset will help determine what music will be effective, how it will be done, and who will lead it.

Joe Smith, in his paper "Understanding Rural Communities," points out the differences between what he calls "rural" and "metropolitan," saying that they are not necessarily connected to population but are, in reality, mindsets. For example, a person with a rural mindset works in a small institution, has little need to learn complex relational skills, and is always aware that life depends on many risks which cannot be controlled personally. The metropolitan mindset person works in a large institution, needs a high degree of relational and communication skills, rarely recognizes anything that affects their prosperity except the actions of people.

Some issues arise from these differences. First, the metropolitan mindset often assumes it is superior. Second, inner-city dwellers often have a rural mindset. Third, a person from the country may go to the city assuming that he/she has a lot to learn; however, when the city person goes to the country, the assumption is that they have much to teach. I would suggest that the same may be true, respectively, for those who migrate from the "heartland" of the United States to either of the coasts, and vice versa.

Cultural differences exist not only between people with differing national origins, but also between people with differing mindsets. The two outlined above are only a sample. Such cultural differences are facts to be carefully considered when assessing the effectiveness of the liturgy and music of a parish.

Other local cultural phenomenon should also be considered. For example, in one rural state, the request for a volunteer song leader in a local parish that had no parish musician met with a seeming stonewall. It was discovered that if the rector had approached a specific person who had the necessary skills, that person would have readily agreed to do it; however, to expect someone to step forward voluntarily and say, "Yes, I would like to do that," was considered, in that culture, to be thinking too highly of oneself. This person's peers would have thought he was "putting on airs." Such discernments are made only after one has gained the trust of the local community. The existing cultural norms must be guides to those who would work in situations where they are not native to the prevailing culture.

Music Leadership Models

In planning to begin Singing for Life a process of assessment is valuable because it educates the parish about itself and its liturgy. Begin by investigating these areas:

1. The demographics of the parish
   a) Develop a parish profile with special attention to ethnic make-up
   b) Summarize the parish history and the generational legacy
   c) Name factors of current community impact: what changes are occurring that might influence the parish
2. The pros and cons of the existing music
   a) Evaluate the choice of music: look for a balance between old and new, styles used, appropriateness to the propers
   b) Describe the musical leadership—its competence and match for the parish
   c) Discuss the appropriateness of music to church size and resources
3. The resources within the parish
   a) Name musical parishioners and leadership other than the formal, if any
   b) List musical instruments available
   c) Determine the amount of financial support possible for musical resources
4. What changes are indicated?
   a) Choose which are needed immediately
   b) Decide what could be changed in a year, two years, etc.
5. What is needed to implement change?
   a) Consider people as well as things and then ask:
      i) Is it available in the parish?
      ii) Is it available in the community?

The following are possible music leadership models in the small parish. There is nothing magical about these suggestions. Some situations may require a combination of models or something else entirely.

- Priest or bishop functions as song leader. This entails teaching and leading hymns, psalms, and/or service music so that the congregation may sing. Therefore, the congregation sings only when a priest or bishop is there to initiate music. In some areas this may be quite infrequent. There is little opportunity to build a musical repertoire particularly where none has been established generationally.

- Parishioner with appropriate skills functions as a song leader/cantor. (See "The Cantor: Leader of Song, Minister of Prayer" a brochure published by Associated Parishes for Liturgy and Mission.)[14] This person may not necessarily have professional training but will have a natural singing ability with a pleasant voice and a strong sense of pitch and rhythm. Leadership of this type is effective even without accompaniment. When the music leadership is no longer one of the jobs of the clergy, there is more opportunity to build a body of music that serves the community.

- Parishioner with appropriate skills functions as an accompanist using some instrument for accompanying—perhaps a melody instrument such as a flute or violin (fiddle), or a chording instrument such as a guitar, autoharp, or keyboard, etc. The congregation will need to be more self-starting once a musical introduction has been played. A small group of people other than the accompanist may offer vocal leadership to introduce new music by singing it through.

- Professional musician who has some other means of livelihood (or perhaps is an at-home mother/father or retired person) may volunteer to help plan music, function as cantor/song leader and/or accompanist. There may be the establishment of a small group of singers as a choir, although this is not always necessary.

- Professional musician who is hired with parish funds to plan and lead the music.

Small parishes need to look carefully at the question of whether to have a choir. Frequently, small parishes think they are inferior if there is no choir. There is a huge myth that a choir is necessary to lead a congregation in singing; however, it has been my experience that unless there is a very specific acoustical situation in the building, most choirs cannot be heard sufficiently during congregational singing for one to rely on it for leadership. It seems to me, especially in small parishes, that strong singers are needed in the congregation, scattered throughout to provide the leadership that may be needed. If a parish has singers who want to get together to prepare music for liturgy, then it seems a good opportunity to use their skill and enthusiasm in this way. Should they want to offer an anthem, they could assemble at the appropriate time at a designated place, returning to their seats in the congregation afterwards.

An important thing to remember is that music in the liturgy is a necessity even if it is just a few simple acclamations sung at appropriate times. If a parish has not been singing at all, begin by learning something like "Glory to God" in *Wonder, Love, and Praise*[15] which could be used as a song of praise at the beginning of worship. The assumption must be made that most people will want to sing when there is effective leadership and music which they can sing with some practice.

A hindrance to Singing for Life is the assumption that worship must have a high level of perfection. While being well prepared is a goal of leadership, the congregation should not feel that they are expected to *perform* the liturgy. When a congregation is learning new music and building its repertoire, it will be necessary to repeat hymns and songs frequently until they are learned. Mistakes will be made until the music and words are taken to heart. The value of looking at the progress made during this learning process is a good model for accomplishing other long-term goals the parish may have.

Musicians must listen and learn from the community about what music will help it prepare to receive the sacraments and to live out its commitment. In this sense, the musician is a catechist—not only a teacher, but also an instrument for prayer. The musician must address his/her own prejudices regarding issues of taste and musical style. To assist the community in preparing to receive the sacraments, the musician may need to choose and/or lead music sometimes that (s)he does not like. This is the nature of servant ministry and must be balanced with the prophetic role of calling people to new experiences and a deeper emotional, spiritual, and/or intellectual understanding of music.

The following are questions to ask parishioners to help determine musical cultural norms:

- What radio stations do you listen to? What kind of music do you listen to at home or in the car?

- What music would you want to include in a very happy event such as a wedding, baptism, major anniversary or birthday, graduation?

- What song or piece of music causes you to remember a particularly important time in your life? For example, people who were involved in the civil rights movement might recall the song "We Shall Overcome." Do this in both the popular culture as well as the religious culture. The music may be the same.

- When has a hymn or song come to mind during some situation at home or at work? How has it been helpful? For example, in one parish, a business executive was observing a high degree of conflict between two project groups. As he was planning a meeting to initiate reconciliation between the two groups, he called the parish musician to find out the text of a hymn containing a phrase which kept going through his mind. It had to do with conflict, and he wanted to use the text in the meeting.

- When you have experienced the loss of a loved one or have had a serious personal setback, what songs or hymns have been comforting to you?

Singing For Life as Ministry

A commitment to Singing for Life is a ministry not only for the musician in a leadership role, but also for the laity of the parish. Singing for Life means that the practice of singing is a good companion to those physical, mental, and spiritual experiences that constitute existence. Singing is something that can be done with good result from shortly after birth until death. Because of the properties of music, humankind turns to musical expression for those moments when words seem less than adequate.

As Christians, we are called, both laity and clergy, to represent Christ and his church. We are also called to bear witness to Christ wherever we may be and to carry on Christ's work of reconciliation in the world while taking our place in the life, worship, and governance of the church. As we have considered The Song, The Singer, and The Singing, three vital components of church music, we begin to penetrate the depth of the musical experience in liturgy. Once we know this wholeness, we can no longer look at music as non-essential to the liturgy or as a gloss added by those specially trained.

Singing for Life as ministry is not the successful constructing of a music program alone. Whenever one chooses a song to sing between the Epistle and Gospel that enables a deeper understanding of those readings, it is ministry. Singing the words "The steadfast love of the Lord never ceases. God's mercies never come to an end,"[16] with strength and conviction is ministry. One never knows when someone standing nearby is in personal crisis. For that person, the witness of The Song and The Singer may be a much-needed reassurance. The commitment of a parish community to assess its musical needs and work for the development of a musical liturgy that feeds the congregation, and encourages them to grow in the faith, is ministry.

Accepting the Context

Singing for Life as ministry can be done in a parish of any size. Greater numbers and more resources simply mean that the way it is done may be different, not better. A feeding program serving a thousand meals a day in a large urban parish is not necessarily better than one serving fifteen meals a day in a small town. The job of feeding the hungry is being done. Somehow, we seem to think that there is a magic list of equipment and resources that is required to have good music. The first mythical, magical requirement is having an organ and the second is having a choir. Many small parishes so desire having an organ that they will buy something quite inferior musically when another solution with greater musical integrity could have been explored. Accepting the context of the parish does not mean settling for less or ceasing to dream or work toward a vision. It means taking a realistic look at the parish and searching for the pathway of authenticity for the gathered community.

Accepting the context of the parish is the first step to becoming successful at Singing for Life. Once the demographics of the parish have been examined, you may need to evaluate the statistics as they relate to the parish mindset before a valid context can be determined and finally accepted.

As an example, consider a mythical St. Warbuck's Church. It is a parish of one hundred fifty members with an average Sunday attendance of fifty-two, one-third of which are children under the age of seven. The neo-Gothic building, which seats two hundred seventy-five, is in the town of Lansdowne, a small but growing, wealthy suburb of a medium-sized city with one large international corporation which employs most of the parishioners. A retired lawyer and his wife, who spend the winter in Santa Fe, want to make a large donation in six figures for a new organ. The part-time parish musician loves to give organ recitals and is thrilled to have the possibility of a performance instrument. St. Warbuck's has a paid quartet as the choir and uses *The Hymnal 1940*.

The demographics of St. Warbuck's indicate that the primary employer of its parishioners is expanding and bringing in many highly-skilled employees with young families from a recently acquired firm in southern California. It is predicted that the town of Lansdowne will double in size over the next five years. St.

Warbuck's has a sizeable endowment and a metropolitan mindset. The rector is concerned about many things at St. Warbuck's including the possibilities for its future. Before the vestry accepts the donation of the organ, she would like to assess the musical needs of the parish. While the paid quartet is wonderful, she knows that the congregation barely sings. She sees the numerous children and knows there are more to come.

St. Warbuck's is at a critical point in its life in many ways. If we were to delve more deeply, we would find other factors with a significant bearing on the future of St. Warbuck's. However, the proposed donation has narrowed the focus to the issues within the liturgical/musical life of the parish. It is difficult to deal with the variety of implications tangential to the obvious dilemma when the pressure to accept such a donation is looming. If you were the rector what would you do?

Calling Disciples

A frequent observation from very small parishes is that there is no one with any musical skills in the parish. If this is true, then there is little hope for the parish. I will need to be convinced that somewhere there is a community of people who never sing "Happy Birthday," who never listen to the radio or TV, who never hum along with a catchy jingle, or who can't learn to sing the round "Row, row, row, your boat." Perhaps this musically-challenged community has such a hard life that they have simply ceased having anything to sing about. I can believe that could happen. But that would be all the more reason to begin Singing for Life.

Often the musical challenge in the small church is leadership. If there is no one who can play the organ or piano, then look for someone who can sing. This is probably easier than finding someone who plays some other melody instrument such as a flute, recorder, or violin. A person who can demonstrate how a song sounds can be taught how to lead a congregation in singing. This may be a high school student who has headphones permanently implanted. Calling forth disciples is part of the ministry of Singing for Life. Unfortunately, we are often unwilling or unsure whether we should go this far down to the lakeshore for the disciples.

In many dioceses there is a training program called "Leadership Program for Musicians Serving Small Congregations."[17] This is a place that can help gather support for the new disciples.

Endowing the Ministry

St. Warbuck's has all the financial resources it needs. It may not have been aware that it also had a small but valuable endowment in the seventeen children under the age of seven. One hopes that St. Warbuck's invests wisely and doesn't bury its gift of talents to await the master's return.

Most small parishes cannot afford to ignore the children in their midst and do quite well including them in the full life of the parish. This is even more important when a commitment is made to Singing for Life. Not only is the gift of music in the context of a loving community a lifelong skill for our children, but it also provides a heritage for a spiritual and theological journey that grows and grows. We ignore it to our peril.

Having come full circle in our discussion, we can dream of the time when another generation of Christians is ready to consider their earliest recollections of music in church.

Notes

[1] From *Ruling Chiefs of Hawai`i*, p. 425, The Kamehameha Schools Press, Honolulu, 1992.

[2] Winter, Miriam Therese, *Why Sing? Toward a Theology of Catholic Church Music*, Pastoral Press, 1984, p. 243

[3] *Ibid.*, pp. 230-231, Dr. Winter's quote includes references from "Doctrine Concerning the Sacrifice of the Mass," an address by John XXIII, and *Music in Catholic Worship*.

[4] *Ibid.*, p. 232.

[5] *The American Heritage Dictionary of the English Language*, Third Edition, Houghton Mifflin Company, New York, 1996, p. 1446.

[6] As quoted from *Music in Catholic Worship* noted above.

[7] Book of Common Prayer, Church Publishing Incorporated, 1979, p. 847.

[8] *Ibid.*, p. 305.

[9] *Wonder, Love, and Praise: A Supplement to The Hymnal 1982*, Church Publishing Incorporated, 1997, # 824.

[10] *Lift Every Voice and Sing II*, Church Publishing Incorporated, 1993. #31.

[11] *Wonder, Love, and Praise*, Op. Cit., #814.

[12] *The Rite Song* CD-ROM, Church Publishing Incorporated, 1999.

[13] Lewis, C. S., "Answers to Questions on Christianity" from *God in the Dock: Essays on Theology and Ethics*, Eerdmans, 1970.

[14] "The Cantor: Leader of Song, Minister of Prayer" published by Associated Parishes for Liturgy and Mission, www.associated-parishes.org.

[15] *Wonder, Love, and Praise*, Op. Cit., #821.

[16] *Ibid.*, #755.

[17] For information about LPM log onto www.lpm-online.org.

The Seventh Fire is the time we are living now. It was foretold that in the Seventh Fire, a new people would emerge, a new generation who would not let all the pain and anger and lies stop them from finding out the truth about who they are and what has happened. It would be a time when the new people would look back over the trail of Tears of so many generations and ask "why." In looking back, they would notice things others had left beside the trail and they would go back and pick them up and bring those things with them in to where we are now. The things that were left behind were the various ceremonies, the medicines, the drums, the songs, the dances, the languages, the stories – all those things that gave meaning to being an Ojibway.[1]

Towards a Lakota Rite

Martin Brokenleg

General Philosophy
The idea in this section is to state assumptions about this process. These are for discussion and thought. Others may be generated.

0. The process is primarily the responsibility of Lakota who are committed to the Episcopal Church. This does not exclude non-Indian interest and participation, nor does it exclude Lakota who are not Episcopalians. It does say that this process is the obligation and product of the Episcopalian Indian community.
1. The goal of the Lakota rite is assumed to be for worship in the Episcopal Church, mindful of the canons, the Book of Common Prayer, and the customs and traditions of the Anglican communion.
2. The Lakota Rite guidelines are optional at all times, and the obligation of the primary clergy who officiate.
3. Lakota culture, particularly the religious and symbol systems, are the basis for the ritual and ceremony of this Christian rite.

0. For example, colors are to be understood in their Lakota context and not primarily in terms of their western rite context.
1. Ceremony (what is done) is understood in its Lakota context. For example, plains Indian music usually consists of a phrase sung to a melody and repeated many times (akin to the Eastern Orthodox style). This musical form will develop in the future to be used in conjunction with the singing of hymns as in the hymnals we now know.

2. Ritual (the words and texts) rely heavily on the Book of Common Prayer, and <u>Niobrara Service Book</u>.

0. Lakota is to be utilized at every service, at least the Lord's Prayer. This practice touches a deep sense of identity and belonging even among Lakota who do not speak the language, and this is now the majority.

1. Every Eucharist should conclude with a meal provided by the congregation. During the meal elders and honored guests will address the congregation in honor of the occasion.

Arrangements

0. Room arrangements assume the *hocoka* of the home (tipi) or alternatively, of the <u>*wiwayang wacipi*</u> (sun dance). All liturgical arrangements and movement should be consonant with this concept. Movement will always be to the right (clockwise), for example. Consequently. A worship space would typically have an arrangement like this.

Furniture

0. The altar should be just large enough for the Eucharist as it is usually experienced in the location (e.g., 3' x 3' x 3'). Normally, the altar would be covered with red cloth. *Sa*, the essential sacred color, connotes beauty and sacredness as well as the color red.

No candles, books (except what is absolutely necessary for the consecration), or flowers are to be on the altar.

0. The lectern should hold the scriptures. It is normally covered in blue. *To* implies an other-than-ordinary quality.

1. Normally, the center of the space will have a fire. This can be accomplished by a cluster of candles in place of an open fire. Four large candles, perhaps in the colors of the directions, will meet this purpose.

2. Because the burning of offerings such as tobacco is normally done at the fire, a candle stand containing sand may he provided in the middle of the *hocoka* for votive candles. This traditional Christian offering is a reasonable alternative to the offerings burned in the fire in Lakota settings.

3. The seating for honored persons (clergy) is at the liturgical west, opposite the entrance and lectern.

Appointments

0. Plates and cups should be dignified and reflect Lakota culture.

1. Corporals and purificators are normally red.

2. Neither veils nor burses are used.

3. A hand fan such as an eagle wing fan may be used to protect the elements from insects during the service. The same fan may be used to "cense" the people at the beginning of any gathering.

4. Bread used at the Eucharist will be made by members of the congregation.

5. Grape wine for the Eucharist is normally red and sweet, and is mixed with water.

Vestments

0. Clergy and ministers will normally wear tunics and broad stoles (e.g. six to eight inches in width). The tunics are not necessarily white. Chasubles are worn by at least the main celebrant and may be worn by all priests and bishops. Note that the vestment colors need not match.

Ritual

0. Directional prayer is used at the beginning of the gathering or at the intercessions.

Ceremony

0. All ordained clergy will normally participate in any service they attend in vestments, taking part as the main celebrant directs.

1. A deacon will participate at every service and will read the gospel, lead the intercessions, and assist with the distribution of Communion, particularly in taking Communion to the sick. Normally, deacons will conduct parish calling.

Notes

[1] From *The Seven Fires: An Ojibway Prophecy*, related by Sally Gaikesheyongai (Sister Vision, Toronto, 1994).

Christianity has traditionally appeared to place its major emphasis on creation as a specific event while the Indian tribal religions could be said to consider creation as an ecosystem present in a definable place. In this distinction we have again the fundamental problem of whether we consider the reality of our experience as capable of being desribed in terms of space or time – as "what happened here" or "what happened then."

Vine Deloria, Jr. (Lakota)[1]

Our Place: Inculturating [Anglo] Liturgical Space

Juan M. C. Oliver

Introduction

The theology of inculturation—a vision of the life of the church deeply rooted in a profound respect for cultural difference and uniqueness—has had a strong influence on the development of our cultural sensitivity in liturgical design. As a result, very few Episcopalians today would balk if we were to suggest that a Hispanic liturgy should look, feel, and sound Hispanic, or that a Native American worship space should be designed to incorporate elements of native ways of gathering.

Like our homes, decorated with an eclectic mix of furniture and artifacts, the liturgical structure of the church is increasingly variegated, a mosaic of cultural expressions of enormous variety and richness. Most of us find this variety at times discomforting, at times rewarding.

However, in our excitement about the inculturation of the liturgy in African-American, Hispanic, Asian, and Native American communities, we have not focused similar attention on our Anglo experience of worship. Rather, we have assumed that American Anglo worship is already inculturated, although our Anglo worship is by and large a creature from another culture—nineteenth-century Britain. The purpose of this essay is to explore the need for inculturating the liturgical space in North American Anglo worship.

I have employed the theological concept of inculturation to discern possible ways to envision qualities desirable in a modern Anglo-American place of Christian worship. In Part I, I review the theological concept of inculturation under its two main paradigms, Incarnation and Paschal Mystery, and explore the church's life in the context of contemporary America. In Part II, I present the role of liturgical architecture in the formation of an "ethnic domain" or "our place" and suggest avenues for the inculturation of the liturgical place of the church. In conclusion, I draw a picture of an American worship space for the late twenty-first century.

Part I:

The Theology of Inculturation:
Incarnation and Paschal Mystery

Beginning in the early 1960s theologians started to use the term, "inculturation" to refer to the need for the Christian message to be fully incarnated in a given culture in order to be able to transform that culture. In 1978, Pedro Arrupe, then General of the Society of Jesus, defined inculturation as,

> the incarnation of Christian life and of the Christian message in a particular cultural context, in such a way that this experience not only finds expression through elements proper to the culture in question (this alone would be no more than a superficial adaptation) but becomes a principle that animates, directs and unifies the culture, transforming it and remaking it so as to bring about a "new creation."[2]

Anscar Chupungco has defined liturgical inculturation as "the process whereby the texts and rites used in worship by the local church are so inserted in the framework of culture that they absorb its thought, language, and ritual patterns."[3]

Incarnation

A theology of inculturation has, as part of its foundation, the Incarnation of God in human history. But a theology of the Incarnation which views God in history as the intervention of God only "from above" may appear to stress the significance of the Word's own Incarnation into first-century Jewish life and thought but actually suggests that there is nothing of value in that culture (or any other culture) apart from what is brought to it by Christ.

Moreover, this view of the Incarnation entirely "from above" does not do justice to another aspect of Christology: the presence, at the core of creation, of the Word in whom all things were made. It is this presence of the Logos in human history that opens up the possibility of a dialogue between gospel and cultures, a dialogue in which the culture is a dynamic element in relation to the gospel rather than a passive recipient of it.

The doctrine of the Incarnation presupposes the presence of the Word in creation. Theologically speaking, the Word is at the heart of all creatures. The Christ who took human flesh is the Word in whom all has been created. This means that he is at the heart of all human cultures, that he is responsible for all that is good in them, and that he makes them vehicles of salvation.[4]

Following Justin's doctrine of the *logos spermaticos*—which asserts that a generative form of truth can exist in limited quantities outside Christian thought—Aylward Shorter suggests that the Word is present in cultures prior to any conscious knowledge of the gospel. But even Justin does not include an explanation of how the gospel can challenge and transform fallen aspects of cultures; the incarnation of the church and the gospel in a specific culture is not the same thing as the assimilation of the church into a cultural system to give that system divine corroboration. There is a redemptive agenda behind inculturation. It is to this transformative aspect of it that I now turn.

Paschal Mystery and Cultural Transformation

In *Christ and Culture*, H. Richard Niebuhr suggested that the relationship of Christianity to culture was one of transformation: Christ transforming culture. Similarly, Shorter suggests that the incarnation of the gospel in cultures has a transformative goal:

> Inculturation implies that the Christian message transforms a culture. It is also the case that Christianity is transformed by a culture, not in a way that falsifies the message, but in which the message is formulated and interpreted anew.[5]

This transformative aspect of inculturation is not limited to the transformation of non-Christian cultures. All cultures are in need of transformation, and thus transformational inculturation needs to occur in Christian cultures as well:

> Culture...is a developing process and there must be, therefore, a continuous dialogue between Faith and culture. Inculturation is as relevant to the countries of Europe and North America, for example, which have been Christianized and now de-Christianized, as it is to the cultures of the Third World in which the Gospel has only recently been proclaimed for the first time.[6]

The dynamic relationship between faith and culture requires that faith challenge the culture to become everything that it can be, and to forsake its dehumanizing traits. Such a challenge makes conflict inevitable—particularly when the Incarnation is the only paradigm used to build a theology of inculturation. Shorter suggests that the paradigm be enlarged to include the whole Christian mystery, with the emphasis shifted from Incarnation to the Pasch. There are several reasons for this. First, it was through the Pasch of

Jesus that his Spirit became universalized and available across cultures. Second, in order to be transformed, cultures must themselves "die" to all that is not worthy of humanity. Third, the church, by seeking the transformation of cultures, must be ready to witness to the Lord, repeating in itself the pattern of his self-emptying and Pasch.

Inculturation and liberation

If the mission of the church is the transformation of the world, the Paschal Mystery embodies the pattern according to which the church carries out this work. In the same way that the Incarnation is a precondition of the Paschal Mystery, inculturation is a precondition of the church's imitation of Christ's Pasch. In this transformative scenario, inculturation—understood as the Christian life fully incarnated in a given culture—becomes coextensive with liberation. As Christian communities confront the cultural evils of their societies, they also transform those cultures towards greater authenticity, dying in order to bring about new life. In this sense the Paschal Mystery is a paradigm for the church's own death and resurrection in its conflict with the fallen aspects of cultures. As Shorter points out, "The liberation of the poor and the oppressed is the fundamental condition for authentic inculturation. Otherwise the dialogue is not with the true Gospel of Christ."[7]

The Inculturation of the Liturgy

If the liturgy is, as Yves Congar has said, "the epiphany of the Church,"[8] it follows that the inculturation of the liturgy is central to the manifestation of the church, not only to itself, but also to the world.

In its "Constitution on the Sacred Liturgy," Vatican II provided for a certain level of adaptation:

> Provided that the substantial unity of the Roman
> rite is preserved, provision shall be made, when

revising the liturgical books, for legitimate variations and adaptations to different groups, regions,
and peoples, especially in mission countries.[9]

However, this adaptation of the Roman rite envisioned by the
Council Fathers does not go far enough in addressing the funda-
mental cultural spirit characteristic of specific cultures, a spirit that
generates externals such as music, color, and instrumentation.
Writing about the inculturation of the liturgy in Africa, Roman
Catholic liturgist E. Elochukwu Uzukwu suggests that,

> It is only when the liturgist starts to grapple with
> the fundamental perception of the universe by vari-
> ous African peoples, their understanding of the life
> of man lived in dynamic relation to ancestors, to
> good and evil spirits, to good and evil people, to
> the physical universe and God embodied in myth
> and ritual; only when this perception of the uni-
> verse is taken seriously and its role as a problem-
> solving mechanism in the real African universe...is
> seen dia-loguing and not duo-loging with a cri-
> tiqued and living, thereby evolving, Jewish-
> Christian tradition...do we have an African liturgy
> in the making.[10]

Uzukwu goes on to distinguish between "hidden" and systematic creativity in the work of liturgical inculturation. Hidden creativity is found in the music, hymnody, readings and homilies, art and
architecture of African churches, even churches with otherwise
markedly "Roman" liturgies. However, he points out that these
attempts are "mere adaptations which satisfy immediate cravings"
and lack "the space to let go of their primitive dynamism which
could transform the structure."[11]

Systematic creativity, on the other hand, springs from a process of theological reflection by the local church, deepening "its apprehension of the Christ-event through courageous and soul-searching reflection on its faith experience."[12] This reflection leads to the embodiment of the conversion experience of the local church in its own cultural context.

Systematic creativity is a matter of discovering and expressing the identity and mission of the local church in a given cultural milieu, rather than the application of cultural expressions onto an otherwise Roman (or "English") liturgy. Assuming, with Uzukwu, that systematic creativity is the goal of liturgical inculturation, and that mere adaptation is at best a remedial, temporary step, a procedural question may be asked: How does liturgical inculturation take place?

Form and Content in Inculturation

Because inculturation is a complex process, writers tend to consider it by making a distinction between content and form. Thus for Peter Schineller, inculturation involves incarnating the Christian message [content] in a particular form of ministry [form] within a culture,[13] while for Chupungco the inculturation of the liturgy involves the incarnation of an unchanging content in culturally variable liturgical forms. Similarly, Shorter suggests that there is an essential content of meaning captured in variable and contingent liturgical forms.

Chupungco proposes that in the process of inculturation a distinction be made between form and content.

> [The Second Vatican Council's Constitution on the Sacred Liturgy, *Sacrosanctum Concilium*] distinguishes "immutable elements, divinely instituted," from the "elements subject to change…. [The liturgy] is made up of an outward shape or form and an inner meaning or content. The distinction in *S.C.* 21 between the immutable elements and

the elements subject to change is built on this perception of form and content."[14]

He goes on to suggest that "the theological content refers to the
meaning of the rite, while the liturgical form refers to the ritual
shape with which the content is visibly expressed."[15] Chupungco
relies on the distinction between content and form to guarantee
the permanence of one while changing the other. He writes,

> Although the two cannot be separated, they can be
> distinguished and hence studied as individual
> units. It is thus possible to apply dynamic equiva-
> lence to one without touching the other.[16]

Shorter also makes a distinction between unchanging and
changing elements in Christianity. Among the unchanging elements, Shorter lists the original cultural context of Jesus, his historicity, the Incarnation and Paschal Mystery, sacramental words
and gestures, and scripture in its primary meaning. He lists previous theological formulations, and the wording of dogmatic definitions, among changing elements. He sums up: "The meaning is
essential, but the forms in which it is expressed are contingent
upon culture and history."[17]

Schineller, Chupungco, and Shorter are at pains to integrate the
unchanging content of Christianity with its changing forms of
expression—two poles of a dichotomy that serves all three writers as
a safeguard to the church's identity in the midst of change. However,
most contemporary theories of ritual suggest that meaning cannot
be understood in an abstract, universal sense, as if a meaning could
be extracted from a text or a ritual and reinserted into a different
form. Meaning is not a self-subsisting reality, independent of different "manifestations." Rather, it is a social construct, engaged in by
persons seeking to make sense out of their experience.

> Within the humanities and social sciences...notions
> of the neutral observer, a neutral language, and a
> world of brute facts are giving way to alternative
> interests and approaches. The task now is to under-
> stand better human expression as it occurs in particu-
> lar contexts and what and how it means for those
> whose expression it is. What this broad shift involves
> for those of us working in liturgical studies is to rec-
> ognize, finally, that the meanings of Christian wor-
> ship are always "meanings-to-someone."[18]

Students of ritual increasingly suggest that the construction of meaning does not happen at an abstract level but in contextual, embodied, ritualistic ways. For this reason, discussing incultura-tion in terms of an eternal, unchanging content incarnated in vari-able cultural forms ignores the fact that meaning and context cre-ate each other. As Catherine Bell has pointed out, "By virtue of the interaction of a body and a structured environment, ritual works to dispense with conceptualizations or articulations of the relation between its means and ends."[19]

It seems more fruitful, therefore, to consider the object of liturgical inculturation to be not a message, content, or meaning, but the "interaction of bodies with a structured environment"—the church doing the liturgy. It is the living, breathing church that, in its liturgy, inculturates itself in a given culture. This inculturation must be based on the church's own freedom and responsibility to be culturally authentic to its context as well as evangelically authentic to its mis-sion. The concern to preserve, let us say, "the identity of Anglican worship" throughout a multiplicity of inculturated liturgies does not properly involve a distinction between the form and the content of the liturgy, but rather between whether a given church community is authentically Christian and Anglican or not.

The issue of the authenticity of the church applies on two dif-ferent levels: cultural and evangelical. Cultural and evangelical authenticity demand a church that is indigenously related to its culture and, at the same time, truly evangelical: proclaiming, by word and practice, the same news that Jesus proclaimed. It is the church, engaged in praxis—liturgical and otherwise—that inculturates itself, and the issue of inculturation therefore needs to be couched not so much in terms of orthodoxy as in terms of ortho- or heteropraxis.

Modern North American Anglo Culture

Into what is the church inculturating itself? The other articles in this volume explore the inculturation of the church and its liturgy in a variety of "ethnic" settings. It is perhaps too easy for the Anglo reader to be fascinated by these inculturation experiments in other cultural settings while forgetting to inculturate the liturgy in Anglo culture. It may even come as a surprise to some Anglos that there is such a thing as Anglo culture, for—in the popular mind—culture is something to be found in other "ethnic" groups, not in one's own.

What is culture? Marcello De Carvalho Azevedo suggests a useful working definition:

> [Culture is] the set of meanings, values and patterns which underlie perceptible phenomena of a concrete society, whether they are recognizable on the level of social practice (acts, ways of proceeding, tools, techniques, costumes and habits, forms and traditions), or whether they are the carriers of signs, symbols, meanings or representations, conceptions and feelings that consciously or unconsciously pass from generation to generation and are kept as they are or transformed by people as the expression of their human reality.[20]

Although much writing on inculturation arises out of the experience of the church in relation to mission and "foreign" (meaning non-European) cultures, the need to address the inculturation of the church in relation to the "Christian" cultures of Europe and North America is a pressing one.

> There is...a need for inculturation of the Christian message also in relationship to cultures which were intimately connected with and inspired by the church and which even could not be understood historically without its Christian background. Deeply reshaped by modernity and not reached by an inculturated church, these cultures cannot responsibly be considered as Christian any more. Most of the meanings, values and patterns that underlie their social practice and their symbolic level are certainly not in accordance with the meanings and values of the gospel.[21]

We must narrow our scope, therefore, to the inculturation of the church at worship in the context of Anglo-American modernity.[22] According to Azevedo, the impact of the technological revolution, and with it the instrumental nature of technological knowledge and its impact on modern consciousness, has produced several areas of concern for the inculturation of the church.

Azevedo's analysis suggests that, in the culture of modernity, the nature and scope of information systems, the reach of biotechnological developments and the scientific worldview itself, married to a capitalist economic determinism which arises from the same foundations as the scientific worldview, have, while stressing human choice and liberty, also worked to drastically reduce these through worldwide systems of oppression. The church must confront these systems and values of modernity on modernity's own terms—the dignity of the individual as shaper of his or her destiny—while affirming the need for openness to a transcendent God.

Several cultural aspects of American modernity must be considered in any discussion of the inculturation of the church's gathering place:

- The global nature of information systems suggests that the church at prayer must be a world-centered church, aware of world issues and actively responding to them.
- The integrity, autonomy, and freedom of persons at worship are a modern cultural assumption. Modern Christians gather to worship because they want to and not because they have to. Belonging to the church is a matter of choice and not a given.
- Modern Christians see themselves as actively involved in the shaping of their lives.
- A pervasive sense of justice/injustice, based on the freedom of the individual, both imbues modern Christians with a desire for a just society and requires their willingness to work for justice within themselves.
- Modern Christians will have to confront the meanings and values of modern American culture at its foundations.
- These five issues will be echoed below as I attempt to delineate an American sense of Christian community and its worship place.

Part II:
Our Place: The House of the (Anglo) Church

Liturgical Place

This section examines inculturation as it affects liturgical space. First, it is useful to note that the troubling form/content dichotomy examined earlier is also difficult to apply to church architecture. It raises questions such as: What is the content or message of church architecture? What aspects of Christian architecture are immutable? Fonts? Tables? Apses? Gothic arches? Pews? And how can we tell the unchanging essential meanings of Anglican architecture from the changing "expressions" of those meanings?

Furthermore, the distinction between form and content may not be applicable to the inculturation of liturgical space in the same way that it may be applied to the inculturation of a text. Whatever Hagia Sophia meant to the crowds gathered there in the sixth century was in all likelihood different from what the house church at Dura meant to the fifty or so people gathered there in the third. It is not clear to what extent we can speak of an essential meaning of the gathering place of the church, unaffected by historical coordinates and their attendant social, intellectual, economic, and political contexts.

Discussions of liturgical space often refer to the sense of the "sacred." As suggested by Rudolf Otto's *The Idea of The Holy* and Mircea Eliade's *The Sacred and The Profane*, the concern for the sacredness of liturgical space is pitted against the risk of its secularization or profanation. However, as Jonathan Z. Smith has suggested,

> Within the temple, the ordinary (which to any outside eye or ear remains wholly ordinary) becomes significant, becomes "sacred," simply by being there. A ritual object or action becomes sacred by having attention focused on it in a highly marked way. From such a point of view, there is nothing that is inherently sacred or profane. These are not substantive categories, but rather, situational ones. Sacrality is, above all, a category of emplacement.[23]

To say that a sacred space confers sacrality through emplacement is to point out the meaning-making ability of the space. For by "sacred" we usually mean the ability of an object, person, or situation to have ultimate claims on us. Just as meanings must be meanings-for-someone, the sacred is always sacred-for-someone. As James Empereur has pointed out, symbols involve us subjectively:

> The validation of symbols can only take place subjectively. One does not create or destroy symbols by intellectual argument. Their persistence can even appear to be irrational. Symbols are adopted because they answer to our subjective needs and are validated in our experience.[24]

It therefore follows that the liturgical place is meaningful not of itself, but in relation to the persons who inhabit it. Liturgical space is "our place." It belongs to a group, not to the priest or the head of the altar guild.

Our Place: Ethnic Domain

The aesthetics of Suzanne Langer may help to elucidate this sense of "our place." Langer suggests that the arts present semblances of reality, each in its own way—an experience of a virtual, "as if" aspect of life. Architecture presents the semblance, she says, of an "ethnic domain":

> Architecture creates the semblance of that world which is the counterpart of a Self. It is a total environment made visible. Where the self is collective, as in a tribe, its World is communal; for personal Selfhood, it is the home.... Symbolic expression is something miles removed from provident planning or good arrangement. It does not suggest things to do, but embodies the feeling, the rhythm, the passion or sobriety, frivolity or fear with which any things at all are done. That is the image of life that is created in buildings; it is the visible semblance of an "ethnic domain," the symbol of humanity to be found in the strength and interplay of forms.[25]

As a liturgical symbol the place of the liturgy is intimately evocative of the "tribe" which occupies it—the church. The building is the visible and tangible expression of the community that uses it. For this reason considerations of liturgical place must go hand in hand with an understanding of the liturgical assembly as the primary symbolic element in Christian liturgy.

Precisely because the place of the liturgy manifests the self-image of the Christian community, it would be a mistake to attempt the inculturation of liturgical space as merely one element among many others (vesture, music, text, gesture) in liturgy. For if liturgy is to be defined as patterned symbolic action then the role of place as symbol involves creating a structured environment in which bodies and all the other liturgical elements will interact. This structured environment will either support or contradict the display of other symbolic structures. A Eucharistic Prayer from the 1979 Book of Common Prayer, for example, means one thing where the assembly is gathered around the table in a circular formation in a modern building with plants and a large skylight, and something else in a Gothic building where the priest says the prayer facing the east wall at the top of a flight of steps, lost in a cloud of incense at the dim end of a dark room.

In the complex of symbols comprising the liturgy, the assembly is the primary symbol, followed by place. Based on the assembly and place, the other symbols, water, bread and wine, oil, and Bible are assimilated. It is in the context of the gathered assembly that the church uses the other symbols in its liturgical action. Liturgical place is above all, the place of the assembly, the House of the Church.

How Anglos Assemble

How is the church to inculturate its meeting places, incarnating in Anglo- American culture, transforming it in the pattern of the Paschal Mystery?

Empereur has sketched several attributes of what an American sense of Christian community would be like. Such a sense of community would be characterized by its being formed "from the base up rather than being territorially predetermined," and "concerned with the quality of life." It would be informed by a Christological pragmatism "in and for the world around us," and exhibiting "pluralism in ritual, structure and theology," while seeing itself as a processual reality, the church as "an event moving throughout history."[26]

This American sense of community parallels what Lawrence A. Hoffman has characterized as a shift away from an "Ottonian" sense of sacred to mean "numinous" towards a new sense of "*communitas*":

> ...a cultural setting in which class structures are removed, social distance dispelled; ...The new master image of community emphasizes the fellowship, the group, what in contemporary Hebrew parlance is known as the *chavurah*. Its vocabulary includes words like "persons," "openness," "relationships," "sharing."[27]

Besides this shift in the sense of the sacred, there is the question: How do Americans gather? The question raises several issues, most notably the fact that Americans do not often gather. Families share a table less and less often and neighbors live for years on the same block without knowing each other. However, when Americans do gather, several characteristics stand out:

- We gather on time, freely, and often in places of natural beauty.
- The event begins fairly quickly.
- Our gatherings, if they are social, always involve food, but seldom singing and dancing (although music is often performed or played electronically).
- Dress, although at times extremely casual, is rarely meaningless.
- We mingle, move around and visit with each other freely.
- We express gratitude by bringing something or by writing or calling the host afterwards.
- Significance in these events is tied closely to aesthetics. A more

"valued" event will likely involve "higher" aesthetic choices—which often, though not necessarily, means more expensive choices.

If we take these elements seriously, we begin to see a clear picture of an Anglo assembly's place of liturgy. Members of such an assembly would:

- be aware of themselves as the central agent of the liturgy and would therefore facilitate the moving around, seeing, touching, and hearing of one another;
- understand themselves to be consensual sources of authority and empowerment;
- foster and display the creativity of members;
- include nature as one of the main foci of the sacred;
- pay attention to the aesthetic qualities of the objects used;
- make provision for singing and dancing (if these were participatory rather than performance pieces);
- take into account that people would bring food, money, and other gifts as expressions of gratitude.

Most church buildings cannot accommodate this assembly. In fact, they facilitate the obverse of this picture, preventing human contact, keeping people's creative powers at bay, and separating them from nature while placing the focus of power and authority almost anywhere except upon the people.

A fully inculturated place of the church would look and feel less and less like a commercial theater. Instead, it would embody the expectation that people do not simply attend the liturgy: they do it. Thus the seating arrangement would surround the ambo, so people might not only see and hear Scripture readings, but also see each other's responses to them. The area around the table might be large and uncluttered, so the people may stand around it with the presider. The font might be placed so that the people can easily approach it from all sides, to sign themselves, to welcome neophytes, perhaps to dance or process around it.

The evidence of the community's work in service to its surrounding world would shape the look and feel of its place. The place would reflect the community's life of justice and its solidarity with the marginalized, including them in the liturgy, insuring accessibility, and perhaps favoring the creative endeavors of marginal peoples and third world cultures.

Such a place might embody a sense of what it would be to live in a just American society: a place where individuals are valued in their relationships to each other as active creators of those relationships; where authority resides in the self; and where differences among selves are experienced as a blessing rather than a threat. Therefore the look and feel of liturgical places will differ from one another, and celebrate that difference rather than aspire to bury the uniqueness of the local Christian community under a generic "Anglican" churchiness.

Thus, the inculturated assembly would leave behind the Romantic confusion that cannot distinguish nineteenth-century England from the sacred. An inculturated house of the church for an Episcopal Anglo congregation may come to express Anglo culture while transforming it with gospel values.

Notes

[1] From *God is Red: A Native View of Religion*, p. 78, Fulcrum, Golden, Colorado, 1994.

[2] Pedro Arrupe, S.J., 1978 "Letter to the Whole Society on Inculturation," in J.Aixala, (ed.) 1981. *Other Apostolates Today: Selected Letters and Addresses of Pedro Arrupe S.J.* Vol. 33, 172–181.

[3] Anscar Chupungco, O.S.B., *Liturgies of The Future: The Process and Methods of Inculturation.* (New York: Paulist Press, 1989) 29.

[4] Aylward Shorter, *Toward a Theology of Inculturation.* (Maryknoll, N.Y.: Orbis Books, 1988), 78.

[5] Shorter, 14.

[6] Shorter, 11–12.

[7] Shorter, 248.

[8] Referred to by E. Elochukwu Uzukwu. 1987. "Liturgy: Truly Christian, Truly African," *Spearhead.* No. 74, Dec., 1987. 29.

[9] *Sacrosanctum Concilium*, 38

[10] Ibid.

[11] Uzukwu, 36. (I utilize Uzukwu's understanding of the work of inculturation as inseparably related to a culture's fundamental perception of the universe in Part II in an attempt to apply inculturation to the area of Anglo liturgical space.)

[12] Uzukwu, 37.

[13] So Peter Schineller, S.J., 1990 *A Handbook on Inculturation.* (New York: Paulist Press) 65 ff. The "Christian message" is the object of inculturation, as shaped by tradition, scripture, and the *magisterium.*

[14] Chupungco, 36-37.

[15] Chupungco, 37.

[16] Ibid.

[17] Shorter, 255.

[18] Michael B. Aune. 1991. "Worship in an Age of Subjectivism Revisited." *Worship* 65,3: 224–238. For the expression, "meanings-to-someone," cf. Ronald Grimes, Ritual Criticism (Columbia: University of South Carolina Press, 1990), 42.

[19] Catherine Bell, 1990. "The Dynamics of Ritual Power," *The Journal of Ritual Studies.* 4/2 (Summer, 1990) 310.

[20] Marcello De Carvalho Azevedo, S.J. *Inculturation and The Challenges of Modernity.* (Rome: Gregorian University, 1982) 10.

[21] Azevedo, 29.

[22] Perhaps it would be more accurate to speak of post-Modernity. However, for the sake of clarity I will keep Azevedo's term.

[23] Jonathan Z. Smith. *To Take Place: Toward Theory in Ritual.* (Chicago: University of Chicago Press, 1987) 104.

[24] James Empereur, S.J., *Exploring the Sacred.* (Washington, D.C.: the Pastoral Press, 1987) 41.

[25] Suzanne Langer. *Feeling and Form.* (New York: Charles Scribner's Sons) 1953. 98–99.

[26] Empereur, 52–3.

[27] Lawrence A. Hoffman. *Beyond The Text: A Holistic Approach to Liturgy.* (Bloomington: Indiana University Press, 1989) 168.

I talk both ways, Indian way and Bible way; if you really know about them, they are the same. But people today don't know about either, and these are the ones causing the trouble.

Joe Flying By (Lakota)[1]

Mother the Earth

William C. Wantland

In Greek mythology, Gaea is the goddess of the earth, sometimes referred to as Mother Earth. Other mother goddesses of that time include Isis of Egypt, Astarte of the Canaanites, and Ishtar of Babylonia. Worship of these goddesses was strictly condemned in the Old Testament. These deities were seen as expressions of the divine power, and were usually part of a pantheon of pagan divinities. Certainly, the worship of these mythological beings is forbidden to Christians as the worship of false gods, condemned by the first and second commandments.

Recently, American society has seen a rise in interest in the worship (or at least respect) given to Gaea, as Mother Earth, both by some environmentalists and by some proponents of New Age neopaganism. Often, non-Indians refer to "Indian spirituality" as embracing respect (and possible worship) for "Mother Earth." Does Indian spirituality embrace this pagan concept of Gaea or Astarte, or is the reference to "Mother Earth" compatible with Christianity?

First, it is necessary to point out that there is no such thing as a unified "Indian spirituality." There are more than 300 Indian tribes and nations in the United States, speaking 200 different languages, each representing a different viewpoint of spiritual understanding. It is appropriate to speak of Lakota spirituality, or Seminole spirituality, or Chippewa spirituality, but not of a generic universal practice of spirituality.

Each and every culture has particular ways of expressing spirituality and beliefs. For example, in the first-century culture of the

Middle East, the symbol of cleansing was the act of washing. Baptism became a spiritual symbol of cleansing of the soul, and hence a rite of initiation into a religious belief system. It was part of the rites by which Gentiles became proselytes of Judaism. Baptism was later used by John the Baptist, and later still by Christians.

By the same token, bread and wine were the staples of diet in the Middle East, as tortillas and pulque were in Central America. Jesus took these cultural symbols and made them outward and visible signs of the sacrament of the Eucharist.

For Christians, these cultural symbols of the Middle East have become universal sacramental signs. What Jesus used, we now use, even if our own ethnic or cultural background did not originally include these sacraments. Christianity, as it spread from the Middle East to Africa and Europe, adapted local cultural symbols to express Christian truth to people who otherwise might not have easily understood the Christian message.

We are familiar with the missionary work of St. Boniface, who ended the pagan German worship of the oak tree by replacing it with the evergreen, which, by remaining green year round, symbolizes eternal life, and so now, as the Christmas tree, represents the Incarnation of Jesus. In the same way, the pagan springtime colored egg became the Easter egg, the symbol of Christ bursting from the tomb as a baby chick bursts from the egg. There is also the Roman practice of celebrating the winter solstice (the feast of Sol *Invictus*) as the rebirth of the sun, but now the date of celebration of the birth of the Son, the Nativity of Christ.

Various Indian cultures have ways of expressing theological concepts which are compatible with Christian understanding, and therefore are excellent teaching tools for the church. Just as early Christians used incense, so do Chippewa people use sweet grass, and Navajo people use cedar. Just as for Europeans, and some Asiatics, a bell calls one to meeting or worship, the ram's horn served that purpose in ancient Israel, so too a conch shell in Hawaii, or an entrance song in Plains Indian culture.

On the other hand, there are cultural symbols which clearly cannot be used by Christians, as they symbolize concepts contrary to Christian belief. The pentagram in the Middle East and Eastern Europe is a symbol of the powers of evil. The Inuit chants to placate evil spirits and the Navajo belief concerning dead bodies and the souls of the dead are incompatible with Christian theology.

There are many ways various Indian peoples might use their own symbols to express Christian truth. But what about Mother Earth? What do Indian people mean when they speak of the earth as our mother? Remembering that we cannot speak for all Indian people indiscriminately, nonetheless, most Indian people would share a common belief in one God, who creates all that is, and would carefully distinguish between the Creator and the created order (the universe).

• • •

Several years ago, an elderly Chippewa woman spoke to a number of male prison Inmates at a Wisconsin state prison. She was not a Christian, but followed the traditional religion. I remember clearly her admonition to the Indian inmates: "Do not be fooled by the white beliefs. Always remember, God is your Father, and the Earth is your mother. Do not confuse the two."

Most Indian people see God as the source of all that is, the Creator. All that is created, including the earth, is part of our extended, created, family. For this reason, many Indian people will speak of "our brother, the deer," or "our cousin, the tree," or "our mother, the earth." This in no way expresses any concept of an earth goddess, or of divinity in the earth. This distinction between Creator and creation, between God as Father and Earth as mother, simply reflects one clear strand of holy scripture, and of Christian spirituality that is present in a great deal of Indian spirituality.

In Genesis, God orders the earth to give birth to all forms of life, both plant and animal: "God said, 'Let the earth produce fresh growth, ... plants bearing seed...'" (Gen. 1: I 1). "God said, 'Let the earth bring forth living creatures ... all according to their kind" (Gen. 1:24). Genesis 3:19 also speaks of all coming from the earth and returning to the earth.

This is paralleled in Ecclesiastes: "All came from the earth (dust) and to the earth (dust) all return" (Eccl. 3:20). Later, in Ecclesiastes, the phrase "Mother Earth" actually appears—"As he came from the womb of Mother Earth, so must he return, naked as he came" (Eccl. 5: 15).

In the opening verse of chapter 40 of Ecclesiasticus, the earth is referred to as the "mother of all": "A heavy yoke is laid on the sons of Adam, from the day when they come from their mother's womb until the day of their return to the mother of all (the earth)."

Too many modern Americans cannot accept that Christianity was not originally expressed in European terms, is not culturally wed to European culture, and can borrow symbols from any culture which may have excellent ways of expressing the universal truths of Christianity. Many Indian symbols may be ways of expressing Christian truth that seems strange to Europeans, but not to those who see through the eyes of other cultures.

Note

[1] From *In the Spirit of Crazy Horse*, by Peter Matthiessen (Viking, New York, 1983, p. xxix.

We sing in order to survive.

An Ojibwe singer[1]

Inculturation:
Not Just A Dairy Product Anymore

Monte Mason

Inculturation is a word apt to be used in certain crypto-liturgical circles, as though people "out there" could not possibly glimpse its magnificence. So, to those not within this circle, it often catches some off guard, like a sudden attack of lactose intolerance, lexicographically speaking. Inculturation is a word full of the richness of these uncertainties, heavily dependent upon the perceived correctness of the person using it or the use to which it is applied. Generally, it is safe to use the word as a term of grateful approbation, received by one culture as a gift from another. Should one wish to avoid the term altogether, one could easily choose from a rather healthy list of words—assimilate, gather, absorb, incorporate, assemble, etc.

Be that as it may, inculturation is nothing more than cultural borrowing or stealing, depending on one's viewpoint. The process is as old as humankind and continues to be a decisive indicator of societal health, establishing norms of cultural refreshment. Its practice seems unnoticed, like an involuntary exchange of perfumed airs. Yet inculturation is not always easy to define, examine, or prove. Examples of its dilatory nature are placed within this paper for consideration and further thought. What follows is a broad discussion of inculturation: its general effects upon the arts in the nineteenth and twentieth centuries as pertaining to the Anglican Church in Europe and America, its effect on so-called classical music, and on the music of hymnody. Along the way, the article attempts a critique of victimization "art" and as a case study of an entirely different sort, discusses musical inculturation in Minnesota, using the hymn "Many and great are thy works" (Lac qui Parle). Finally, there is a how-to commentary for the aspiring musician.

As the contents of this book should indicate, this article is by no means exhaustive, nor should it be. Its main purpose is to be both descriptive and provocative, for what at first may seem to be inculturation may be something else, and what is not assumed to be inculturation may in fact, be just that. Further complicating the issue is the understanding that inculturation exists on several planes, running the gamut from very superficial to the most profound.

Entry into this confusing arena is perpetrated by the following list, gleaned from the author's imagination and a general sort of music history. The list is selective and does not even include the very real instance of the inhabitants of a small south seas island, who upon discovering airplanes in places they thought only birds could fly and clouds could float, fashioned models of these machines and placed them on upwardly jutting promontories.

Specimen #1: In 1954, Jacqueline Smith brings back a straw mat from an earthen community in Africa. She had such a good time there, was moved by the beauty of the land, the strength of its people, and wished a *carte de visite* from same to remind her that indeed, travel was broadening. She placed this carefully selected memento, a mat of fine weaving, upon a wall in her living room, the space already tastefully decorated in a fashionable Danish modern Sante Fe. There the mat remains to this day, reminding not only Jacqueline, but all whom she invites to her home, of her good fortune in having the wherewithal to go to Africa in 1954, or was it 1955; it's been such a long time.

Specimen #2: The famous Turkish Janissary bands take eighteenth-century Europe by storm. For the first time, Western composers and public are exposed to the sound of timpani, bass drums, cymbals, and triangles.[2] Western music has existed for quite a few centuries without much knowledge of these instruments and the need to use them. Yet after exposure to *banda turca*, before long the likes of Gluck, Mozart, Haydn, von Weber (*Turandot*), and Beethoven (*Ruins of Athens, Ninth Symphony*) start to use them. Since sound shapes form, the discovery of the percussive color of these instruments has changed Western musical thought forever and made drum and bugle corps possible (go, *Blue Devils*).

Specimen #3: Similar circumstances occur with the arrival of Javanese gamelans to the Exposition Universelle, Paris, 1889-1890. Other such ensembles are to follow. The sound, rhythms, and formal structures of the gamelan delight Debussy and Ravel. Debussy includes whole stretches of gamelanian music in his piano compositions, Ravel in *Mother Goose*. Timbres, rhythms and repetitive features of this music continue to influence Lukas Foss and Oliver Messian several decades later. These concepts become the ideological darlings of the minimalist school of composition in the last third of the twentieth century.

Specimen #4a: Louis Moreau Gottschalk, the American Liszt, so to speak, incorporates Creole melodies into his compositions, some of them quite dazzlingly fine, and plays them to enraptured audiences in North and South America. Debussy and Ravel also pick up strands of American popular music, common to the dance hall and bistro. Yet another Frenchman, Darius Milhaud, finds himself in New Orleans, the better to understand American jazz forms and ethos.

Specimen #4b: The influence of jazz and related idioms upon the compositions of the so-called classical mid-twentieth-century American composers weighs heavily upon likes of Copland, Gershwin, Bernstein. This is so well known that to mention it at all borders on overstating the obvious. Yet, further comment is needed, because the esthetic of American musical identity clearly places these composers within a *floraisance* of nationalistic identity.

Since this classification speaks to understanding of inculturation, we look further.

Inculturation from Within: America and Europe

Although European artistic styles were clearly stamped with nationalistic identities centuries earlier, what is now understood to be an esthetic of clear nationalistic expressions of them were not promulgated until roughly the 1860s. It was around this time that artists, composers, playwrights, etc., sought national identity by relying on indigenous inspiration from nature or folk motifs, be they febrile, visual, aural or textual. They sought identity and value in the Ur nature of a primitive simplicity, of local geography and landscape. In the visual arts, we have such examples as the grouping, *en famille*, of Scotsman Charles Rennie Mackintosh (1868-1928), architect Louis Sullivan (1856-1924), gardener Gertrude Jekyll (1843-1935), and the decorator William Morris (1834-1896). Additional expressions of natural or domestic landscapes were provided by the playwrights Henrik Ibsen (1828-1906) and Anton Chekhov (1860-1904).

In the United States and England, the various expressions of most of this esthetic have been called the Arts and Crafts Movement. Although the manifestations of the ideas promulgated by it took slightly differing turns on either side of the Atlantic, it was essentially the same, for the stylized expression of natural forms expressed not a patriotic nationalism so much as it did a geographic one: a pride of place and earthly origin. We may thus view the contemporary and congruent rise of interest in the use of natural, or folk, music within the same esthetic, even though the name of the Arts and Crafts movement seems rarely applied to it. Nevertheless, it is well represented by a venerable host of composers—Grieg, Sibelius, Smetana, Dvorak, Mussorgsky, Stanford, Holst, Vaughan Williams, McDowell, Respighi, Bartok, Copland, Gerswhin, etc. All of these composers were heavily influenced by folk music or the depiction of folk stories. Since utilization of this material varied from superficial to basic and formal, we look at two composers and compare the manner in which they incorporated folk music into their compositions. If the reader accepts the author's line of reasoning, then both will have concluded, *a due*, that it is not always easy to spot superficiality of intent, even when much is to detect. Herewith a discussion of the music of Edward MacDowell and Antonin Dvorak.

We take first the American, Edward McDowell (1861-1908), for instead of hewing steadfastly only to the then current pieties of divine European inspiration, he sat in his proper Bostonian back yard, the one infested by the ivy of the same name, and produced his "Orchestral Suite #2," subtitled and often know as *The Indian Suite*, in the year 1897. This work incorporates conscious applications of Native American melodic structures and represents a thoughtful treatment of native music by someone "outside" of its milieu. Lest we view the connection too favorably in light of this discussion, it should be said that the entirety of McDowell's work might be better characterized as a composer's response to Adirondackian sympathies, and his excursion into the Native American milieu likened to an elevated appreciation of the use of birch bark as wall paper.

The last decade of the nineteenth century also contained Antonin Dvorak's three-year visit to the United States, spent mostly in New York, New York. However, a side trip allowed for a summer in the Czech community at Spillville, Iowa, in 1893. That same summer, he partook of the relative nearness of Minneapolis, 150 miles north, and once there, the opportunity of visiting Minnehaha Falls (named subsequent to Longfellow's 1855 poem, *Hiawatha*, and never know by that name by local Indians). His impressions of this journey are well know and have been recorded elsewhere.

Much notice has been given Antonin Dvorak's compositional use of American idioms, especially of black materials. These are most famously found in the "American" quartet and quintet, Op.

96 and 97, both written in Spillville. His use of of black motifs and/or inspiration in the *New World Symphony* is also widely known. Less appreciated is his interest in Native American materials, but in at least one instance, a *Sonatina* for violin and piano, Opus 100, we find a native melody, whose slow theme was penned, we are told, whilst at the falls of Minnehaha, and so great was the double excitement of (1) experiencing this joyous cataract and (2) the almost simultaneous hearing of an Indian tune, that having no paper upon which to write same, Dvorak was forced to make notation of the melody upon an article of clothing, namely a portion of his shirt.

This tired nineteenth-century cliche of the tune-on-the-shirt-cuff is assigned to many such composer stories and is here given weight by its inclusion in the Minnesota Historical Society exhibit dealing with Dvorak's visit to Minneapolis and the melody in question. And, as he wandered about the bosky dells and sun-kissed fields of Spillville, oft times sans sketch book, it does seem he was wont to write on many, presumably accessible, portions of his shirt.[3] The veracity of Dvorak's inclusion of the Native American "air" need not be treated so lightly, however, for the interactive exhibit not only displays the music, but plays it at a touch of a button.

Other than the refreshing freedom that allowed them to appreciate a good tune wherever they found it, Dvorak and MacDowell would seen to have very little in common. Yet there are similarities which they shared with the good company of others, Grieg and Sibelius included: a keening romanticism which had its roots in the nineteenth century. They were all lured by the siren call of trolls and wispy things behind dark trees. The deep woods represented a gloomy Gothic glamour, if you will, to such sensibilities and finds similar expression in the period's landscape art as well.

It is difficult to charge the two composers with many more substantial similarities than these. Dvorak's use of American folk material, black or red, is not nearly as indicative of a love and desire for things American than it is an attempt to inform a Bohemian understanding of musical nationalism. It is most definitely not a very loud transatlantic sort of hello. His Gothic romanticism (*Silent Woods*, "Goblin's Tale," etc.) leaves room for the possibility that any American music could, at the time, be considered part of the fantastic and exotic world of romanticism, no matter whence its inspiration. Dvorak's use of folk idioms was informed by an already deeply felt expression of Bohemian nationalism and identity. So great was his gift for assimilation that he could have visited the Canary Islands and written charming fishing songs for piano four hands. But the artistic result would still be a Bohemian identity, not a salmagundi of Canary sea bass.

MacDowell had a much different esthetic: his forte was the elegant and descriptive miniature and, for this, his language was best kept to the programmatic romance of field, woods, and sea—*Woodland Sketches, Forest Idylls, Sea Pieces, From an Old Garden*. But again, it is not at all a stretch to continue the list with *Orchestral Suite #2, The Indian*, for German romanticism cared more about the fearfully exotic than it did about rescuing a particular native air from oblivion.

The above comparisons lead to some distinctions concerning inculturation. In both cases, historic examples have been brought forth from the last decade of nineteenth century America and at a time when America itself was awakening to its possibilities in the name of the Arts and Crafts Movement. The esthetics of the two composers are equally satisfying and compelling; their music more so—nevertheless, their use of Native American or Black materials was incidental to their esthetics. One receives the decided impression that the eastern European composer did the better job with American assimilation than did the American; but, as stated earlier, Dvorak's esthetic led to deeper applications of a Czechoslovakian nationalism. MacDowell's borrowings were informed by his understanding of a translated Teutonic romanticism.

Given this short analysis of one type of superficial inculturation, it is clear that restraint needs to be exercised before calling such and such inculturation. Yet in other areas, it is quite possible to place the American use of its indigenous idioms within the same stream of European nationalism discussed above, and it was only a matter of time, MacDowell notwithstanding, before Gershwin, Copland *et alia*, began to express these ideals in ways that readily filled American culture with its iconic flavor. To accomplish this, Copland used folk music of the Appalachians, the cowboys, and Mexico. Gershwin's inspiration was found in the popular music that had its roots in the complex mixture of American minstrel shows, camp meetings, and black music of the nineteenth century.

England Again Turn Insular

For the purpose of hymnology and congregational song, we turn to other expressions of nineteenth-century assimilation. Because our topic is the inculturation of hymnody and things ecclesiastically useful, we speak of English Hymnody, and about this topic, so much has been said that it need not be said again, except that the British Isles also underwent a nineteenth-century recognizance of its folk music.

One of the first Anglican manifestations of the import of its folk tradition in relation to hymnody is found in the 1871 publication of *Christmas Carols, New and Old*, edited by Henry Bramley (text) and John Stainer (music). This slim volume contains many tunes that were latterly made famous by their inclusion in the *Oxford Book of Carols* (1928) and other such volumes.

Christmas Carols, New and Old, gave public notice to the value of Scottish, Welsh, English, and Irish folk material, and it was soon learned that once in published circulation, these tunes—even the ones on the bawdy side of secular—could be adapted to the use of the church. What was more, their elegant simplicity, born of decades of "long-term composing" (*fide* George Pullen Jackson) had a means of gaining quick public approval. The interest in folk melody carried Englishmen beyond their borders; Cecil Sharpe became well known for his travels to America, the better to report back the news of what had happened to British tunes, now that they had been visiting in the colonies for awhile.

Such was their appeal, that a corpus of folk music of the British Isles began to appear in other English collections, most notably the Martin Shaw/Ralph Vaughn Williams/Percy Dearmer collaborations, *Songs of Praise* (1931). They garnered further popularity in Methodist and Presbyterian publications, as well as *The Hymnal 1940*.

Another way to look at the rediscovery of British Isles folk hymnody and song is that this interest began to show itself at roughly the same time as did the Oxford Movement, which in turn was concurrent with the beginning of the chant reforms of Solesme. The monks of Solesme urged a return to a musical historicity through the study and historically informed performance of plainsong. Founded in 1833, by Dom Gueranger, as a center for plainsong study, Solesme hit its stride with the 1881 "Les Melodies gregoriennes, d'apris la tradition" by Dom Pothier. The English desire to rescue its vast treasure of folk music is thus placed in a much broader context—a nineteenth-century European desire to uncover roots and to place those roots within historical imperative.

Historicity – A fad of the centuries

One hundred and fifty or so years later, we find that this drive towards historic authenticity continues, stronger than ever. It is present in architectural reference, archeological unearthings, liturgical retrieval of sacred texts, and the study of historic norms that surrounded their presentation. The obvious fault of this movement is and was that the point of the correctly perceived origin is faddish at best, utterly confusing at worse.

From which time-chest do we choose, and can we justify rethinking liturgical norms of the thirteenth century while the fifth century beckons with the far greater riches of earlier opprobrium? And why is it so important to rediscover and replicate, for example, third-century liturgical norms when we fail to insist that accompanying simulations of authentic music and art do not also accompany them? The deeper we dig into historicity, the more the tendrils of its extremes tend to include stunted growths, such as the demagoguery that uses an aberrant form of historicity to justify changes in liturgy, abandoning current practice for the sake of 246 A.D., all in the name of The More Historic Christ.

The opposite, or the curse of historicity, seems to fuel much of the Mega-Churches' energy, and has most certainly given so much power to many renewal movements of times gone by. Both these phenomena tend to abandon any pretense to organized church affiliation. Such an approach disavows the historicity of the Church, consigning it to the closet of singular reproach. To deny this identity implies that faith must perforce be based on a history, that Jesus is alive now, and that his historic presence cannot, for example, vivify the presence of God within our twentieth century, post micro-chip lives.

Yet the drive towards authenticity and the kiss of its intellectual/cultural approval is indicative of a great yearning. This cannot be denied, even given the seeming success of efforts to do so, for there exists an obvious human drive to improve upon the present through assimilation of the urgencies of the past.

From Within
While we may be thus comfortable with the idea that inculturation is a process based on a superimposed external commodity, we are less comforted by the idea that the need (or process) of inculturation is primarily based upon internal stimuli, and the proposition that there may be, indeed, an abundance of such stimuli. A culture discovers anew its own wealth and brings it back to the mainstream—the historic approach. Yet it might, at the same time, also welcome ahistoric forms of material even while spinning off bits of stuff to other cultures, such as a star gathers material into something, which through the course of history is then subsumed

into the pantheon of necessitated icons, dusting it off now and again to see if it might perform double duty as something more than a museum piece.

We have already discussed the case of the Anglican Church and its nineteenth-century assimilation of British folk music. That this should have happened is not too surprising. In the eighteenth century, the Anglican Church was vivified anew by the curious necessity of the bodies politic and cleric—Mother Anglia dropped the Brothers Wesley from her social circle, perfectly thrilled with the idea that she could officially ignore the pests if only they would agree to let themselves in through the back hall. Anglican hymnody was agreeably stimulated by this arrangement and we cannot today imagine this body of hymnody were it not for those pesky Methodists and their not so secret admirers.

As to the United States of the mid nineteenth century, many would be surprised to find that some of our most cherished nineteenth-century offerings (or abominations; the cheerful reader must decide) have been assimilated from the Lowell Mason/William Bradbury/Stephen Foster repertoire, originally designed not towards the inculcation of adult spirituality, but to the inspiration of our little dears, the angels in the Sunday School Department.

Francis Densmore and Her Famous Wax Cylinders
[While reading through this next section, the reader may well wonder as to its inclusion. While not immediately obvious, its import will be made clear in a later discussion on the practical merits of applying resources from one culture to another.]

It is a source of continuing fascination that technology often precedes artistic development. Such developments often follow the same tendency in the acts of inculturation and it is interesting to explore the rise of interest, study, and documentation of folk music once the phonograph and wax cylinder had been invented. This invention is generally dated to 1877, the year of Edison's famous non-electric recording of "Mary had a little lamb." Musical anthropology was thus ushered into a period of unprecedented opportunity; instead of relying on fallible notational devices, it could, without electricity, carry recording devices and blank wax cylinders into the field, recording note for note the music of van-ishing peoples or their changing ways.

Heretofore, the exacting complexities of non-notational systems had eluded even the experts, for the western system of notation was not adequate to the display of micro-tones and micro-rhythms. Newer notation attempted to deal with these inherent problems, but served rather to negate the freedom of understand-ing and performance.

Into this new world of sound saving devices entered Minnesota's own Frances Densmore, who notated, recorded, and analyzed the music of various North American tribes at the turn of the century. In the case of the Ojibway, her major work was published in two volumes in 1910 and 1913. It is now simply called *Chippewa Music*. These volumes were compilations of her field work at the Red Lake, White Earth, Leech Lake, and Lac du Flambeau reserva-tions, covering vast tracts of lake and forest in the northern half of Minnesota. These places are still somewhat remote, at least con-ceptually, from the rest of the state. They were extremely remote in the early days of the century, when travel to them was purchased by the rigors of former ox carts on logging roads. To achieve her studies, Frances demonstrated levels of devotion we might now fail to appreciate, and her activities are thus all the more remarkable.

Her work took her elsewhere in the states, and her studies of other native music were just as impressive. She always took great care to place an understanding of native music within its cultural and societal framework. In the case of the Ojibway repertoire, she was even able to ascertain in some cases what strand of tradition, which Ojibway band "owned" what music, and even to place a particular song within historical context in terms of newer or older traditions. This latter discernment could help her understanding of a song and whether it had become "tainted" by fads, white influence, extra-tribal influence and so on.[4]

Like the artists Eastman, Catlin, and Curtis, Frances Densmore arrived in the nick of time to record the practices of presumed dying cultures. Using the same cultural hegemony to collect what was laid to destruction, Densmore fits into the same category of painters, photographers, and archeologists wishing to preserve bits of foreign cultures rapidly disappearing. Today we might call that morally reprehensible. But there is an ambiguity in such a statement, because cultural artifacts were then, and are now, understood to have historic, cultural, and emotional values, reflexive upon the culture which gave birth to, or inherited them. Further, these artifacts are sometimes identified by other cultures as unique restatements of their values and are changed or molded to reflect notice within the new culture. They thus become cross-cultural or multi-cultural. But once this occurs, there is yet another transference, this time from the culture which co-opts another's expression. In order to become subsumed into another culture, that culture must first at some level, analyze the artifact's availability as to its use as metaphor.

Metaphor – Finding the Muse in the Maze

The fact that cultural co-opting has gone on for millennia with little notice need not deter us from trying to analyze it. In fact, the conundrum ought to motivate towards the direction of more quick thinking. If the reader may bear with the example, let us consider the hopelessly over-used icon of American religious fervor, "Amazing Grace," and consider it in the light of inculturation.

Other than the certain branches of the Orthodox, there is probably no American Christian sect that does not "own" the text and tune to "Amazing Grace" aka *New Britain*. Like most stories of creativity, the hymn's genesis is fascinating. Its text was written by John Newton, prior to 1779, and in autobiographical response to his conversion. It explores, albeit obliquely, the tension between his conversion and his former life as a sea captain of many slave ships.

The poem was not originally matched to the music we now associate with it. Apparently, other melodies were sung to this text. It was in Spilman's shape-note hymnal, *Columbian Harmony* (1829) that the famous tune was printed. In 1835, the text and tune first kissed each other, in Walker's *Southern Harmony*, also a shape-note hymnal, and where the tune was first named by its identifier, *New Britain*.[5]

Regardless of its printed date, it is highly probable that the melody had been circulating in a previous extant form as part of aural tradition.[6] Like other borrowed tunes from the folk tradition of the British Isles, it was to find a new life and purpose amongst the English speaking settlers of the New World. Other than their obvious function and historicity, it is generally assumed that the early shape-note hymnals (of which only two are mentioned above) give credent historical documentation to the contemporary extent and practice of English folk hymnody as transformed by its American colonists. As such, we may safely say that variants of certain materials in these hymnals are indicative of a pre-existing repertoire that may stretch back several centuries and have their origins in relative antiquity of the British Isles.

This then may explain some of *New Britain's* inherent musical appeal, for the tune, in some form or other, is probably much older than its text and has thus had a good chance at the rather long-term composing side of the table. This is not an isolated example of English folk hymnody transplanted to America; it is an exemplar of dozens of tunes or tune families from the British Isles which have now entered the American hymnic pantheon.

Let us ask what else might be the appeal of this hymn: Do the words move us? Is the juncture of text and tune particularly apt? Was, or is, the issue of racism addressed in any way in the singing of *Amazing Grace*? Since there is absolutely no reference to it in the text, what right do we have to insist that it might be? Does the performance of the hymn by a white congregation bring it closer to the black community? Does the performance of it by a black community bring it closer to the white community or to its own? Would a common understanding of its textual or musical origins be helpful to "normal" people, choose your race, in the pews?

Beyond the bizarre tortures endured by the obsessive and compulsive performance of this hymn by cinema and television, thereby assuring the entire known world that there is only one hymn sung by Americans, ever, world without end, is there a universal application of this tune to the American religious experience? Or has it suffered the fate of Grant Wood's painting, *American Gothic*, so that whatever charming and useful iconic power once possessed has been reshaped, *ad absurdam*, by the culture of horrid fascination?

The broadest answer to each of these questions is no. But narrower answers might be yes. It is clear by its wide acceptance, that hymn and tune possess a certain "American universality," and that the application, or borrowing, of it on so many different levels, by so many divergent groups, corroborates this claim. Aspects of ownership are quite high, yet, there are contentious border disputes going on over who owns the purest tradition of its performance.

What makes everyone get it and decide it is THEIR song? Surely it is not just the pretty tune and the nice words, for the world is full of wonderful hymns, all of which by definition possess the same attributes. This author even remembers a Methodist childhood that seemed complete, even though *New Britain* was curiously missing from it.

The answer is that the inherent constructs which allow inculturation's usefulness and aggrandizement thrive not always on specific usage or understanding of how such might be applied, but rather on the usefulness of the metaphor which the artifact represents. In other words, it is not the words, not the notes, and not the combination of the two that sets the metaphor, although they do contribute. The culture has already set up the paradigms for the metaphor and it is to the degree that poetry and music combine to form overarching metaphor that the thing succeeds. (If one accepts the definition of folk music as having been long-term composed, then one must also consider the very real probability that a culture, in some inchoate form or other, continues to invent, inform, and process its definition of itself via specific means, including the use of metaphor.)

More important, then, is the possibility of transfer of metaphor from one culture to another, and whether the transference will possess a spiritual usefulness to those participating in the adoption. The specifics of the questions above are now seen to be inconsequential, for they do not allow for the application of metaphor to explain them. If there is transference of metaphor, the rest will follow and the adoptive culture is then free to decide its usefulness.

We do not need to know the origin of this text, nor is it all that important to know the provenance of the music. The text is ultimately about sin and redemption, and it is finally this metaphor that speaks to the soul, not the circumstance or culture in which the "I" of "I once was lost..." was first penned. Layers of melodic antiquity combine with a certain universality of text, forming a synergy available to all wishing to participate in it, and we find that overarching beauty and transforming power of *New Britain* to be the metaphor, not especially the hymn itself.

• • •

Let us take another hymn of a different sort, one whose roots place it within a different realm of understanding, yet entails in its final analysis an appropriate metaphor of inculturation. *Lac qui Parle* is the only native American hymn known to broad acceptance of different cultures in America. Like *New Britain*, it is powerful in its own right without explication, yet since much less seems to be known about it, we present some in-depth information as to its origin and import to the Upper Midwest region. This includes short lessons in Minnesota geography, history, cartography, and the origins of the hymn's creation.

The ascribed author of text and tune of *Lac qui Parle* is Joseph Renville, born about 1779, the offspring of a French trader and

Dakota mother. As a child, he spent some time in Canada, where he received education in the French language and Catholicism. He was later to serve as guide to Zebulon Pike in 1805, traveling with his party from Prairie du Chien (Wisconsin) to Mendota, immediately south of Minneapolis and St. Paul. Renville was also a British captain in the War of 1812. In the year 1822, he founded the Columbia Fur Company, then selling it in 1827 to the much larger American Fur Company.

It was about this time that he established a sort of trading center at the southern end of Lac qui Parle, a relatively long and narrow lake, lying northwest to southeast, close to the present border of Minnesota and South Dakota.[7] At the time, the present delineations between Minnesota, North, and South Dakota did not exist, and the international border with Canada had only become established in 1823, from the Red River of the North east to approximately the northern center of the state, at Lake of the Woods.

There seemed to be some doubt as to the border's validity; for Lord Selkirk's vast northern land grant, acquired through the beneficence of Hudson's Bay Fur Company in 1811, had obviously existed prior to the 1823 settlement, and since it was thought that it had previously extended as far south as Big Stone Lake and Lake Traverse, only a little north of Lac qui Parle, the border question and the implications of its control, or lack thereof, were of no mean concern.[8]

Amid the uncertainties of this border turmoil grew the community of Fort Renville, at the southeast foot of Lac qui Parle (Lake that Speaks), where the dictates of a smaller geography demanded that all within its relative proximity must pass through, seeking news, company, and trade.

It was from this settlement that, in 1835, Joseph Renville made his annual trading journey to Fort Snelling at Mendota. This fort, built in 1819, was some 200 miles east, at the confluence of the Mississippi and Minnesota Rivers and near what is now Minneapolis and St. Paul. At the time of building, Fort Snelling was essentially the entire American presence in the upper Midwest, or northwest, as it was called at the time, and had as its responsibility the control of the entire northern regions of what is now the state of Minnesota, and parts of North Dakota, South Dakota, and Wisconsin.

It was during his 1835 visit that Renville was persuaded by the fort's agent, Major Taliaferro, to allow a missionary presence at Lac qui Parle. This was in immediate response to the threat of ongoing struggle between Ojibway and Dakota on the western plains—a problem Agent Taliferro wished to deal with by way of Renville. Since he agreed with Taliferro's suggestion, the idea obviously appealed to Renville in some manner.[9]

Historians continue their conjectures as to why Renville allowed missionaries to come to Lac qui Parle and propose explanations by appealing to the reality of Renville's Christian training in Canada, and the decidedly uneasy conflicts between the Ojibway and Dakota that were taking place near Lac qui Parle at the time. They mention, too, with memories of the War of 1812, the implied chance of British advance through Lord Selkirk's domain from the north, taking advantage of the lack of completed international boundaries.

It is known that Indian Agent Taliaferro entertained "occasional Suspicions as to the part Mr. Joseph Rainville (Renville) was and had been acting," and proposed to invite the missionaries "Rev. Mr. Williamson and his family and also Mr. Huggins as agriculturist with his family at Lac qui Parle. For this purpose I invited Mr. Renville to dine with me, and after detailing to him the advantages which would result to him and his large family from having such a valuable acquisition as Doctor Williamson and his family, he readily consented and he offered his protection, and every facility in his power if they would go."

William Folwell, from whom the above is quoted in "A History Minnesota," Vol. I, continues in his own words: "On June 23 (1835) Williamson and Huggins with their families, provided with passports from the Indian agent, departed in Renville's caravan for Lac qui Parle, where they had been 'from motives of policy permitted to locate for *Missionary purposes* and agricultural for the benefit of the wild Indians of that place and vicinity.' It was by such human means that Providence sent Williamson to a station relatively as far away from (Minneapolis and St. Paul) as the Yukon River would be today."

Thus, with passports in hand, the missionaries took part in an experiment in cross-culturalism the likes of which the prairies had not seen. In terms of printed material, this unlikely community of Lac qui Parle brought forth a wealth of material, astounding in its breadth, magnificent in concept—a Dakota/English dictionary, Dakota translations of the Bible, a Dakota grammar, a Dakota translation of "Pilgrim's Progress," school curricula in Dakota, a Dakota newspaper, and a Dakota hymnal, *Dakota Odowan*. This last volume survives in use, with little change, to this day.

While we admit the strength of the Lac qui Parle enterprise, and take pains to indicate none of it would have been possible without the cooperation of Joseph Renville, wife, children, grandchildren, and other relatives, the missionaries themselves were quick to say they made no mistake of their own endeavors, that they had but one intent: to better the lives of the locals only in order to be able to convert them to Christianity. They believed this to be their single and important objective, and one may say that in this pursuit, they were indeed single minded and, at least linguistically, effective.

With the addition of Stephen R. Riggs to the staff, the missionaries, all sponsored by the Presbyterian church, performed the linguistic aspect of inculturation brilliantly; they were far less successful when it came to other aspects of English/Dakota inculturation. Even though Renville had practiced some forms of agriculture before the arrival of the missionaries, missionary-taught farming methods did not gather a majority of followers. Additionally and not surprisingly, conflicts arose between red and white practitioners of the medical arts, and elements of trust suffered. Joseph Renville and his familial legions seemed to take more readily to the white ideas, but even here, they appealed more to the women than the men.[10]

Similar and subsequent attempts were made to assimilate natives at the Upper and Lower Sioux Agencies along the Minnesota River. History has shown that at least outwardly, all these attempts met with tragic failure in the Dakota/White conflict of August, 1862, which signaled the beginning of the plains wars as they spread further west.

What, if anything, can be gained from a study of this extraordinary encampment at Lac qui Parle? First, we may observe that this community was peopled from several cultures each forced to form the means where they might, on some level, cooperate with each other. English, French, Dakota, and various combinations of these all met here for commerce and livelihood. For it to have lasted even twenty years, the community would have had to spend an enormous amount of energy in order to keep an uneasy peace and the rewards towards this enterprise must therefore have been understood to be greater than the alternatives.

Second, the musical rewards are still to be had in *Dakota Odowan*, a hymnal in Dakota and using, for the most part, nineteenth-century English hymnody in Dakota translation. This hymnal was originally published, words only, in 1841. Sometime after 1854, a music edition was published and the book has flourished ever since—a more recent printing in 1969 accompanied by photographs of the Dakota at prayer and community.

Third, is the small body of narrative music found in *Dakota Odowan*. Six of the 108 hymns are of Dakota derivation and the missionary journals proclaim they were written by Joseph Renville himself. Be that as it may, it is more likely that they were arranged by Renville from preexisting Dakota materials.[11] It has been suggested by Raymond Glover, in *A Commentary on New Hymns*, that the tune to *Lac qui Parle* is in fact a funeral song, sung in procession, and thus by implication an arrangement by Renville of preexisting native material. It also maintains that only the text was writ-

ten by Renville and that the melody was extant before its application to the text. A major eye-witness to Renville's creativity was
Stephen Riggs, who indicates only that "... the hymns were composed by Mr. Renville," or "Mr. Huggins and Fanny sang an
Indian hymn made from the 15th chapter of First Corinthians."
John Williamson, a son of another missionary at Lac qui Parle,
and who grew up there, wrote in his biography: "The early missionaries felt their need of a hymn-book, and before many years
published a small collection, some of their composing, some by
the Renvilles and others. These were sung mostly to familiar hymn
tunes, some to French and some to Dakota native airs."[12]

It would seem that Renville's ability to write hymns was mentioned in its relationship to text and the merits of his (or his family's) ability to fit Dakota Christian texts to existing music. John
Williamson's comment about use of French and Dakota "airs,"
while not at all conclusive, lends some credence to the earlier asser-
tion of the possibility of French influence upon native Dakota
music. But we might also turn this argument around by stating
that Dakota music influenced the performance of French music in
that region.

Of the six native tunes in *Dakota Odowan*, only *Lac qui Parle*[13]
is well known outside of the Dakota culture. Known better by its
first line, "Many and great are thy works" it appears at #385, *The
Hymnal 1982*.[14] There is an interesting discussion of this hymn in
The Hymnal 1982 Companion at entry #385 of Vol. Three B,
emphasizing the sociological importance of this hymn to the
Dakota people. It also includes a facsimile of the hymn itself.

The hymn's fourth gift to us, in terms of encompassing
metaphor, is that while it is indeed most honored among the
Dakota, its provenance would seem to indicate that it comes not
from one tribe, but from many, that it represents the interface of at
least three major cultures. The fact that many of the Dakota were
not at all enthralled with this interface is at least partially irrelevant
to its result as an artifact of cross-cultural activity.

Lac qui Parle, then, may be understood in some regard to be not only a song of singular racial identification, but as one of racial integration—inculturation at its most moving. Naturally, individuals will make of this statement what they will, but it is irrefutable that the hymn is not English, European, or African, but American. *Many and great* sprang from the steppes of central north America, singing a duality of racial identity and inculturation, and as an example of authentic American folk hymnody, stands to the prairies as does highest grass to the sky.

Guidelines to Musical Adaptation

The editor of this volume has requested some practical guidelines to the musical adaptation of indigenous music, the better to serve the purposes of a thoughtful liturgical presentation. Here follows that request, based as it is upon the author's many years of shameless borrowing from other people.

If one may cultivate a sense of detached endeavor, removed as much as possible from personality, it quickly becomes obvious that there is only one rule: theory and sensitivity provide the grounding for any such act of liturgical inculturation. In essence, this means that there are no rules, except to approach the entire endeavor with a set of exquisitely honed sensitivities. There is no substitute for an educated compassion.

These simple rules will eventually lead a composer/arranger to this realization—never, ever, write anything for tubular chimes. Or anything else that equates with the auditory equivalent of pink flamingos. This conclusion has been enjoined by the author's life-long (so far) opportunity to discover that our most important musical stewardship should be primarily about maintaining a sense of place of the musical origins of the folk materials being applied. Naturally, tubular chimes will have nothing to do with this, or if they do, sensitive souls will demand the perpetrator to lay down his mallet and leave the room and go to his rattle.

A student of Densmore's *Chippewa Music*, cited above and about which readers were assured the logic of this arrangement, will readily learn that the corpus of Ojibway melodies almost always starts on a high note and descends, by means of larger to smaller intervals, the further into descension the melody moves. One of the most important intervallic sequences is thus the falling minor third and major second. Conveniently for us all, these intervals also figure prominently in plainsong, appearing in similar units. It is thus a relatively simple matter for an astute church musician to attempt some sort of common ground, having the potential to appeal to whites and Natives alike.

Congregational responses were fashioned in this manner for the Eucharist at the Minnesota Diocesan Convention in Duluth, October 27, 1996 (Appendix 3) and adapted from Densmore's book. For this event, the melodic cell was taken from No. 153, "The Thunderbirds," *Chippewa Music*, Vol. II, and consists of a typical falling pattern—CAGE, transposed. These two successive and falling minor thirds are also typical of the Ojibway song repertoire. The falling minor third, or its outline, is also typical of Western chant repertoire, especially collects, simple responses, etc., and so the use of this melodic cell, and by implication, its metaphor, seemed to present no major hurtle to either culture.

By all reports from the Convention that day, these melodic scaffolds performed their function admirably and "felt" common to all. This service music has been sung at subsequent liturgies and reports of these have also been positive.

On the other hand, a drum Eucharist, in which a centonization from Densmore was made and presented as a Sanctus and Benedictus (at the annual conference of the Association of Diocesan Liturgical Music Commissions in 1983 at the Chapel of Assisi Heights, Rochester, Minnesota) met a different reaction.[15] The planners of that liturgy, which included an Ojibway deacon and a fine liturgist within the same person, worked diligently to present what we congratulated ourselves beforehand as a thrilling liturgy.

And so it was; the use of sweet grass in place of incense, fancy dancers leading the entrance rite and the offertory procession, and the incomparable artistry of Henry Greencrow and his musicians made a powerful ceremony even more so. People were brought to lavish outpourings of tearful emotion as it was realized that some of the great powers of art and the Holy Spirit had enjoined a trans-formation of wondrous energy and mystery. At least this was the effect for most of us in the Midwest and western prairie states. For the white folks from the south, the east, and west coast, the reac-tion tended toward being only marginally supportive, the feeling being: why would you think we would like this sort of thing, or, what ever made you think this was going to be good liturgy?

But the most consequential criticisms were received from Native Americans who were also Episcopal priests and who felt that Native American music and trappings had no place in Anglican liturgies and it was a travesty upon both cultures to assume that the two had rightful bearing upon each other. This argument, then and now, had some validity, and indeed, the two missions at Red Lake, Minnesota, represent the antipodes of liturgical incultura-tion: one prefers to keep itself separate from native culture, the other prefers to experiment with amalgams from both cultures.

(Lest this seem to the uninitiated just a little outside the sphere of normality, we would do well to recall the mostly white cities and towns where the Missouri Synod church is across the street from those less oppressive ELCA sorts and, just down the block from that building, there is the German Catholic Church which only lately think it's OK to have picnics with the Irish Catholic church across town and the Episcopalians—well, they're mad at each other and some of them are talking about becoming Methodists or driving 80 miles for an authentic traditional Hymnal 1940 sort of celebration, they haven't made up their minds, even though the Season of High Dramas that put such a damper on things was already eleven years ago.)

• • •

Here are some gentle points of etiquette the would-be incultura-tor might wish to consider.

1. If you have the privilege to observe the culture from which you have borrowed first hand, it is wise to assume nothing and observe everything. Understand that while your work may be appreciated by others, this appreciation may not be shown in the style of its reception. It will most likely be changed to suit local purposes and expectations. Thus, it may therefore be impossible, and quite undesirable, to establish a definitive version of performance. However, one could hold that a certain group sang such a song and that it is believed to be definitive of performance practice by that particular group.

For instance, unless you had discussed linguistics with someone familiar with the reservations of Northern Minnesota, you would probably have no idea that there are differences in Ojibway pro-nunciation between the White Earth and Red Lake reservation, yet their borders are separated by only 30 miles. You might also find yourself unwittingly hampered by the strictures of your culture, and that "looking in" on another, you might, at first, not even be able to detect, entertain, or admit the encumbrances that are your personal-pan emotional and cultural property.

Densmore found, for example, that the insouciant manner in which many of the songs were seemingly presented tempted her to consider that the Ojibway repertoire was based in large part upon improvisation. She, in fact, found that there was no such artistic lassitude, that multiple recordings of the same song by the same singer, performed in immediate succession, or separated by some time, revealed that the songs were performed with only the minute variation that could be expected in a performance of any song in any culture. This finding describes a very deep cultural under-standing of musical norms and their application to the creation of a song, as well as to its performance.

2. Be extremely careful to extract adaptations of non-religious religious music from widely differing societies; the metaphor that is about the metaphor will not hold. It is one thing to adapt a Ukrainian carol to Christmas Eve in Denver, it is quite another to sing a Palestrina motet in a sweat lodge at Red Lake. The effect of the first would be charming while that of the second, appalling. The Ukrainian Carol was already Christian, but the place where the motet was performed was not, the space being dedicated to the religion of the Medicine Lodge. The first instance was respectful of origin and utilized common metaphorical parameters, the second found none, and the result was shockingly disrespectful to both.

3. Adaptations will not necessarily mean the same thing to the adaptee as they do to the adaptor. An artifact of cultural significance may lose its power in transference and mean not at all what was intended. Look for the usefulness of common cultural metaphors, not the thing itself.

4. The composer/arranger, liturgist, priest, etc. also need to keep in mind that an immediate attraction to an artifact, musically or textually, is only one criterion for inculturation, and it is not necessarily the most useful. Millions of cursillistes have been thrilled with the music of the Cursillo renewal movement, only to be rebuffed by a glacial or hellish response (or both, at the same time) when it was offered up on a Sunday morning. The reasons for this are many, but one of the biggest is surely the fact that, intentionally or not, it set up a we/they dynamic in the manner of its style, usage, and experience—something diametrically opposed to the whole needs of a worshiping community. We are not talking about musical taste here, but rather appropriateness of intention, and whether the ground-work has been laid prior to introduction, in order that people may welcome and receive a new piece of music. Without the ground work, the metaphors are in danger of rejection and/or understanding, and the result is a disappointing scene of dissension, rather than community.

5. The attempts to uncover hidden meanings at the interface of art and life have increased in direct proportion to the shifting of the understanding of art itself. One result of this has been the recent rise in the likes of so-called victim-art, and which purpose seems to better understand the pain of the unfortunate and downtrodden through recreations—not necessarily of their lives, but of their pain. Other than an article by dance critic Arlene Croce in the *New Yorker* magazine ("Discussing the Undiscussable"), this movement has seemed to garner little critical attention, and such is long overdue.[16]

Heavy on emotional content, the intellectual construct of victim-art comes up wanting on several counts. No matter how much the latest Holocaust Cantata might improve our understanding of the wretchedness of the human condition, it is a poor substitute for its unreal reality, and the Holocaust Cantata cannot, in fact, atone for the sins of those who perpetrated it, nor is it able to assuage the accreted guilt of those who have been visited by it. To even suggest that it can trivializes the detestable enormities of the Holocaust itself, for in celebrating the angst on stage, its recreation can not safely be separated from the sickening possibility of participation in a form of macabre entertainment. The earnest perpetrators of this victim-art are cast in failure, for the original concept is a flawed metaphor, no matter how well meaning or purely driven the artistic concept might be. And theologically speaking, thus is the stupendous meaning of sin and redemption ultimately denied.

What then, may one say about Picasso's *Guernica* or Penderezcki's *Threnody to the Victims of Hiroshima*? Some would say they are removed from the criticism of the vacuities of victim art, because the artistic vision was broadcast at the point of original creation, not execution, and it did not seek the sensational aspects of the very narrowest form of *feelings* (one should probably place an aura of quotations around this word to indicate that the intellect has been eviscerated from them). While *Guernica* may indeed have been painted in response to and in protest of a specific occasion, the layers of metaphor immediately inform the viewer that the depiction is not just the terror of one war, but of evil. The representation on canvas, while descriptively horrid, is yet highly stylized, removed from the pratfalls of a dialectic realism. The painting thus works intellectually and emotionally—one of its finest dissonances being the constant interaction between these two levels; and the meaning of it all is spun beyond evil, beyond pain. Analysis of Penderezcki's *Threnody* reveals the same tight control and layered use of metaphor.

By definition, if there is one, the intent of victim-art is to engage a sense of the profound. Yet victim-art perhaps most closely falls within the genre of performance-art, where one is able to observe an "artist" posting a month-long livelihood in an igloo on Madison Avenue, or a kitchen made entirely of cheese, or a take-off on an iconic pose of the Virgin Mary, constructed entirely of little sardines. While these activities and resulting artificats may be interesting and/or horridly fascinating, their commentary is of a social nature, and the discussions of them lend themselves nicely to party-time titillation.

This may be an unfair comparison, yet victim-art and performance-art share the same confusion in that the metaphors employed are ultimately limited to an already limiting expression and do not engage beyond what is. Suzanne Langer ("Feeling and Form") might argue that they lack significant form. At this point, one might easily interject that tales of Christ's passion are also theatre, albeit of a sacred sort. This would be quite true, but its layers of metaphor—of time, of God, of death, of resurrection, of redemption, of logos, of suffering, of Moses, of Mary's vigil at the cross—these, and too many more, speak so much better, and richly, than does a ballet choreographed by someone who has AIDS and is about "the AIDS experience."

Victim-art also dangerously courts the arena of political correctness and because it does so, invites the inevitable banality of comparison—is a ballet choreographed by someone who lost his legs in the Viet Nam War more authentic of particular suffering than an opera performed by deaf mutes? It is as though victim-art must be equated with exquisite levels of suffering and that without them it can not possess artistic validity or purpose.

While this discussion may seem callous and unfeeling, it is not. It could be quite interesting and emotionally satisfying to discover how the Viet Nam vet would deal with a non bi-pedal range of movement. The point here is that the pain/suffering duality, while excruciatingly real, is not necessarily a good indicator of ultimate artistic merit or content, and we should not allow ourselves to believe that it is, despite what performers "out there" devoutly believe to be true. Like anyone else, artists are not always to be believed, especially when passion overstates their case.

A closing word on the subject includes the problem that without an underpinning of sacred esthetic, victim-art must seek to invent a paradigm for a secular belief system. As it tries to create the levels of metaphor necessary to ground this system, its putative beliefs become twisted and confused. Since suffering is attached to the cherished beneficence of the recently invented metaphor of victimhood, and since, at least on one level, victimhood virtually demands that it may be extended only so far as the parameter of a particular victimhood will allow it, there is little hope of allowing the metaphor of victimhood to be "owned" or appropriated by the more universal application of sin and suffering.

The desire toward expression is common to all—this sort of confusion is understandable, but it often goes without notice and appellations of quality are frequently awarded to its practice. Yet the most forceful artistic creations receive their clarity in direct proportion to the degree to which this desire is implicitly removed, existing as art, not ideology. One of art's inexplicable conundrums is that the less it seems to deal with political issues directly, the more it connects to a proper relevance and succeeds in being political.

This, then, is a very long way of saying that if inculturation is undertaken in the name of victimization, it should be resisted, for it will in time be seen as the passing fad that it is; the metaphors are too narrow and will get us back to the Motet-in-a-Sweat Lodge or Song of the Crystals by the Sea sort of thing again.

> **6.** As to musical arrangements of preexisting tunes—from any repertoire—historic knowledge of that repertoire is essential. Not because of historicity, *per se*, but because knowledge of historic models, coupled with known aspects of historic performance practice, stand a good chance of keeping the would-be arranger from inserting too much of him or herself into the music. This is important if the arranger is outside the breadth of a tradition, and will ensure a certain honor to the tradition that is being utilized.

A case in point is found in the Appendix, where the author, on the whim of self-appointed challenge, attempts an arrangement of one of the other melodies in the Dakota hymnal, "La Framboise."[17] For the sake of comparison, it is given as in *Dakota Odowan* as well.

The arrangement does manage to do some things reasonably well:

- It resists the temptation to smooth out the rhythms in a notation that could possibly be more easily grasped if notated differently. Instead it honors the exact rhythmic notation with the exception of the end, which is implied by the breath that would be taken between stanzas anyway. The reason for letting the rhythmic notation stand lies in the fact that after looking at the other Dakota melodies, the arranger believes that in comparison to them, the specific rhythmic notation of this particular hymn is unusual enough to warrant its almost exact presentation as printed.

- The harmonic arrangement avoids a certain amount of Western harmonic methodology in favor of one that has a sort of shadow relationship to the tune, thereby letting any harmonic implication of the melody speak for itself.

- Rhythmically, the arrangement is interesting and supports the irregular accentuation of the melody.

- As a whole, the arrangement is conceptually simple, imparting a sense of accompaniment to the melody, doing so as to make color or timbral contrasts to that of the melody—essentially a form of counterpoint. Although the accompaniment consists of only two voices, they operate together, remaining discrete, never overpowering an already powerful tune.

While quite satisfied to have accomplished all this, the arranger is nevertheless aware of potential failure in the following areas:
- If one disregards the fact that a boring harmonization of "La Framboise," published in 1877 for the *Dakota Odowan*, is already indicative of historic performance practice, the possibility arises of dishonor to the tradition of the volume's four-part Victorian harmonization. Yet this very presentation may perhaps dishonor the older pre-contact unisonal singing. The choices are far from obvious; to include any new harmonization runs the risk of violating the traditions of the older layer of the ancient aural tradition in unisonal style.[18]

- The decision to pitch the tune down a whole step was made so that white congregations would be more comfortable singing in a slightly lower tessitura. However, the arranger's observations include that the Dakota repertoire is less concerned with a fear of high notes than is a gathering of Caucasians and that there is wide-spread admiration of their effect, for the Dakota welcome notes beyond a "comfortable" range as an opportunity for vocal color changes and display.

This simple transposition then carries with it something of a dilemma and becomes not such an easy choice. Does one wish for practicality in presentation—and of acceptance by a wider audience—or accuracy of intent and presentation? It is not always possible to have both.

- A major problem to the arranger is his ignorance of Dakota performance practice in terms of tempo, phrasing, and breathing. He has fashioned his accompaniment on the hunch that the tempo is at least not extremely slow and that the rhythmic drive continues between phrases. But if his hunch is wrong—if the tempo is moderate to slow, and includes a relaxed attitude about breathing between each of the four phrases, or if the tempo is at least perky but still includes a relaxed attitude about breathing, allowing each phrase to come to a full stop—the implied rhythmic drive of the composer's arrangement will be lost, and the arrangement will have failed. It will have done so not because it is an intrinsically bad arrangement, but because the arranger did not know the parameters of proper performance practice and so did not know to what degree he had deviated from it. In other words, the creative concept is possibly flawed at the outset, allowing the composer to insert too much of his own personality in the process, and thereby overwhelming the original identity and use of the music itself.

Diversity and the World

One of the most encouraging things to happen to music, sacred or not, is the trend towards the appreciation of what might be called music of the world. This has been documented elsewhere is this article and is understood as a given by any student of its influence upon Western culture. Yet it has gathered more energy of late, so we explain world music as being indicative of the folk traditions of a country that seem to be superb expressions of that culture, something which stamps a particular music with the imprimatur of ethnicity and of an aggregate long-term compositional history.

If we were looking toward music from the Hawaiian Islands as a means for inculturation, we would have to rule that ukulele music is not really an indicator of long-term Polynesian cultural health, even though Hollywood and the Hawaiian tourist industry tell us it is, and we would turn toward the far more ancient Polynesian changes, dances, and instrumental usage. In any case, Ukulele Masses would be sure to follow, if indeed, they have not already, and it takes little imagination to believe they would pop up in the Continental 48 as examples of expressions and proof of our peculiar love of Pacific culture. That such a thing might actually dishonor the *Ur* context of Polynesian music would not necessarily stop it from happening.

This aside, we also note an increasingly wider acceptance of folk music and its application to the needs of congregational song, and, as it provides a refreshing antidote to the oft lamented inanities of the oxymoronic by-products of the Christian music industry, its ameliorative use becomes an invaluable tool toward an informed response against it. Such folk music represents a vivifying clarity to congregational song—it is tuneful and interesting, it bears repeating, it is transparent enough to be performed in many presentations and situations, yet it always retains an air of authenticity. Our discussion of the aforementioned *Amazing Grace* comes to mind in this matter.

We hear the oft-repeated cry for the necessity of the celebration of multi-ethnicity, especially in communities in which such need is not readily apparent. Why we should celebrate otherness in communities that cannot even worship effectively by themselves, does remain a bit of a mystery.

Yet it is equally myopic to insist that the only proper way to pray is in English, with English thoughts, with English metaphors, and with English sounds. Accordingly, this author has carried out a quiet crusade against English As The Only Language. His small suburban parish choir has thus sung occasionally in Latin, Old Church Slavonic, French, German, Hebrew, and Spanish. This multi-lingual approach is justified on many grounds: 1) whenever possible, choirs need to learn the feel and sound of another language, 2) struggling towards the creation of these timbres creates a better understanding of other cultures, 3) the effort to learn something totally different conditions the soul, 4) such a challenge makes singers better musicians in the long run, and 5) a translated vowel does generally perform nearly as beautifully as it would in the original language.

Lastly, as mighty as the struggle might be, as sometimes fruitless the effort may seem, the process of trying to sing in another language is transforming. One of this writer's attempts at such a project was a Cameroonian processional song, in French. Dance steps to the procession were given in the score. When it was announced that not only were we going to sing it in French, we were going to learn simple dance steps, too, there arose a great gnashing of incredulity as though the director, merely by this announcement, crossed all boundaries of propriety. Since compulsiveness is at least partly one of the many blessings of the director, his insistence on the matter wore them down and, we may rest assured, the piece was performed with some celerity.

But the point is that the choir did learn to dance and sing at the same time, did perform the music as an offertory procession, and element bearers bringing up the procession in the rear also decided on the spot to dance as well. And, *mirabile dictu*, all learned that there is fulfillment in exploring adventure and furthermore, the choirmaster got a chance to work in a few lessons on coordination and counting, something that many choirs desperately need. In taking the choir beyond the perception of its membership, toward a discovery of a very different perception of its abilities, the choir succeeded in transforming itself. The metaphor of "choir" was improved upon and changed forever.

One of the reasons for the success of the song from Cameroon lay in that aspect of the Holy Spirit that is almost always over-looked and under-appreciated: charm. The delight and surprise of charm may be likened to an unexpected sign of friendship or find-ing a new flower in the garden that you had forgotten to plant or in fact, did not plant. When it comes to the desire or necessity of change, charm is one of the church musician's best allies, and other than choice musical selections, it is observed that anything with a child, Orff instrument, hand bell, or off-the-wall percussion instrument (excluding tubular chimes) will charm people into notions of acceptance that they could not have imagined possible.

As it assesses the use of metaphor, charm is indeed one of the very values upon which inculturation may into account, and to the extent that charm appears, is a valuable measure of the living force of the Holy Spirit. And finally, through this charm, we are brought to the understanding of a deeply felt sense of spirituality, for it is rather the divine sweetness of that which we share. Inculturation is then merely a walk through the market of exquisite possibilities, the menu incomparably long and full of fortaste of the divine feast of God's love.

Note on Frances Densmore: I had occasion to speak with writer Ted Hall a few years ago about Frances Densmore. Ted grew up in the Frontenac/Red Wing area of the state. Ms. Densmore main-tained residency in Red Wing for many years and Ted had made his acquaintance with her there. When asked by me to describe her, Ted responded by saying that she was reserved and "rather aus-tere." It was perhaps precisely this distance that allowed her so much credibility with others.

Note on *Lac qui Parle*: It is interesting to note a performance at a Pow Wow at Prairie Island, Minnesota, in July of 1, 1997. A Pow Wow always includes a Flag Song. Ray Owens, well-known resident at Prairie Island, explained to me that there are at least four or five distinct melodies for this text and each is somewhat variable according to performance of the drum group's specialty and geographic location. In this case, the Flag Song was from North Dakota because it was performed by a group from that state. The song was repeated several times. Included at the same place in each "verse" was the unmistakable melodic material as found in the tune *Lac qui Parle* above the text of the words. This corresponded to the melody that fits to the words: "thy hands have set the heavens with stars" (*Hymnal 1982*, #385).

Note on *Lac qui Parle*: Hymnal 1982 fortunately contains another hymn which elicits notions of great North American native sensibility. This is Brebeuf's Huron carol, *'Twas the moon wintertime*, #114. While we admit the hymn's luster, the sheen of argument to put it in the same category as Lac qui Parle is somewhat tarnished since the tune itself is demonstrably a French Noel used by many French Baroque composers as a theme in their compositions. Yet a somewhat different case could be stated – that the Noel traversed the Atlantic, was used for easily transferable purposes, and that the success of this transfer argues that its metaphor was accepted by the new culture. What is of far more interest, for our purposes, is that the possibility exists for more materials from this Huron repertoire and that there seems to be no available information about it.

APPENDIX – "Many and Great"
APPENDIX – "Music from Diocesan Convention Eucharist, Duluth, 1996.
APPENDIX – The author's harmonization of *La Framboise* and harmonization as included from Dakota Odowan.

Acknowledgements

The Rev. Michael Forbes for thoughtful encouragement, criticism, valuable commentary and information on the hymn, *Lac qui Parle*.

The Rt. Rev. Mark McDonald for encouragement, friendship, support and the opportunity to write this article.

Bibliography

Books

Balmori, Diana. *Beatrix Farrand's American Landscapes.* Sagaponack: Sagapress, Inc., 1985.

Barton, Winifred. *John P. Williamson – A Brother to the Sioux.* Minnesota: Sunnycrest Publishing, 1980.

Blom, Eric, ed. *Grove's Dictionary of Music and Musicians.* New York: St. Martin's Press, 1970.

Carley, Kenneth. *The Sioux Uprising of 1862.* St. Paul: The Minnesota Historical Society, 1976.

Davis, Barbara. *Edward Curtis – The Life and Times of a Shadow Catcher.* San Francisco: Chronicle Books, 1985.

Densmore, Frances. *Chippewa Customs.* St. Paul: The Minnesota Historical Society, 1979.

_____. *Chippewa Music, Vols. I and II.* Washington: Smithsonian Institution, Burea of American Ethnology, Bulletin 46, Government Printing Office, 1910 and 1913.

Folwell, William Watts. *A History of Minnesota, Vol. I.* St. Paul: The Minnesota Historical Society, 1956.

Glover, Raymond. *A Commentary on New Hymns – Hymnal Studies #6.* New York: Church Hymnal Corporation, 1987.

Hampl, Patricia. *Spillville.* Minneapolis: Milkweed Editions, 1987.

Holmquist and Brookings. *Minnesota's Major Historic Sites.* St. Paul: The Minnesota Historical Society, 1972.

Jackson, George Pullen. *Spiritual Folk Songs of Early America*. Locust Valley, New York: JJ. Augustin, 1937.

Malm, William P. *Music Cultures of the Pacific, the Near east, and Asia*. Englewood Cliffs, New Jersey: Prentice-Hall, Inc., 1967.

McDermott, John Francis. *Seth Eastman's Mississippi: A Lost Portfolio Recovered*. Urbana: University of Illinois Press, 1973.

Nute, Grace Lee. *Documents Relating to Northwest Missions, 1815-1827*. St. Paul: Minnesota Historical Society, 1942.

Riggs, Stephen, ed. *A Dakota – English Dictionary*. Washington: Department of the Interior, 1890.

Riggs, Stephen R. *Mary and I – Forty Years with Sioux*. Boston: Congregational School and Publishing Society, 1887.

Riggs, Stephen R. "The Dakota Mission." *Minnesota Historical Society – Collections, Vol. III (1870-1880)*, 115-128. St. Paul: Committee on Publications, The Minnesota Historical Society, 1880.

Ross, Alexander. *The Red River Settlement*. 1856. Reprint, Minneapolis: Ross and Haines, Inc., 1957.

Thompson, Oscar. *Debussy – Man and Artist*. New York: Dover Publications, Inc., 1965.

Hymnals, Carols, & Songs

Bramley & Stainer, eds. *Christmas Carols, New & Old*. England: Novello & Co., 1871.

Williamson and A. Riggs, eds. *Dakota Odowan*. New York: The Dakota Mission of the American Missionary Association and the Presbyterian Board of Foreign Mission, American Tract Society, 1896.

Williamson and A. Riggs, eds. *Dakota Odowan*. Oradell, New Jersey: The Dakota Mission of the American Missionary Association and the Presbyterian Board of Foreign Mission, 1969.

Davidson, ed. *Kentucky Harmony*. 1816. Reprint, Augsburg Publishing House, 1976.

Glover, Raymond, ed. *The Hymnal 1982 – Companion, Vol. Three B*. New York: The Church Hymnal Corporation, 1994.

Sharp, Cecil, ed. *Nursery Songs from the Appalachian Mountains*. London: Novello & Co., 1921.

Dearmer, Vaughan Williams, Shaw, eds. *The Oxford Book of Carols*. London: Oxford University Press, 1964.

White and King, eds. *The Sacred Harp*. 1859. Facsimile of third edition. Nashville: Broadman Press, 1991.

Poston, Elizabeth, ed. *The Second Penguin Book of Christmas Carols*. New York: Penguin Books, 1970.

Dearmer, Vaughan Williams, Shaw, eds. *Songs of Praise*. London: Oxford University Press, 1931.

Walker, ed. *Southern Harmony*. 1854. Reprint, Los Angeles: Pro Musicamericana, 1966.

Notes

[1] quoted by Michael McNally in *Ojibwe Singers,* (Oxford, New York, 2000, p. 20)

[2] See William Malm, *Music Cultures of the Pacific, the Near East, and Asia*, pp. 56-57, and *Grove's Dictionary of Music and Musicians*, Vol. IV, fifth edition, p. 585.

[3] See Hample, *Spillville*.

[4] See Densmore, *Chippewa Music*, vols. I and II and Francis Densmore note.

[5] See Raymond Glover's *The Hymnal 1982 Companion*, Vol. Three B, pp. 1236 and following, for a fuller discussion of this hymn.

[6] See George Pullen Jackson, *Spiritual Folk Songs of Early America* in this regard, particularly the opening rising interval of a fourth melodic leaps and tessitura.

[7] Lac qui Parle is a prairie version of the finger lakes in New York.

[8] The north eastern international boundary question, east to Lake Superior, was not settled until 1842.

[9] See William Folwell, *A History of Minnesota*, Vol. I, pp. 190,192, and 213 for this and remainder of discussion as it relates to Renville and border issues. See also Joseph Nicolett, *On the plains and Prairies*, and Alexander Ross, *The Red River Settlement*, and Grace Lee Nute, *Documents Relating to Northwest Missions*, 1815-1827, for more information and related topics.

[10] See *Minnesota Historical Collections*, Vol. III, 1807-1880, p. 121 and Stephen Riggs, *Forty Years with the Sioux*, pp. 136-137, 126-127 as well as passages throughout.

[11] Given what we know of the French voyageurs who introduced French folk music to anywhere they trapped furs, and that Renville, being half French and half Dakota was an exemplar of this cultural millieu, it is not possible categorically to exclude the possibility of some French influence within this Dakota repertoire.

[12] John Williamson, *A Brother to the Sioux*, pp. 250-251.

[13] Stephen Riggs, *Mary and I: Forty Years with the Sioux*, p. 53 and 108 respectively.

[14] *Lac qui Parle* appears as a tune name in various guises, such as *Lacquiparle*, or *Dakota Hymn*.

[15] ...Appearing now in *Wonder, Love and Praise* at #855.

[16] For a discussion of victimization and its effect on racial quota systems, see Shelby Steele's article in the November 2002 issue of *Harper's* magazine, "The Age of White Guilt and the Disappearance of the Black Individual."

[17] This title probably signifies less the fruit than the fur trader by the same last name. He and his family were well known to George Catlin in 1835, where on the Coteau des Prairies, the painter "found a welcome at the comfortable trading house of Joseph Laframbroise" (Folwell, p. 121). According to Folwell, he was also known to Agent Taliaferro at Fort Snelling. By the inference of the name's appearance in the hymnal, we may reasonably assume that Laframboise was also well known to Renville, *et alia*, at Lac qui Parle. According to Ray Owens, a well known resident at Praire Island Reservation, descendents of Laframboise are still living on this reservation.

[18] The fact that there is today some contemporary experimenting with harmony, is not really to the point. This experimentation has been taken up within the Indian community and it may indeed by best left there, letting its members decide if they like it or not.

Many and Great

98 DAKOTA ODOWAN.

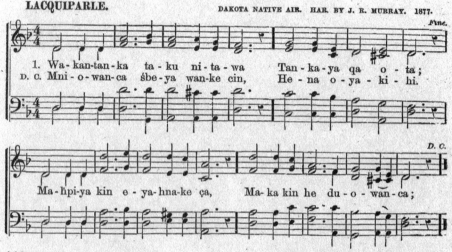

LACQUIPARLE.

DAKOTA NATIVE AIR. HAR. BY J. R. MURRAY. 1877.

1. Wa-kan-tan-ka ta-ku ni-ta-wa Tan-ka-ya qa o - ta;
D. C. Mni-o-wan-ca śbe-ya wan-ke cin, He-na o-ya-ki-hi.

Maḣpi-ya kin e-ya-hna-ke ça, Ma-ka kin he du-o-wan-ca;

141.   Jeremiah 10 : 12, 13.

1. WAKANTANKA taku nitawa
   Tankaya qa ota;
   Maḣpiya kin eyahnake ça,
   Maka kin he duowanca,
   Mniowanca śbeya wanke cin,
   Hena oyakihi.

2. Nitawacin waśaka, wakan,
   On wawicaḣyaye;
   Woyute qa wokoyake kin,
   Woyatke ko iyacinyan,
   Anpetu kin otoiyohi
   Wawiyohiyaye.

3. Adam ate unyanpi kin he,
   Woope wan yaqu;
   Woope kin awaḣtani qon,
   Miye dehan teḣiya waun,
   Jesus onśimayakida qa
   Miyecicajuju.

4. Anpetu wan en yahi kin he
   Wootanin tanka,

Oyate kin hiyeye cin he
   Iyoyanpa wicayaya;
   Jesus waonśiyakida kin
   Unniyatanpi kta.

5. Wicoḣan wan unyaqupi kin
   Jesus amatonwan;
   Woyute wan woyatke ahna
   Mayaqu kin yuwaśte wo;
   Unnaǧipi untancanpi ko
   Unyuecetu po.

6. Miceḣpi kin woyute yapi
   Itancan kin dee,
   Mawe kin he woyatke wakan,
   Ehe ciqon, wacinwaye:
   Nitatiyopa kin he wacin,
   Jesus onśimada.

7. Woehdaku nitawa kin he
   Minaǧi kin qu wo;
   Maḣpiya kin iwankam yati,
   Wicowaśte yuha nanka,
   Wiconi kin he mayaqu nun,
   Owihanke wanin.   J. R.

Music from Diocesan Convention Eucharist, Duluth, 1996

Fraction Anthem: *Christ our Passover*

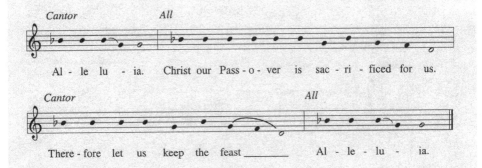

Setting: Monte Mason, from *Red Lake Mass*.

La Framboise, author's harmonization

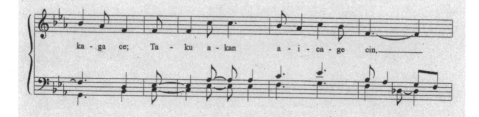

La Framboise, from the Dakota Odowan

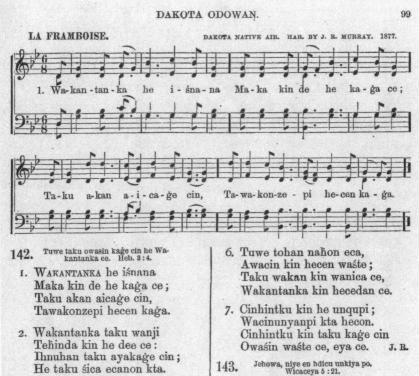

DAKOTA ODOWAN.   99

LA FRAMBOISE.   DAKOTA NATIVE AIR. HAR. BY J. R. MURRAY. 1877.

1. Wa-kan-tan-ka he i-śna-na Ma-ka kin de he ka-ġa ce;

Ta-ku a-kan a-i-ca-ġe cin, Ta-wa-kon-ze-pi he-cen ka-ġa.

142. Tuwe taku owasin kaġe cin he Wa-kantanka ee. Heb. 3:4.

1. WAKANTANKA he iśnana
Maka kin de he kaġa ce;
Taku akan aicaġe cin,
Tawakonzepi hecen kaġa.

2. Wakantanka taku wanji
Tehinda kin he dee ce:
Ihnuhan taku ayakaġe cin;
He taku śica ecanon kta.

3. Wakantanka token econ
Unśipi kin he dee ce;
Tuwe canniyeniye cinhan,
Itkom taku waśte econ wo.

4. Tuwe napin okihi kin,
Taku waśte wanyake kta:
Taku wacinyanpi ota kin,
Wanji ohiiçiye kta ce.

5. Tuwe napin yukcan kinhan,
Tawacin kin wanjidan kta,
Wakantanka kin Cinhintku kici,
Tawakonzepi awacin kta.

6. Tuwe tohan nahon eca,
Awacin kin hecen waśte;
Taku wakan kin wanica ce,
Wakantanka kin hecedan ce.

7. Cinhintku kin he unqupi;
Wacinunyanpi kta hecon.
Cinhintku kin taku kaġe cin
Owaśin waśte ce, eya ce.   J. R.

143. Jehowa, niye en hdicu unkiya po. Wicaceya 5:21.

1. NIYE ekta hdicu mayan,
Wakantanka oyakihi:
Wanuni kin he imamna
Wau kta tka omicikpani.

2. Nitacanku owotanna
Wiconi kin iyahdeya:
Nitacanku uncinpi śni,
Waunnicihtanipi tanka.

3. Otokahe iyececa
Anpetu de pawiyakpa;
Anpetu ska, iyojanjan:
Waduwaśte kin he waśte ce.
     J. P. W.

Ah! Grandchild, really, really we just hold onto the Bible always, and I do it myself. Perhaps he is waiting for us. I wonder why nobody has made a sound for so long, he says! If we sing, just make a sound, up in heaven he will hear us. That's what the preachers used to teach, and there were a lot of people staying with them, you see. That's what they call a lot of shouting. And then when we saw a lot about it we learned more about it; it was really very new and interesting to us. The Bible itself is just like a man talking to us about it. If we search for it hard, it will be good, maybe. Now he lives, he is alive, he himself, they say, is going to come back, he will come back down from heaven, they say, and really the ones who have learned of him he will take back then, just those who know him, who have learned the way, he will take them and go with them to that place, that is the way it is. Do that way, do that way, really, really, time is short. What the Bible says will happen is all happening right now.

Belle Herbert, Gwich'in[1]

Planning with Native Americans for a Shared Worship Experience

Steve Charleston

Several years ago, when I was the national executive for Native American ministries in my denomination, I received a telephone call from a local leader. The lady on the other end of the phone was asking if there were any "Indians" who could participate in Sunday worship. She assured me that the congregation was very interested in Indian people, and that they had once sent some used clothing to help those on the reservations. Finally, she said that she would appreciate it if the Indians who came to church could "dress up" for the occasion, as many of the children would like to see the buckskin and the feathers. Did I know of any Indians who could do that?

My answer was no, I didn't know any Indians who could do that. Understanding that answer is the first step toward respecting Native American people in worship. It is the first step toward respecting the Circle.

The Circle

Let me explain what I mean by the Circle. Almost every cultural community in the world has a symbol that expresses its unique identity as a people-certainly every major religious community does. For Buddhists it may be the lotus; for Islam the crescent moon; for Christians, the cross; for Native American people, and for their theology, the Circle is the symbol.

The Circle expresses the sense of wholeness, of harmony, unity and mutual interdependence that is at the heart of Native civilization. The Circle is a powerful metaphor for the special insights and gifts that Indian and Eskimo people bring into the Christian Faith as part of their ancient cultural heritage. The Circle affirms that there is more to Native society than just exotic forms of dress to amuse Western audiences.

A glimpse at the importance of the Circle helps to explain my answer to the lady on the phone. There is something perversely voyeuristic about the attitude many churches take toward Native Americans. Many congregations like to bring Indians out of the closet on Thanksgiving to add decoration to their seasonal festivals; some see Native Americans as quaint curiosities for Sunday school classes; others want to parade their own social consciousness by an occasional reference to the plight of the first Americans. While all of these circumstances may seem perfectly legitimate and well-intentioned on the part of White congregations, to Native men and women it is a clear signal that the racist stereotypes of the John Wayne movie are alive and well in suburban Christianity. It is a sign that most White Christians neither understand nor respect the values, theology, and wisdom represented by the Circle of Native life.

Only recently have these attitudes begun to change. As more Native American leaders assume positions of responsibility in our churches, as more clergy become aware of the depth of Native theology, as more lay people reject the old racist images of the past, then the bridges for real cross-cultural understanding begin to be built. This is a task that takes two teams working together from opposite sides. From the Native American side, it takes Indian and Eskimo Christians who are willing to become missionaries into the dominant society. From the White Christian community, it takes people who are willing to roll up their sleeves and work with Native counterparts on an equal basis. The days when used clothing drives were enough are over. The time when mutual respect and cooperation are called for has arrived.

Shared Worship: Some Guidelines

This mutual respect can assume one of its best forms in the area of worship. Much of the bridge building occurs when the people of God, Indian and non-Indian alike, come to prayer and thanksgiving. It is appropriate, therefore, for Christian congregations to join together in sharing their common faith. The question is not whether we *should* do this, but *how* we should build these bridges.

The answer is *with respect*. Non-Native congregations must recognize from the very beginning that using Native American symbols, music, and art is not a matter of liturgical decoration. Rather, it is a step across cultural frontiers to touch another people at the very core of their spiritual life. When Indian or Eskimo people share their culture, they are entrusting something precious to another group of people. Just as White Christians would be horrified to discover that the cross was being treated with disrespect, so too will Native Americans recoil at seeing the many elements of the Circle misused.

In a moment, I want to outline a few of these elements; I want to suggest some of the specific Native symbols that can enrich Christian worship. However, before doing so I think it is important to sketch some basic issues that any non-Native congregation should examine before incorporating those symbols into a worship experience.

- **Motive:** Any congregation should begin by self-examination. It should ask what its motives are in wanting to invite Native American participation, whether in person or through symbol. If the motivation is to "dress up," then something is dangerously wrong. On the other hand, if the motive is to honestly learn from Native people, to accept the gifts these people have to share, and to receive the information in a respectful way, then a sound foundation will have been laid.

- **Direct involvement:** How involved are Native Americans in planning the worship experience? Note the words, "in planning," not just "in participating." Effective cross-cultural worship is a two-way street; it takes both teams working together. If the worship is to have real integrity, Native people must be included from the word go.

- **Sharing:** Very often White congregations like to invite Native Americans into their parishes because it is a clean, antiseptic way to "see the Indians" without really having to rub shoulders with them. The question is, will the church members be just as willing to share in worship in the Native community? Will they leave the confines of their own church to venture into an Indian or Eskimo setting? Will the worship be first in one community and then the other, or is this seen as a one-shot arrangement where Native people are just visiting?

- **Learning:** Earlier I said that Native people need to be willing to become missionaries to the dominant society. A major piece of that job is evangelism; Indian and Eskimo missionaries can bring the gospel to White communities where non-Indian Christians can see Christ through new eyes. Done properly, Native word and worship can renew, revitalize, and educate any congregation. The need, therefore, is to consider what learnings can occur from the shared experience.

- Finally, **bonding:** If everything just described is in place, we shall see worship serving as an initial force in Christian bonding. As a tool to overcome racism, suspicion, and isolation, worship can help unite the many parts of the Body of Christ into one cohesive community. Certainly, **this kind of ongoing process should be the goal of the whole worship effort**. A bridge that no one ever uses may be pretty to look at, but it will be worthless. Worship should start a long-term dialogue between Indians and Whites, not just becoming a last word between them before they go their separate ways.

Worship Elements

With this kind of blueprint before us, we can look to some of the elements that make up the variety of worship opportunities in the

Circle of Native religious life. These will only be a few, but they may spark some creative thinking:

1. **The drum:** The use of the drum can become a powerful focus for shared worship. In Indian country, the term "drum" means more than just the physical instrument itself. It implies the singers who are seen as an organic part of the music; they are also the instruments of the drum. Their songs can express the complete range of liturgical statement: from joy to solemn reverence. The drum, a perfect representation of the Circle, embodies the heartbeat of the body of Christ.

2. **The four sacred directions:** Within the Circle, the points of spiritual compass indicate the four sacred directions of God's creation. These directions represent the eternal balance, harmony, and goodness of the world. They can be illustrated by different colors, depending on the tribal tradition. Finding out which colors should be used, and how, will require the leadership of the Native American planners involved in the design of the worship experience.

3. **Our Mother, the Earth:** Here is an aspect of Native American theology that is very precious; one that must be accorded great respect. Speaking of the Earth is not done casually in Native worship; rather, the living Earth shows the nurturing, sustaining power of God in all its warmth and beauty.

4. **The Pipe:** The use of the Pipe in worship is an ancient sacrament of many tribal people, particularly the Plains nations. Unless there is a qualified, acknowledged Native person to share the Pipe in a worship setting, it will be best only to illustrate this part of Native theology. It demonstrates the unity of all life, of human beings and all the kindred creatures God has set on the Earth. It carries our prayers to God as it is passed around the Circle of God's creation.

5. **Sweet grass:** Many tribes have a form of incense used to purify the place of prayer and worship. Part of the planning should be to identify what these are and how best to incorporate them

into the experience. Again, local Native leadership will be crucial to doing this with respect.

6. **Native hymns:** A great many traditional Christian hymns have been translated into Native languages. These are familiar tunes and familiar words; however, singing them in the Native dialect can be a real benefit to White congregations. It helps to bridge the gap between us by reminding us that in Christ Jesus we are all one.

7. **The traditional feast:** In the early church, a community meal was often part of the worship experience. The same tradition still remains as an active part of Native spirituality. This can be a simple but effective way to help the bonding between communities begin.

8. **The giveaway:** In the New Testament, there are many references to a right attitude toward finite wealth and position. A graphic illustration of this Christian truth is the traditional Native American "giveaway." It is just the reverse of the White practice, in that when a person is honored he or she does not *receive* gifts but gives gifts away to others. The symbolism of the giveaway can be a great lesson in Christian stewardship.

These are only eight elements for possible use in shared worship. There are, of course, many others to choose from. Each Native community has its own special symbols, liturgies, music, and arts. Discovering which ones are right for a shared Christian worship is part of the challenge of this cross-cultural ministry.

To get started, a non-Native congregation should first learn which Native communities are nearby. This may seem self-evident, but the truth is many White parishes exist in the midst of Indian people without the least idea of who these people are. Recently I spoke to a White congregation that was literally across the street from the Yaqui reservation. I am not Yaqui and I live hundreds of miles from this particular parish; and yet, here I was being asked to explain "what the Indians think."

There are Native American communities (both urban and rural) in almost every corner of North America. The number of White congregations that can honestly claim that there are no Native people nearby is infinitesimal. They are the exceptions that should turn to national church agencies in Indian ministry for assistance; the vast majority should seek out a living relationship with their Native American neighbors.

Two Caveats

Some of these Native American neighbors may be Christian, others may not. A major part of the respect to be shown in developing a shared time of worship is to begin with that awareness. There are at least two primary things that should be borne in mind by the planning team emerging from the White church.

First, Native American Christians have varying attitudes towards using traditional forms of worship. By "traditional," I mean the elements of word and worship that are parts of their own tribal heritage. For example, some Native Christians welcome the use of the sacred Pipe in worship, while others would prefer not to use it. Non-Native planners should never assume that all Indian people are alike; they should definitely not presume that the Indian congregation down the road will be eager to bring the drum into the sanctuary. This is why careful planning, mutual involvement, and learning become so critical to the success of worship. Native American and White Christians need to explore just which liturgical practices are best for their own relationship.

Second, traditional Native Americans (that is, those men and women who worship God in their own tribal fashion) must be approached with a sense of historically informed respect. The truth is, these people have endured generations of religious persecution. Both the federal government and the Christian church have been guilty of denying them their right to worship God in their own way. It is not hard to understand, therefore, that many of these faithful people may feel cautious about invitations to share their lives with others. We must never forget that it was only on August

11, 1978, when the United States Congress passed the American Indian Religious Freedom Act, that many of these people were legally free to practice their religious convictions. Prior to that time, they were worshiping in an underground fashion much the same as early Christians, despite our American Constitution. Consequently, bridging the religious frontiers between Christians and traditional Native people requires special sensitivity, trust, and patience.

Inviting traditional people into a Christian setting is not something that should be done in an abrupt manner; asking medicine persons (the spiritual teachers and leaders of a traditional Native community) to share in worship is an interreligious relationship that demands careful dialogue, mutual understanding, and sufficient time to establish a basis of trust. Examining the motivation of the Christian congregation will be absolutely critical; recognizing the dark history of abuse that traditional people have suffered will be crucial; and accepting the fact that many of the spiritual practices of traditional persons are not for public display will be of primary importance.

Sharing Our Spiritual Gifts

These words of caution may discourage many White Christians from attempting a shared service of worship. To be honest, that's just as it should be. In the past, the tendency has been to take it for granted that Indian people didn't mind being called on short notice to bring their cultural-spiritual gifts to display before others. The result has been that many Native people have been treated as extras in a kind of Buffalo Bill Wild West Show; Indian men and women have been asked to talk, dance, and sing while White audiences have sat back and watched. The hard question we must all ask is this: Was that the kind of sharing of spiritual gifts that Paul had in mind?

As both a Native person, and as a Christian, my own answer has to be a resounding no. We *have* to be cautious. We must admit that some congregations will have to be discouraged, especially if their motivation and planning is inadequate to the new adult relationship between Indian and White Christians. We must announce that things have changed. It is much more likely now that the White congregation will have to leave its church walls to step into the Native worshiping community as guests. When Indian or Eskimo people do come to the White setting, they will not be coming as performers, but as missionaries and evangelists. The reciprocal relationship between our two communities (that bridge-building image we have stressed in this article) is the model we will be using from now on.

For those who are not discouraged by this new vision of Native word and worship, I invite you to explore the opportunities for renewal available to you in the Native American community. The word you hear will be the gospel of Christ Jesus, but spoken in the language of Native America. The worship you experience will be in praise of God, but in the sights, sounds, and symbols of Native America. I believe this is the kind of sharing Paul had in mind. I believe this is the true Body of Christ in action. I believe this is respecting the Circle.

Note

[1] From *Shandaa*, University of Alaska Press, 1992, pp. 179-180; these words were spoken when Belle was estimated to be between 105 and 127 years old and living in Chalkyitsik, Alaska.

You become what you believe

Faith Moyer (Inupiat Elder)

The Alaskan Orthodox Mission and Cosmic Christianity

Michael J. Oleksa

The Alaskan Mission

Two hundred years ago this September, the first overseas mission of the Russian Orthodox Church arrived at Kodiak Alaska, founding what would become in 1970, the Orthodox Church in America. Just as this movement began in the west and moved eastward, in exactly the opposite direction as the rest of North American history, the Alaskan experience, in fact, contradicts many stereotypes of Christian missions and missionaries.

Although the monastic clergy in 1794 were sent to minister to several hundred employees of the fur trading company in the region, their primary goal was the conversion of the indigenous peoples of the Aleutian and Kodiak Archipelagos. When they discovered that the former were exploiting and oppressing the latter, the missionaries sided with the Natives, whom they called "the Americans," protesting the abuses of their Siberian compatriots to the civil authorities in Irkutsk and St. Petersburg. Under house arrest for nearly a year, most of the monks either returned to Russia to report directly to the governor and Tsar, or moved out of harm's way by relocating elsewhere. By 1812, Father Herman, one of the elders of the original delegation, had moved to *Elovoi* or Spruce Island and established a hermitage, a chapel, and, later, an orphanage there, three miles from the Kodiak settlement. Thanks to the linguistic talents of the Tsar's personal representative, Priest-monk Gideon, the Kodiak parish operated the first bilingual school in the territory, teaching over a hundred Alutiiq children to pray, sing, read and write in their own language. Within a decade, ten thousand converts had been received into the Church.

Modern historians often ask why, if the Siberian frontiersmen in this early period so brutalized them, have the Aleuts remained so devoted to the Russian Orthodox Church. Part of the reason lies in the sympathetic and supportive stance of the original missionaries, their heroic defense of the Aleuts despite the hostility of the company administration and its employees. Another reason for the continued Aleut dedication to Orthodoxy is the identification of the mission with the indigenous culture and language, its willingness to use the aboriginal languages liturgically and to train local leadership for the church. But the most fundamental reasons for that continuing devotion are deeper, more theological, more spiritual.

Nine months after their arrival at Kodiak, Archimandrite Joseph, the head of the mission team, wrote a lengthy report to his igumen (abbott) back in Valaam, on Lake Ladoga from where the eight volunteers had been recruited. He detailed the religious beliefs of the Kodiak people, reporting that they had already had many of the Ten Commandments of Moses in their spiritual tradition. They had a story of the Great Flood in the time of Noah. They believed that all people were descended from the first parents, although they ascribed no names to them. In short, the missionary wrote, there is ample evidence that the Holy Spirit has been active among these people, and this should come as no surprise, since He goes wherever He wishes.

The Cosmic Gospel

This openness to the possibility, indeed the probability, that a so-called "pagan" culture would contain within itself certain fundamental truths which Christianity could and should affirm, echoes the most ancient attitude of the Church toward society. The Apostolic Church entered the Greco-Roman world of the first millennium AD opposed in many essential ways to the values and worldview of that time, and yet willing to express its message in words and symbols intelligible to the people of that age. There was then, and is now, no other choice. To communicate anything, one must employ a common vocabulary. The Church struggled for eight centuries to fill the original Greek words with Christian meanings, to redefine what the words themselves meant. Greek, for example, had such terms as "god," "time," "reason," and "will," but the Christian experience of all these was radically different from what classical culture understood. Entering a culture in which the world was seen as a balance of conflicting forces without any over-all order of purpose, and in which, therefore, human beings were left at the mercy of these capricious powers and had to control or manipulate them in order to survive, the church faced a tremendous missionary task. In the first nine centuries of the Christian era, she undertook to articulate her own worldview, in which the cosmos is governed by a supreme, transcendent, omnipotent and all-wise God. Christian saints denied the personal existence of the old pagan deities, but insisted that the "natural" forces they personified were, indeed, sacred realities, worthy not of worship, which is due God alone, but of reverence.

During the centuries called the "Dark Ages" in Western European history, the Eastern Christian Church dealt with many issues the Western Church is only now beginning to address. In the seventh century, for example, one of the central theological themes on which Christian thinkers reflected was the spiritual importance of the created universe. John 3:16, for example, in the original Greek says, "For God so loved the cosmos that He sent His Son..." Ephesians 3:9 refers to the mystery which had been hidden "in God who created all things by Jesus Christ," who, according to Ephesians 1:23 "fills all in all." Colossians 1:15-20 goes further:

> For by him were all things created, that are in heaven
> and in earth, visible and invisible, whether they be
> thrones or dominions or principalities or powers; all
> things were created by him and for him: He is before
> all things, and by him all things consist; and he is the

> head of the body, the church: who is the beginning,
> the first born of the dead; that in all things he might
> have pre-eminence. For it pleased the Father that in
> him should all fullness dwell.

As well, the Paschal Gospel reading, John 1:1-17, proclaims a cosmic dimension to the coming of the Word made Flesh. In the eastern Christian tradition, the coming of Christ is not necessarily understood as the direct result of the Fall, of sin and evil. Adam and Eve were created to grow toward spiritual perfection and maturity, to develop in cooperation with God, and to nurture the earth according to His will and plan. Instead, they used their god-given and god-like freedom to develop in the opposite direction, with disastrous consequences for the whole creation. Even if they had not rejected their original purpose and goal, they could not have attained full spiritual maturity without God's direct, personal assistance. Christianity believes that while human cooperation and devotion is essential, it will never in itself be sufficient to fulfill all that God demands. His standards are higher than humanity can reach exclusively by their own perseverance or effort. Sin threw the whole process off track, but the incarnation, at least in the opinion of several ancient Greek saints, was part of the original divine plan all along.

Having refused to submit to God's plan, human beings received the earth as His gift but exercised their dominion over it without reference to His Will. Christ not only fulfills the Will of the Father, but also reveals the "mystery hidden from all eternity." That mystery is namely that He is the unifying and vivifying personal principle from which everything and everyone derives their origin, life and ultimate purpose. He is the Logos, the Word, the Reason, the Plan and Purpose of "all things."

Do the lilies of the field communicate a spiritual reality? Do the heavens declare the glory of God and the firmament his handiwork? Does "nature" have a spiritual importance? Yes, said the Eastern Church fourteen centuries ago. The Word of God is "embodied," St.

Maximus explained, first in the entire visible universe, then in the Holy Scriptures, and finally and most perfectly in Emmanuel, Jesus Christ, the Word made Flesh. It is the same Logos, the same Word, the same Reason and plan "embodied" each time. In the first "embodiment," it is, as C.S. Lewis once wrote, as if the message were written in letters too large for us (in our fallen condition) to read. In the Old Testament law and prophets, the message becomes more intelligible and focused. And finally, in Christ, the "mystery hidden" is revealed.

Sacred Materialism

This vision, this understanding of the created universe required Eastern Christian missionaries to approach "pagan" spirituality with a good deal of openness and discernment. No, there is no god Zeus or goddess Athena, but the reverential attitude toward the sun, the sky, the earth, which these mythic deities were meant to promote can be affirmed by the Church, once they are given their true name: Christ. He is the "Sun of Righteous," as the Christmas Troparion (theme hymn) proclaims. Those who worshiped the stars are taught, as the hymn continues, "by a star to adore thee..." On Epiphany, twelve days later, the faithful process to a nearby stream or seashore to perform the "Great Blessing of Water," during which all the uses to which God has put Water in the Old Testament, and some of the prophesies about how He will continue to use it, are read. These include the first creation of the world, (Genesis), the deliverance of the child Moses in the Nile, the escape of the Hebrew nation from Egyptian slavery by passing through the Red Sea (Exodus), Gideon's fleece (Judges), Elijah's contest with the priests of Baal (1 Kings), Naaman's cure (2 Kings), as well as wonderful passages from Isaiah 12:

> Therefore with joy shall ye draw water out of the wells of salvation. And in that day shall ye say, Praise the Lord, call upon His Name, declare His

doings among the people…Sing unto the Lord; for
He has done excellent things: this is known in all
the earth.

The readings culminate with the gospel account of Christ's baptism, where, once again, the Spirit of God is on the face of the waters, this time to bless, renew, and sanctify them, restoring them to what the whole creation was in Eden: a sign of God's presence, power, and love.

Eastern Christians believe in sacred materialism. God uses physical objects and visible elements to communicate with His People. The created universe is the means by which we enter into communion with Him. He chose food as the most perfect way to enter our lives. And what is the bread? Flour, yeast and water, baked to a certain temperature? No, it is much more, for to create bread, one needs the whole world. The earth must turn, the rain must fall, the soil must be fertile, the sun must shine, night must come, the wind blow. If all this is in harmony, and humans interact with it appropriately, tending the garden as God originally planned, bread can be baked, communion with God restored.

The pagans deified the fertility principle, named it Dionysius or Bacchus or a thousand other names. The wine harvest was their celebration of this life-affirming cosmic mystery. They were not entirely wrong. They were, however, mistaken about the identity of the Life-force they worshiped. It is all Christ. He chose to make water into wine as his first miracle, but He is always doing that, in every vineyard since time began. Some say this is merely physics and chemistry, the "laws of nature," natural processes which operate without reference to any spiritual principle. Others say it is the work of fertility gods of goddesses who must be placated, appeased, worshiped or manipulated to assure future harvests. For the Christian, it is all Christ, who only does the work He sees His Father do. The Word made Flesh only does in His Incarnate Form what the Word, embodied in the whole creation, has always done.

Cosmic Salvation

Orthodox Christians are not pantheists, but they are *pan-in-theists*. The universe, taken as a whole, is not God, but He is "everywhere present and fills all things." It is His will, His presence, His power that creates and sustains everything and everyone at any given time. Creation is not only an event in the distant past but the reality of each passing moment. "Grace" is not a supernatural substance, "amazing" or otherwise, transmitted to the otherwise graceless world by certain religious actions or under certain liturgical circumstances, but the very energies, the action of God in the world. All is Grace.

In Alaska, the Valaam monks found that the Aleuts believed that the life force which animated the sea mammals they hunted was a sacred reality which had to be treated reverentially. Their Eskimo and Indian neighbors to the north and east shared this belief. The Church could affirm rather than condemn this humble, respectful, attitude toward life, for Christ is the life of all things, not just all people. The Church blesses by putting His Name, proclaiming His sovereignty, not just over human life, but over the entire cosmos. It is at this deeper, essentially spiritual level, that the Christian Gospel, proclaimed and celebrated liturgically and sacramentally within Eastern Orthodoxy, converged with the pre-Christian spiritual tradition of ancient Alaska.

This is the good news the Russian monks brought to Alaska two hundred years ago. Their message affirmed all that was, "true, honest, just, pure, lovely and of good report" (Phillipians 4) and sought to introduce Christianity as the fulfillment rather than the destruction of what the people had always believed. When, thirty-two years later, Father John Veniaminov and Aleut Chief Ivan Pan'kov translated the gospel of Matthew into Aleut, literacy became a popular sensation. Literate, educated Aleuts assumed responsibility for, and leadership positions within, the Church decades before the sale of the Alaska territory to the United States in 1867. Rather than casting off the supposedly "imposed" religion of their former oppressors, the Aleuts joyfully took the initiative of evangelizing Eskimo and Indian tribes on the mainland. The Alaskan Church grew from less than a dozen chapels at the time of the transfer to nearly a hundred today, thanks primarily to Aleut missionary outreach. The indigenous Alaskan Orthodox Church was born.

Identifying with, suffering with and for their flock, respecting their languages, cultural norms and ancient spirituality, educating them in the ways of the gospel, and preparing them to take responsibility for their Church, all contributed to the success of the Alaskan Orthodox mission. Perhaps most important, however, was the theological vision and liturgical celebration of the creative universe as fundamental to Christian spirituality. In an age where many are seeking a religious tradition that will integrate their reawakened ecological sensitivity into a comprehensive spiritual vision, Eastern Orthodoxy alone offers a Christian alternative to the various Gnostic/ "new age" movements which attract them in large numbers. The mission of the Church includes, but also extends beyond, the conversion of people to a liturgical/doctrinal/ethical system or code. It extends beyond the building of church structures, temples, schools, seminaries, or the publishing of theological books and spiritually-oriented periodicals. It extends beyond the celebration of services, the valid administration of sacraments, beyond preaching, teaching, converting and forgiving.

To accomplish this whole, this complete, this "catholic" missionary task, our theologians must articulate the cosmic understanding, the faith and practice of the ancient undivided church, in terms intelligible to people from all nations, and all religious, non-religious and even anti-religious traditions. Our parish clergy and people must celebrate this vision with a common understanding of what their *leitourgia*, their *work-on-behalf-of-the-world*, really is: "on behalf of everyone and for every thing." It is only with this cosmic vision, this full comprehension of what the Church is actually doing, that all the various educational, sacramental, liturgical, and charitable activities become worthwhile, meaningful, worthy of allegiance, dedication and sacrifice.

It was in that spirit that the first Orthodoxy missionaries came to Alaska two centuries ago. It is in that spirit that we, individually sinful and unworthy, must collectively, as the Holy Church, continue their work into the next millennium. There is, indeed, a plan, a purpose, a goal to the created universe, and it is *all* Christ. We can conform our lives to Him and thus live in harmony with that all-embracing Plan, the pre-eternal Logos or not. We will be judged accordingly. We can include within that vision, by blessing and sanctifying it, all that was made in Him and through Him and for Him, or we can exploit, destroy, pollute and desecrate the cosmos which He so loves. We will be judged for that as well.

International Anglican Liturgical Consultation Or Compass Rose Liturgical Tourists?

Juan Quevedo-Bosch

Most of us started arriving at the International Anglican Liturgical Consultation (IALC) in palm-fringed Kerala through the ultra modern Cochin airport about 70 kilometers from Kottayam, India. We covered the considerable distance between them during a harrowing two-hour "kamikaze" run. Our driver, seemingly possessed by a death wish, careened around cows, people, and trucks at top speed. An Australian couple was sharing the cab with me. We soon realized that overtaking on curves was mandatory. We passed many churches, mosques and Hindu temples, as well as what we believed must be the world's largest concrete replica of Michelangelo's Pietà.

The Kottayam Incident

As soon as we settled in Kottayam (pop. 65,000), an important center for "Saint Thomas Christians," news reached us from the local Kottayam police of legal problems concerning our visas. For two days it was not clear if we would be able to stay. After some negotiations the authorities agreed to let us stay. We would become what I refer to as "Compass Rose Liturgical Tourists", and our Consultation effectively became downgraded to something rather different than I had expected.

During the preparatory months leading up to the meeting we

had received two different and conflicting sets of instructions about our visas from our Indian counterparts. As a result of the confusion, some delegates had their visa applications denied, while others were on tourist visas.

For some of us either coming from, or currently living in, the Industrialized North, the necessity of reconciling opposites is an imperative. In Eastern thought, holding together what seem to be contradictory notions poses no philosophical dilemma—so Indian theologian Raimundo Panikkar tells us. When such opposites go unreconciled with regard to the arrangements for an international meeting, however, it can spell disaster, and very nearly did.

Our Liturgical Consultation took place in the middle of a national election campaign which had been called after plans for us to meet in India had already been finalized. Although I could not even attempt to grasp the complexities of Indian democracy, I can say that when I asked a Christian woman staying in my hotel for whom she was voting, she said with surprise and anger, "Congress, of course!" I prodded, stating that I had heard that the Congress Party had been widely charged with running a corrupt system for many years, to which she replied: "Yes, that is true, but they do not mess with religion." Her response reflects a particular concern in the State of Kerala, a state that has been first to attempt many things in India. For example, women's rights legislation, a social policy of religious tolerance, and a literacy program, have all been enacted there. It is also the state with the highest percentage of Christians.

At the time of the Consultation the Communist party was in power in Kerala, however, I believe the Keralites have since elected another government. The BJP, a pro Hindu party, was in power at the national level, and shortly after we left, the Indian electorate re-elected them on a nationalistic and religious (Hindu) platform. During the electoral campaign, we witnessed racial slurs towards Sonia Gandhi, the Italian-born widow of former Prime Minister Rajiv Gandhi.

I am spending time on the context of the Consultation because it is my opinion that it became a primary element in our deliberations.

It is as though the situation shook us violently and made us deeply aware of the fact that we were, as a group, having to deal with real and pressing issues in the so-called *Third World*. After our run-in with the local Indian police, we could not pretend to be merely liturgical tourists with India simply as the backdrop to our deliberations. We were yanked from the heights of affluent arrogance and forced to see and deal with our surroundings far more attentively and respectfully. Context and inculturation are always essential for liturgy, and our experience at this consultation profoundly made that point.

For the benefit of the uninitiated, allow me a small detour into the mysteries of International Anglican Liturgical Consultations. IALC is the brainchild of a group of Anglican members of *Societas Liturgica*. (*Societas*, born in Europe as the Liturgical Renewal Movement, is an ecumenical society of liturgists.) IALC began as the caucus of Anglican members of this group, made up mostly of professors, staff, and pastors interested in liturgy. Since its inception, the scholarly members of *Societas* have worked tirelessly, sometimes using their own funds, to bring representatives, every two years, from the rest of the Anglican Communion to share in discussions and to produce position papers on liturgical issues.

The initiative and funding for these consultations has mostly come from two sources: the United Kingdom and North America. After the Toronto Consultation in 1991, it became apparent that the same level of funding would not be available every two years, at which time the Steering Committee decided that full Consultations would be held every four years, with every effort being made to ensure the widest possible representation. Preparatory conferences are held during the intervening two-year period with a group composed chiefly of Anglican members attending *Societas Liturgica*.[1]

The clashing of icebergs

In 1999, a large group of Anglican scholars mostly from the North Atlantic, and pastoral liturgists from all over the Communion met in

Kottayam. I believe the meeting was a historical watershed, whatever the final assessment. In these thoughts on the Consultation, I am using a metaphor of "cultural icebergs" coined by Eric Law, a Canadian-based consultant and facilitator on the issue of cultural diversity, inclusion and difference. With this metaphor, apt in our context, he suggests that floating above the 'water level' of our perception is our awareness of ourselves, i.e., the things we know that make us different from others. He points out, however, that there is far more beneath the surface: our cultural assumptions and patterns of behavior, things which are often hidden even from ourselves.

The historical importance of Kottayam '99 lies precisely in its effect on the minds of the largely scholarly constituency from the Industrialized North (IN) which has been, not surprisingly, a guiding force in our deliberations. The cultural effects, however, were also felt by those of us from the Developing South (DS). We experienced, and were profoundly challenged by, the overall Indian context, and specifically by the ancient forms of Indian worship, both Christian and Hindu.

Kerala put us in contact with liturgy and history unique to Eastern Christians in India. It provided us contact with a history that *is present* in the practices and faith of the "Saint Thomas Christians" (Mar Thoma). This is a living community, a cultural minority, in a dynamic relationship and tension with the majority Hindu culture.

One of my frustrations at these meetings (which I have been attending since Toronto '91) has been the fact that I live, personally, between worlds. As a Cuban studying in Canada (for whom Kerala's landscape and climate almost hurt because of their resemblance to home), I cannot help but detect the cultural iceberg lying just below the surface in many of my colleagues from the IN of the First World. I see how aesthetic preferences, cultural presuppositions, social class, and even expertise can become hindrances to an effective dialogue with the majority of the Anglican Communion, which is now largely in the DS. Furthermore, suffering from my own cultural autism, I find myself often unsuccessful in bridging the gap to make connections, in comprehensible and acceptable terms, with both the IN and other culturally diverse parts of our Communion in the DS.

I'll offer an example of what I mean. The topic of the failed *full* Consultation in Kottayam was to be the "Ordination Rites." A preparatory Conference was held on the same topic in Jarvenpaa, a lovely Finnish town and the last residence of the composer Sibelius. During the Jarvenpaa meeting we dealt with ordination rites through the presentation of a number of papers and lively discussions. I particularly recall the mention of the "rugby scrum." To begin with, I did not have any idea what a "rugby scrum" was. Our national sport in Cuba is baseball. Rugby is as alien to us as roast beef! The gist of the critique was that the crowding of people around the presbyteral or Episcopal candidate in the ordination liturgy can distract from the centrality of the sign of the laying on of hands, which is better demonstrated by one person laying hands upon another person laying hands upon another, or by individuals laying hands upon the candidate(s) one at a time.

The argument for the necessity of "seeing" the laying on of hands, I contend, might be apt in the North American or European (IN) context as a marker of what is to be perceived and understood. In such matters, though, we often make decisions because of our own aesthetic preferences, only then moving on to find support in history. The shortening of the aesthetics of minimalism, middle class abhorrence of messiness, a post-industrial revolution desire for order, along with the post-modernist suspicions of hierarchies are all under-the-water chunks of ice (to use the cultural iceberg analogy) in positions like the one expressed by IN participants regarding ordination rites, .

Delegates from the south who are used to making their way in packed transportation systems, many living under various systems of authority with every-day experiences of extended families and large human groups, perceive "the rugby scrum," this crowding of people, quite differently from those who grew up under different circumstances.

Moreover, people from the South live in "abiding astonishment" (a phrase I borrow from Walter Bruggeman, who defines "abiding astonishment" as the celebration of an enduring miracle), not a concept generally-occurring among those who manage the media and institutions of higher learning, who monopolize control of the state, who create and transmit proper "facts," and who explain cause and effect to the masses. The experience and articulation of "wonder" tends to occur by word of mouth in simpler social units. "Abiding astonishment" happens among those who yearn for and receive miracle, who live by gift since they have little else by which to live, and who are sustained only by the slippage and gaps in the dominant system of power[2].

The corn cob or the Caribbean stew?

The dialogue between culture and gospel is one that has been better dealt with by a number of very proficient theologians and is a topic that I, as a novice, cannot appropriately cover in this article. However, I will say that I prefer a paradigm, or model, of relationships between culture and gospel that follows the example of the Incarnation. If we understand the Incarnation as dynamic by nature, then culture and gospel come together in a process of give and take, of natural selection, successive periods of growth and pruning, challenge and embrace. This is a process put in motion by Jesus himself,[3] and one that has been continued by the disciples and the Church ever since. The study of inculturation as a process has already taken place in the Church and is important to an understanding of where we are and where we may be going.

As Anglicans today, we find ourselves with many of the same concerns as those involved in earlier exchanges, for instance between Pope Gregory and Augustine, and today, between the Archbishop of Canterbury and other Bishops regarding the diversity of customs in Anglicanism and how best to evangelize. Taft tells us that:

> As a historian of Christian liturgical traditions, it is
> my unshakable conviction that a tradition can be

understood only genetically, with reference to its origins and evolution. Those ignorant of history are prisoners of the latest cliché, for they have nothing against which to test it. That is what knowledge of the past can give us. Knowledge of the future would serve equally well, but unfortunately that is not yet available to us. This does not mean that our ignorance of the future leaves us enslaved by our past. For we do not know the present; and in the present the past is always instructive, but not necessarily normative. What we do today is ruled not by the past but by the adaptation of tradition to the needs of the present. History can only help us decide what the essentials of that tradition are, and the parameters of its adaptation.[4]

One has to understand that the history of the Christian tradition begins within the Palestinian cultural paradigm. It evolves within the Mediterranean antiquity and takes shape for the West within the northern European cultural tradition. What happened when the gospel went to the rest of the world? Why did the same process of creative incarnation seem to stop in the its tracks when Western contact was made with the local cultures of Asia, Africa and Latin America? I suspect that some of the answers to these questions lie in the issue of power differential between the West and local Asian, African and Latin American cultures. Colonialism at its inception and Globalization today are part of the same process and share the same dynamics.

So, when we speak about the past of Christian liturgical traditions we are making a cultural statement, since there is no such thing as the gospel devoid of culture. Nor can one successfully peel off the cultural cob to find an authentic kernel of gospel truth. The process of interaction between the gospel and surrounding cultures is one that cannot be undone. What I am asking for is the continuation of this historical process in which local cultures become valid interlocutors with the gospel, and not just the Carmen Miranda of liturgical backdrop.

The paradigm shift necessary to foster an understanding of local cultures is a tall order. That shift would require the acceptance of an embodiment of knowledge and insight in different media than what the West has been accustomed to: music, dancing, and possession as opposed to various Cartesian concepts such as sages, oral traditions, as well as elders instead of books and academia. Phenomenology, a very western intellectual tool, might be helpful in understanding cultural differences since it postulates a suspension of judgment and invites an openness to the phenomena observed and described.

Signs of hope and challenges

Kottayam '99 was the first meeting of the IALC outside the IN, and is, I believe, a milestone in the history of the IALC, not so much for the work done as for the impact the life of Indian Christianity had on the IALC participants. There were many moving and sincere attempts on the part of some of the IN delegates to listen and understand what the people of the DS have to say. Although the majority of IALC delegates are from the IN, our northern partners have fostered the increasing participation of delegates from the DS. This will not, of course, be without consequences.

The movement to organize regional consultations and provincial workshops should gain strength and should include Asia and Latin America. Events such as these between IALC meetings will provide opportunities for closer contacts with local cultures and with the many challenges that Anglicans in the South face daily. These local events would not only enhance liturgical education, but would also foster mutual understanding and strengthen, beyond IALC, the partnership of scholars and pastoral liturgists.

IALC is a fundamental part of a global dialogue within Anglicanism that will redefine our identity by pushing further the boundaries of the Eurocentric, English-speaking paradigm. This process, I believe, is already well underway.

Notes

[1] For further information you may wish to consult: Paul Gibson, "International Anglican Liturgical Consultations: a 14-year review," 1997, available at the Lambeth Conference site http://www.lambethconference.org/reports/report4.html.

[2] Walter Brueggeman, *Abiding Astonishment*: Psalms, *Modernity, and the Making of History* (Louisville: Westminster/John Knox Press, 1991)p. 42.

[3] Mark 7:24ff the syro Phoenician woman.

[4] Robert Taft in *The Liturgy of the Hours East and West*, pp. xivv-xv.

APPENDICES

Recommendations Towards the Inculturation of Lakota Catholicism

Lakota Inculturation Task Force
Diocese of Rapid City

Introduction

We, the members of the Lakota Inculturation Task Force, developed the following recommendations in response to many Lakota deacons and lay leaders who have used Lakota symbols and ceremonies in the Liturgy of the Church and in response to a growing desire among Catholic Lakota people to identify with their past traditions while honoring their Catholic faith. We recognized that there has been a growing sense among the Catholic Lakota people that these symbols and expressions of a common faith should become a regular part of any Liturgy celebrated in a Native community.

We realize that the inculturation of the Liturgy is a controversial issue among the Lakota people. We do not intend any disrespect to Traditional Lakota people in any of the recommendations we make. The Second Vatican Council states "Let Christians, while witnessing to their own faith and way of life, acknowledge, preserve and encourage the spiritual and moral truths found among non-Christians, also their social life and culture." (Nostra Aetate #2) We make this statement our own. We affirm our respect and reverence for the Lakota tradition. At the same time, we assert that as Catholic Lakota people we have a right to use the symbols handed down to us in both the Catholic and the Lakota traditions. As Lakota Catholics, after prayer and discernment, we choose to use these symbols to enhance our spiritual life and our relationship with God.

Missionaries of the past, being people of their time, did not approve of Lakota religious traditions and in fact forced people to abandon their traditions if they became Catholic. Today, we recognize the sincere efforts of some contemporary missionaries to come to a respectful understanding of Lakota symbols and rituals. We acknowledge and are grateful for their good work and we are determined to build on their effort. The time has come, however, for us, Lakota people, in union with the Bishop and the Church's teaching, to advise on these matters, and to use these ceremonies where we judge appropriate.

We selected three phases for the process of inculturation. Phase 1 is an examination of what Lakota ritual items can be used in liturgical services and prayer services. Phase 2 is an examination of religious elements in Lakota life and ceremonies, which prepare the way for the reception of the Gospel and its expression in the Church. Phase 3 is an examination of Lakota philosophy and theology.

Part 1 of Phase 1 contains our recommendations for the Liturgy of the Eucharist; these recommendations represent an initial effort to make a regular inculturated Liturgy of the Eucharist available. We will also consider the Sacraments of Baptism, Confirmation, Marriage, Reconciliation, Anointing of the Sick, Holy Orders, Communion Services, and Funeral Rites in order to find more culturally appropriate ways of celebrating these rites.

This process is ongoing. We recognize that the work of inculturation is never completed once and for all. We realize that these recommendations will need to be refined as information is gathered from the experience of the inculturation process. We welcome any comments or suggestions that would help produce an acceptable, regularly inculturated, experience of the Sacraments and Rites of the Church.

It is important to note that every Liturgy is meant to be an inculturated Liturgy. We acknowledge that any single form of inculturated Liturgy is not for everyone. Given the diversity of Native communities on and off the reservation, it is essential that a variety of inculturated liturgies be available in order to reflect the diversity of cultural expressions in the contemporary Native community. Practically, this means that when the following form of inculturated Eucharistic Liturgy is celebrated, another Eucharist must be made available to people who are not able to attend this Liturgy or who do not wish to do so.

We encourage the local community's advice and recommendations regarding the implementation of this inculturated Liturgy. For instance, the members of the local community must choose when it is appropriate to do the Cannumpa Yuha Wocekiye (Sacred Pipe Ceremony). Moreover, local people have to provide readers, singers, people to do the Azilya (incensing), and respected Catholics to do the Cannumpa Yuba Wocekiye. In this document, we do not insist that all of the symbols recommended be used at a given Eucharistic Celebration. Rather, the members of the Task Force want to affirm that these symbols and ceremonies may be used if a local community wishes to do so.

Finally, we affirm that the religious symbols and traditions of the Lakota have been entrusted to the Lakota people alone. It is only the Catholic Lakota people who have the right to advise Church leadership on the use of these symbols. It would be inappropriate for a non-Indian priest, deacon, religious, or lay person to use Lakota religious symbols or ceremonies, e.g., Sacred Pipe, Feather, or incensing. By taking this position, we are not attempting to infringe on the right or responsibility of bishops, priests, or deacons to fulfill their appropriate roles in the Liturgy. We affirm that a Native bishop, priest, or deacon ought to use these symbols.

We ask non-Native bishops, priests, and deacons to refrain from using these symbols for important pastoral reasons. First, the symbols belong to people of Lakota heritage. The symbols are an expression of their culture and are most appropriately used by them. Second, at the present time there is great resentment and anger in the Lakota community because many non-Indians have appropriated these sacred symbols for themselves and use them in inappropriate and irresponsible ways. This is insulting to all Lakota people, who find it very difficult to understand how a non-Lakota person can appropriate their religious symbols. Third, by insisting that only Native people use these symbols, the Task Force wants to encourage the development of leadership, *ordained and non-ordained, among the Lakota people.*

We, the Catholic Lakota members of the Lakota Inculturation Task Force, make the following recommendations with confidence and a strong desire to pray in this manner.

Phase 1: Ritual
Part 1

1. Guidelines for the Liturgy of the Eucharist

Recommendations

1. Catholic Lakota Leadership

Lakota people in leadership roles, ordained and non-ordained, are a necessary foundation for the inculturation of the Church and the development of an inculturated Liturgy. It is important to foster Lakota leadership in every area of the Church's life—social justice, catechetical, and liturgical.

2. Language

At the heart of inculturation is use of the Lakota language. It must be recognized that not everyone is able to speak or understand the language; nevertheless, it is important to use the language when it will enhance the prayer experience. In the Liturgy of the Eucharist, when a Lakota speaking priest is not presiding, the following could be done in the Lakota language:

1. Form C of the penitential rite.
2. The homily—given by a Lakota deacon or repeated by a Lakota speaker.
3. The prayers of the faithful.
4. The readings.
5. Lakota hymns.
6. Traditional Lakota songs—melody, drum beat.

3. Space

A circle may be incorporated into the celebrations of the Liturgy and prayer services in the present structures where and when possible.

For the purposes of Azilya (incensing), water blessings, distributing communion, etc., ministers move in a sun wise direction—clockwise.

4. Ritual Time and Priorities

In Lakota ritual the focus is not on clock time, the focus is on the activity itself. It is better to think of Lakota ritual time in terms of order—doing things according to priorities. A ceremony takes precedence over all other activities. People sacrifice other activities in order to be present for the ceremony. They place themselves in a proper frame of mind and the ceremony takes as long as it takes to do it correctly. Length of clock time, short or long, is irrelevant.

In the same way, the Liturgy of the Eucharist begins when the people assemble and lasts as long as it takes for the prayer. No other event takes precedence over the Eucharistic celebration. The people's first priority is to be present at the Eucharist with a good heart.

5. Music

Song is at the heart of the Lakota religious way of life. It is essential that music be part of the Eucharistic Liturgy. There are two types of music which are recommended:

5.1. Hymns

Lakota hymns, e.g. "Jesus Chante," "Jesus Jesus El Mau," are part of the Catholic tradition and should continue to be used. These songs were translated from English and Latin and use organ music. They have been used by the St. Mary and St. Joseph Societies. Translation of modem hymns into Lakota is also encouraged.

5.2. Lakota Olowan (traditional music)

The use of traditional Lakota music, a drum, an eagle bone whistle, and a gourd may be used in the Liturgy. The Lakota people, while observing the traditions of making new songs, are encouraged to pray for new lyrics and melodies that can be used in the

Liturgy. These new songs must follow the conventions of Lakota sacred music: e.g., ceremonial songs, Inipi Ceremony songs.

These conventions are:

5.2.1. Use few words and vocables—e.g. repeat "Jesus iyotancila," or "Jesus Wastecilake," (Jesus, I love you).

5.2.2. Use Lakota drum beat—drum roll at beginning and end.

5.2.3. Use Lakota singing.

5.2.4. Use Lakota lyrics.

5.2.5. Use Lakota rhythm—one two beat.

5.2.6. Use Lakota melody.

6. Cannumpa Opagi Na Cannumpa Yuha Wocekiye (The Pipe Ceremony)

6.1. Public Use

6.1.1. The Sacred Pipe is meant to be used in public.

6.1.2. The Sacred Pipe Ceremony should be a normal practice in the Eucharistic Liturgy.

6.1.3. When the Pipe Ceremony is used in the Eucharist, notice must be given ahead of time so that people may decide if they wish to attend.

6.1.4. This form of inculturated Liturgy must be an option and not the only Eucharist available.

6.1.5. Rules regarding the Sacred Pipe Ceremony must be respected.

6.2. Who Should Do a Pipe Ceremony

The Pipe can be used by any Lakota or Native person who has been given a Pipe and has learned the ceremony. Within the context of the Eucharist or other sacraments, the person must be a Lakota Catholic. It should be a person of good reputation who uses the Pipe in a respectful manner. It should be someone who is recognized as a leader by the Catholic community—leader in the sense that that person can bring people together.

6.3. Place of Sacred Pipe Ceremony in Order of Worship

6.3.1. The Pipe Ceremony should be used within the order of worship of the Eucharist.

6.3.2. The whole Pipe Ceremony is—fill the Pipe while singing the Pipe Loading Song, light the Pipe, smoke the Pipe, sing the song honoring the Pipe. The Pipe remains present throughout the whole Liturgy. A Pipe carrier, usually a woman, carries the Pipe in procession—entrance and recessional.

6.3.3. The most appropriate place for the Pipe Ceremony is at the prayers of intercession.

6.3.3.1. The tobacco represents an offering of all things to God.

6.3.3.2. When each person smokes the Pipe he or she makes a prayer of petition.

6.3.3.3. The smoke rises and brings *the prayers* of the assembly to God.

6.3.3.4. At each Eucharist people are designated ahead of time to smoke the Pipe—e.g., the celebrant, concelebrants and deacons, the Pipe carrier, Eucharistic ministers, others.

6.3.3.5. After the Pipe is smoked, it is placed on a Pipe rack beside the altar.

6.3.3.6. After Communion, when the sacred vessels are put on the side table, the Pipe may be emptied, taken apart, and put back in the Pipe bag.

Note:

A blessed Pipe is not to be used as a decoration nor is it to be put on display. If it is taken out of the pipe-bag, it must be used. If it is used in a sacramental setting, i.e., the Eucharist, it is to be present through the entire ceremony.

7. Tate Topa Olowan (Four Winds Song/Prayer)

The Four Winds Song/Prayer comes from the Inipi Ceremony. When the Pipe is not present the Four Winds Song/Prayer can be done.

7.1. This ceremony may be done at the penitential rite or at the prayers of petition. It has elements of involving God's great work on behalf of the people. It would be similar to form C of the penitential rite. It also has elements of petition, so it could be done at the prayers of petition.

7.2. The Four Winds Song/Prayer is offered by a Catholic Native person of good reputation.

8. Azilya (Incensing)

8.1. Introduction
In a Native context, incensing with sweet grass, sage, or cedar should be a normal practice at the Eucharistic Liturgy.

The smoke represents a prayer. It is a prayer of cleansing and purifying and blessing of people and objects used in ceremonies. Sweet grass, sage, and cedar are used for incensing. Sweet grass is used most often.

8.2. Place in the Order of Worship
Incensing may be done at one or all five of the following places in the Liturgy of the Eucharist:

8.2.1. Penitential rite: the people are incensed as a sign of cleansing and purification in preparation for participation in the Eucharist.

8.2.2. Gospel: the Book of the Gospels is incensed as a way of honoring the Icon of the Word of God.

8.2.3. Offertory: the offerings are incensed and the altar is honored as an Icon of Christ. As the smoke rises, the offering prayer is carried to God.

8.2.4. After the altar is incensed, the people may be incensed.

8.2.5. During the Consecration, the Body of Christ and the Blood of Christ may be incensed, as they are elevated.

8.3. Who Should do the Azilya

8.3.1. At the penitential rite, any Catholic Native person of good reputation may incense the people.

8.3.2. At the Gospel, it is appropriate for a Native deacon to incense the Book of the Gospels. If a Native deacon is not present then the deacon incenses the Book of the Gospels with a bowl only while a Native person(s) incenses with a bowl and an eagle feather.

8.3.3. At the Offertory, it is appropriate for a Native bishop or priest to incense the offerings and the altar. If a Native bishop or priest is not present then the priest incenses the offerings and the altar with a bowl only while a Native person(s) incenses with a bowl and an eagle feather.

8.3.4. A Native person(s) incenses the people.

8.3.5. A Native person(s) incenses the Body of Christ and the Blood of Christ at the elevation during the Consecration.

Note:

Incensing is done in a clockwise direction.

9. Cunli Wapahte (Tobacco Ties)

Tobacco Ties may be placed in a basket at the entrance of the Church. They are brought up at the offertory procession and placed near the altar. They should be burned after the Eucharist is over.

10. Handshake

The traditional handshake is a sign of peace and unity. It should be a part of each Eucharistic celebration. For the present it is *recommended* that it remain at the *time of the* "Sign of Peace."

11. Eagle Feather

The eagle feather is wrapped in a red cloth and can be placed on a table next to the altar.

12. Symbols that can be used in the Eucharistic Liturgy

The following list is not meant to be exhaustive, others may be added:

    12.1. eagle feather

    12.2. staff

    12.3. four colors

    12.4. flags in the four directions

    12.5. vestments with Lakota designs

    12.6. Altar and Churches decorated in Lakota designs

    12.7. Sacred Vessels decorated in Lakota designs

    12.9. The color of purificators, and corporals may be red

    12.10. When they are being used in the Eucharistic celebration, Sacred Vessels should be covered with a red cloth. It is also appropriate for the reserved Eucharist to be covered in a red cloth.

Appendix A

The Task Force recognizes that many Lakota people use the Sweat Ceremony as a means of purification and as a way to pray for forgiveness and healing. It also recognizes that the Naming Ceremony and the Tying of the Plume Ceremony have been used in the context of the Eucharist—usually after Communion and before the final blessing.

The Task Force has just begun its work. It will investigate the following ceremonies and their relationship to the Liturgies of the Sacraments and the worship of the Church.

The members of the Task Force continue to reflect on the following ceremonies:

1. Naming ceremony
2. Making of relatives
3. Buffalo singing ceremony
4. Vision quest
5. Spirit keeping
6. Ball throwing ceremony
7. Sacred meals/feasts—including Christmas and Easter
8. Wiping of tears ceremony
9. Give-away

AZILYA

There was a clarification on the use of the azilya at Mass. The azilya may be brought to the people at the Penitential Rite. It is used at the Gospel. It is used for the offertory gifts—it is brought to the people at this time only if it was not used at the Penitential Rite. In other words, it is brought to the people only once in a Mass. The most appropriate time is at the beginning of the Mass.

Keeping of the spirit

The members of the Task Force want to amend the discussion of this topic from the last meeting in which it was indicated that only the person keeping the spirit was in mourning. The members think that it is traditional Lakota practice that if a family decides to keep the spirit, all immediate family members are in mourning. The whole family has to honor the tradition. The principle is that the members of a family keeping the spirit of a dead relative can't enjoy themselves for a year until after the memorial feast. It is also the custom that the mother or wife dresses in black. Sometimes some of the relatives cut their hair. The members of the family, while they may attend a Pow Wow, would not dance at one.

Wiping of Tears

Wiping of tears ceremony can happen a few days after someone is buried or it can happen at the memorial or both—there is no set time to do it. It is done when requested by a family member or relative. Food is usually served. People comb the hair of the mourners and feed them. They give them tobacco and drinking water. It can be a public or private ceremony. It can be done for the whole family or an individual member of the family.

The Wiping of Tears is done at religious gatherings e.g. Sioux

Indian Congress, mini-Tekakwitha Conference, memorial feasts, and healing services. The Task Force recommends that it be offered on holy days, e.g. Good Friday, All Souls Day, All Saints Day and Easter.

Wake

1. When the family is willing and able they should be encouraged to be involved in the Wake service. They can do the readings, prayers of petition, and songs. Sometimes the family won't want to do any of these things. In such circumstances the Christian community, attentive to the Lakota tradition and Church tradition, must take these roles.

2. When there is only one night of wake, a combination of the Rosary and the Wake service from the Order of Funerals may be used.

3. It is important to rediscover Lakota hymns and traditional music and use them at the Wake Service, e.g. a Lakota hymn or traditional song after each decade of the Rosary.

4. In some places the coffin is closed during the meal. This depends on the custom of the community and on the desire of the family.

5. Relatives and friends may be invited to talk about the deceased during or after wake services. However, an open microphone in not appropriate for the funeral service.

6. If the deceased is a veteran the honor guard will have the Roll Call and read prayers.

7. Corrections to the last document:

   7.1. Leadership:

   The members recommend that the sentences, *"Two Types of leaders are needed. Traditionally, when someone dies in a community a member of the Tiospaye is designated to oversee the services. We recommend that people be trained to work with the Tiospaye leader and when necessary actually become the master of ceremonies for the funeral rites,"* be changed. They should read, "Two types of leaders are appropriate, the first is a person designated by the Tiospaye to act as the contact person and master of ceremonies. The second is a lay leader, the Church's contact person, who works with the person from the family. If necessary, the lay leader could become the master of ceremonies."

The Reverend Mark Francisco Bozzuti-Jones members also recommend that the sentence, *"It is important that the members of these teams, people in good standing in their communities, get the formation they need to do this work well,"* be changed. This sentence should read, "It is important that the members of these teams be made up of people who are respected in the community and the Church, and that they get the *formation* they need to *do* this work well."

7.2. Items placed in the casket: Change "food" to dry food, add pictures, rosary, and a cross.

7.3. Sursum Corda: The Wake Service in the old Sursum Corda should not be used. Rather a translation should be made of a Wake Service from the Order of Funerals.

7.4. It is recommended that the talks at wakes be more instructional. Different members of the team could prepare a talk on different aspects of Catholic life and traditional life.

7.5. Give away: the correct spelling is wihpeyapi.

Funeral

1. The Four Winds Song:
The Four Winds Song can not replace the Song of Farewell. It could be sung at the beginning of the service or before the Song of Farewell.
The Song of Farewell could be translated and the drum could be used with it.

2. Veterans:
   The flag is removed from the coffin during the funeral or covered over by the star quilt.
   At the graveside the honor guard will read prayers and fold the flag and present it to the family.

3. The ribbons worn by the pallbearers can be pinned on the star quilt before the coffin is lowered.
   The Iclowanpoi, the Going Away Song, or the traditional Farewell Song is sung either in the Church or at the graveside.

4. The members of the Task Force did not want to mention anything about the use of the eagle whistle and eagle feather at funerals. People will use them when they want to. However, since the eagle feather is a sign of life it is not traditionally used in the presence of a body. The members of the Task Force suggested that in light of the Christian understanding of death, a statement be developed to demonstrate the possible use of an eagle feather at Catholic funerals.

5. There was some discussion about using sweat rocks at a funeral and painting the face of the deceased. This discussion needs more development.

Book of Etiquette

The members of the Task Force suggested that a book of etiquette be published which would spell out expected behavior in Church and at wakes and funerals. This discussion arose in connection with getting children to behave during services. The members feel that parents do not know what is expected any more.

Blessing of the Stone

The blessing of the stone takes place when the family is ready. It is it's own ceremony.

Marriage

There seems to have been very little ritual with traditional Lakota marriages. The members of the Task Force simply listed observations.

1. One member observed that at a traditional marriage during a Sundance, a blanket was put on the ground. The man conducting the Sundance was the minister. The couple stood at the entry of the arena and everyone went around and shook hands with them.

2. Sometimes a Pipe Carrier performs the ceremony. Sometimes a Sacred Pipe Ceremony is used at the traditional wedding.

3. The family of the groom gives gifts to the bride's family. The family of the bride gives gifts to the groom's family. This was the formal engagement. They were now related. They became members of each other's family and the families themselves became related. In the tradition, marriage was an exchange of gifts; e.g. warriors had to have horses to give to the family of the bride. Marriages were civil ceremonies. There was not much religious ritual used in them.

4 Some members have seen a church wedding followed by a traditional wedding in the home.

5. The Task Force would like to develop a rite of engagement that would incorporate the exchange of gifts and the joining of families. This rite would be followed by preparation for marriage. The couple would be instructed about the Christian meaning of marriage and about Lakota values. This would be a type of marriage catechumenate.

6. The members felt that Task Force needs to address the follow issues:
    6.1. Marriage preparation.
    6.2. Rules for dealing with in-laws.
    6.3. Irregular marriages and convalidations.
    6.4. Annulments.

7. Civil marriage today.

The BIA superintendent issues a marriage license. The civil marriage takes place in the tribal court before a tribal judge. A judge, recognized clergy, or a traditional leader can perform the ceremony. The people make the contact.

Tokala Societies

Some members thought it would be good to discuss the revival of Tokala Societies. These societies were made up of people who dedicated themselves to helping others. This discussion needs more development.

Chapel

The Task Force talked briefly about a new chapel at the Center.

1. The chapel should be in the form of a circle. Although it is possible to have a square building with a circle within for the worship space.
2. It should be made out of logs to match the Center.
3. It should include Lakota artwork.
4. The altar clothes and vestments should be of Lakota design.
5. Lakota people join prayer and action. The worship space needs to have room for motion.
6. The altar should be in the middle. It should not be stationary. The seating should be all around the altar.
7. It should have central heating and air.
8. A soil engineer needs to check the soil.
9. The roof will have a slight pitch.

Practical Implementation

1. The Bishop needs to see and approve the recommendations concerning the use of the Pipe and smudging.
2. If the Bishop approves, set up meetings on each reservation with the pastoral teams and explain what we are doing and the recommendations we have made. Make it

clear that we want people to have a choice. We realize that an inculturated Liturgy is not for everyone.

3. Set up meetings on each reservation to explain what we are doing to Native people who are interested. Try to work with at least one priest on each reservation in order to provide an inculturated Liturgy each Sunday.

4. The members feel a certain urgency to implement some of the inculturation recommendations.

5. There will be a need for ongoing education. People need to know what we are doing, that it has been approved by the Bishop, and that it has the support of the priests.

The Pipe Ceremony

Introduction

The members of the Task Force want to make it clear that the Sacred Pipe is just that—the Sacred Pipe. It is not Christ nor is it a substitute for Christ. It has a similar symbolic value for ancient Lakota people as the Cross has for ancient Christian people. However, it does not have the same meaning as the Cross and it ought not to substitute for it. The Pipe does have a place in Lakota Christian worship since it is a religious symbol provided by God to the Lakota people.

The meaning of the Pipe does not have to be transformed in order to be incorporated into Christian Liturgy and prayer. The Sacred Pipe Ceremony arises out of an ancient Lakota tradition. It was a way in which God chose to communicate with the people before the Gospel was preached. Just as Jewish Christians kept some Jewish customs and incorporated them into the Liturgy, in the same way Lakota Christians want to retain the Pipe Ceremony.

An incidental remark:

In the 1970's, Fr. Bill Stolzman entered into dialogue with medicine men on the Rosebud Reservation. One of the questions asked of these leaders was how do you explain the importance of the Pipe. This was a difficult question for them to answer because it was not their way of proceeding to explain sacred ceremonies. They said that just as Jesus Christ was held sacred to Christian people so too the Pipe was held sacred to Lakota people. They meant this in an analogous way. However, people then began to say that the Pipe was equal to Jesus. Today, in the minds of some, the Pipe and Jesus compete against each other. The intention of the medicine men was to try to get across the idea that the Pipe was a sacred ceremony. The intention was not to pit one against the other.

Public Use

In the 1960's and 1970's there was a tendency to emphasize the sacredness of the Pipe to the point where *no one* or only a very few could touch it. Ben Black Bear Sr. said that if the Pipe became too sacred it would disappear. It is meant to be used by the people. Anyone can use it and anyone can smoke it.

The Pipe is meant to be used in public. It is used at the beginning of a Tribal Council session and at other civic gatherings. It has to be used in public or else it is meaningless. At these meetings, the Pipe is wrapped in sage and the people are smudged with sweet grass. This protects the Pipe from evil. It is also possible that this would protect the Pipe from the power of a menstruating woman.

Symbolism

The Sacred Pipe Ceremony is basically a sacrifice. In the Old Testament, the first fruits of the crops were sacrificed on the altar. In Lakota tradition, instead of food, tobacco is used to represent everything to be sacrificed. When the Pipe is loaded and the tobacco burns, it becomes a sacrificial offering.

The Sacred Pipe Ceremony developed over many centuries. Three hundred years ago, the Lakota people, trying to figure out the meaning of life, looked around for the most sacred thing in nature. That most sacred thing was conception of new life.

The Sacred Pipe Ceremony reenacts the most sacred thing that God does for the people—conception of new life. Whenever conception takes place, new life begins. The people of long ago did not understand it and people today do not understand it. It remains mysterious and wonderful.

The Lakota people understood that God was communicating himself through *conception*. So the people tried to imitate as closely as possible this activity of God so that they could communicate back to him, God communicated to the people through life. They communicated back to God in the best way they could.

It is the symbolic reenactment of the beginning of life:
>Tobacco is used instead of food (plants or animals)
>Pipestone—female
>Pipe stem—male
>The stone and stem are kept separately. The only time you join the stone and stem is when you get ready to load tobacco into the Pipe.
>Fire—God
>Smoke—life. It ascends to the heavens. It carries prayers to God.

Having a menstruating woman present clashes with the symbolism. Her presence is real and overshadows the symbolism. That is why it is a problem to have a menstruating woman standing in the presence of the person praying with the Pipe. She is the real thing and negates what is being done symbolically.

An incidental remark:

Life begins at conception—that is really what the Sacred Pipe Ceremony is about. When the Pipe is loaded and the fire is lit, it is the reenactment of conception itself. The fetus in the womb is a human life. The Lakota people have traditionally held the fetus sacred, so much so, that their most sacred ceremony represents life in the womb.

Women and the Pipe

The rule is that a menstruating woman cannot be present when there is a Sacred Pipe Ceremony.

It is important to understand the historical underpinnings of the rules that surround ceremonies.

Two hundred years ago, a woman during her period was separated from the community for four days. She lived in isolation and did not associate with the community. The rule for a menstruating woman not being around the Pipe was part of that more exclusive rule. Now the rule exists without the historical context or reasons. Sometimes the rules for using the Pipe are overemphasized. The historical and practical reasons for these rules need to be studied. In many cases, the reason for the rule has disappeared but the rule has not.

Observations:

1. To have a menstruating woman present at a Sacred Pipe Ceremony is not bad or evil. The reason they are asked not to participate is that their real presence overshadows the symbolism.

2. It is possible that the Pipe can be protected in the presence of a menstruating woman and kept holy and sacred in several ways:

   2.1. Smudge the participants with sweet grass.

   2.2. Wrap the Pipe in sage.

   2.3. Place flags with the four colors at the four directions in order to create a sacred space in which sacred things are used and the Pipe can be protected.

3. Individual pipes take on individual meanings and are used for different ceremonies. Not all pipes have the same meaning. A person might use a particular pipe for the Sun Dance and for no other purpose. Different pipes have different customs. For instance, the leader might offer a particular pipe to be smoked by only elderly people and, at another time, he might offer a pipe to be smoked by everyone.

   The Sacred Pipe in the possession of the Keeper of the Pipe at Green Grass holds a privileged place among pipes. The rules could apply to this pipe in a stricter sense.

4. Usually, a woman carries the Pipe to the place of the ceremony. She can smoke it but the man loads it.

5. A woman can load and smoke the Pipe when she is by herself and for her own use.

Who Should do a Pipe Ceremony

The Pipe can be used by any Lakota person or Native person who has been given a Pipe and has learned the ceremony. It should be a person of good reputation who uses the Pipe in a respectful manner. It should be someone who is recognized as a leader by the community—leader in the sense that he can bring people together and put them in a frame of mind that they are united. He will use the Pipe as an instrument of unity and peace.

Use of the Pipe in the Eucharist

1. The Pipe is used to help people see that they are praying together. The smoking of the Pipe is a sign of unity. Sometimes everyone present smokes it. Sometimes designated people, representing the other people present, smoke it.
2. The Pipe is not to be used as a decoration nor is it to be put on display. If it is taken out of the bag, it must be used. If it is used in a sacramental setting, i.e., the Eucharist, it is to be present throughout the entire ceremony.
3. The person leading the Pipe Ceremony within the context of the Eucharist or other sacraments must be a Lakota Christian. He needs to be a leader from the Christian community.
4. The Pipe Ceremony can be done by itself. It is basically a way of praying. Instead of simply using words, a person prays with an instrument. The Pipe Ceremony is incorporated into all Lakota Ceremonies—Sweat Lodge, Sun Dance, Naming Ceremony, etc. It should be incorporated into Catholic Ceremonies.

Incidental remarks

The Pipe as a sign of unity is not meant to compete with the Eucharist as a symbol of unity.

1. The Pipe is spoken of as a sign that people are of one heart and mind, and that they are at peace. The Pipe Ceremony does not bring about unity and peace although it may be

used to pray for those things. The story was told of a meeting between the Lakota and some army officers. They gathered to sign an agreement. The group gathered in a circle and the Lakota leader prayed with the Pipe and offered the Pipe to the entire circle. The first officer wiped the Pipe with a handkerchief then smoked it. The next officer would not smoke it. The Lakota leader took the Pipe back and the ceremony was ended because there was no unity of minds and hearts.

The Eucharist is a sign of unity and peace; but it also brings it about. The Eucharist is the Risen Lord reconciling all things to himself.

2. The leader of the Pipe Ceremony will designate certain people to smoke the Pipe. The purpose of smoking is to offer prayers to God. At the Eucharist all who can receive.

3. The Pipe Ceremony is similar to the "Kiss of Peace," which is a sign that everyone is united in the community. It does not compete with the symbol of the Eucharist but rather externally expresses a hoped for result of the Eucharistic activity.

4. Matt. 5:23-24 – The Pipe can be seen as a way in which we practically implement this passage in Matthew. Before approaching the Altar, we should be reconciled with one another.

Important Considerations

1. Advanced notice needs to be given when a Pipe Ceremony is going to be used at the Eucharist or in the celebration of other sacraments or prayers. This way people who cannot attend or who feel uncomfortable will be able to gracefully excuse themselves.

2. Attending a Eucharist with a Pipe Ceremony is optional. A Mass should be available for those who feel they do not want to attend a Eucharist with a Pipe Ceremony. The Pipe Ceremony shouldn't be an imposition but a real option.

3. The rules regarding the Sacred Pipe Ceremony should be respected.

Education is very important

1. Before the Eucharist, the Pipe Ceremony should be explained. The rule regarding menstruating women should be explained—preferably by a woman elder.
2. There needs to be an educational process that includes more than brief comments before Mass. It is important to enter into dialogue with communities on the reservations.

    2.1. Explain the Eucharist and symbols such as the cross.

    2.2. Explain the Sacred Pipe Ceremony and why we want to use it in the Eucharist.

Entrance Rite

Two ideas were talked about:

1. Need to look at the normal way people gather. As people come into the church, let them greet one another with a handshake. When the time arrives for the Liturgy to begin, the presider calls the community to worship and the opening hymn begins. The smudging occurs during the penitential rite.
2. Gather in a separate place. At the time for the Liturgy to begin the whole community enters the church led by the drum and a Sundance song. The smudging takes place during the penitential rite.

During the smudging, flags would be put up in the four directions to establish sacred space. It is also possible that the four-direction song could be sung at this time.

The Episcopal Church has the option of substituting a song of praise for the Gloria. The Roman Rite does not have that option. However, since the four-direction song is a song which commemorates the omnipresence of God and the wonders that God has done for the people, it can easily be used as the third form of the penitential rite which generally recognizes God's powerful intervention on behalf of the people.

The drum and a Sundance song could be used in the entrance and recessional. The Sundance song would be one without words.

Music

1. Members of the Task Force will put together melodies and Lakota words for the Gospel Acclamation, the Holy Holy, the Memorial Acclamation, and the Great Amen.
2. Members will also try to record an entrance song.

Coming of Age Ceremonies

Puberty is a major change in the lives of young people. It is a time of great physical and emotional change for girls and boys. It presents an excellent opportunity for education.

There are two coming of age ceremonies:

Buffalo Singing Ceremony: coming of age ceremony for young women.

> The first menses of a girl is extremely important. At that time the grandmother or an older woman teaches the girl how to take care of menstruation, important facts about sex, important principles of married life, ways to raise children and she instills in them correct values. It is psychologically a good time to teach these things to young girls. It is an opportunity to infuse in them ways to behave and ways to live. This includes customs and religious teachings. It is an opportunity to teach young girls something that will stay with them the rest of their lives. Even though they may not understand completely everything they are being told, they will eventually remember it as their lives unfold.
>
> After the time of instruction, the Buffalo Singing Ceremony is conducted for the candidate. In this public ceremony, she is presented to the community as a young woman. The grandmother or older woman is required to be her mentor and protector until she marries.

Vision Quest: coming of age for young men.

> When a boy begins puberty, the Grandfather or older man leads him through his first sweat, teaches him how to take care of himself, and how to relate to others—especially women. The boy is taken on a Vision Quest.

He is taught values and ways of behaving. Whatever he is taught at this time, and whatever activities he does, will become part of his life. Through the Vision Quest, he will learn spirituality, which will become a habit and a way of life.

Observations
1. The Buffalo Singing Ceremony and the Vision Quest could be combined with preparation for Confirmation.
2. We need to discuss ways in which the public ceremonies could be conferred at the time that the Sacrament of Confirmation is conferred.
3. The group felt that if this was initiated it would be well received by the Catholic Lakota youth.

Celebrations at Christmas and Easter

The members of the Task Force felt it would be worthwhile to re-introduce a form of the Christmas and Easter celebrations. These celebrations would be a way in which the communities could remember the good things of the past with the hope of bringing people together.

These celebrations would give the communities one more opportunity to take control *of* their own spiritual lives. It would give them an incentive to build a celebration that would enhance Christmas and Easter.

Leadership is needed: someone to bring the community together.

Christmas

In the past, the celebration was basically a public feast with a Christmas flavor. All the people cooperate to get it together. There are presents, apples and oranges and candy for the children. Everybody celebrates together.

Some aspects of the Christmas celebration:
1. The celebration begins with the Liturgy of the Eucharist.

2. After the Liturgy, orations are given by pre-selected individuals, each from different families, on six symbols, which were given to them the year before. These symbols are a star, triangle, circle, cross, crib and ____? The symbols are made out of cedar boughs. They are used to decorate the Church.

3. Children sing Christmas songs.

4. The celebration is led by an announcer. It is up to the announcer to organize the program. He chooses the next orator with a symbol or calls for a song from the children.

5. The celebration is conducted in Lakota.

6. At a designated time in the celebration Santa Claus appears. He distributes presents and candy to the children. The Santa Claus never speaks at these celebrations. The announcer speaks for Santa. The announcer makes up funny stories about Santa's journey. The Santa uses a mask and old clothing such as an old overcoat or fur coat. He is not dressed in red like Santa Claus. It is Santa's job to pick the leaders for next year's celebration by giving the symbols to six different families. This means that they will be in charge of organizing next year's celebration and giving the orations on the symbols.

7. The feast continues with the distribution of food. The distribution begins at the door and proceeds clockwise until all the food is distributed. Men and women sit separately. The men sit to the North and the women sit to the South.

If the feast takes place outside everything is done according to the Four Directions. Everyone sits in a circle. Starting with the West, the food is distributed clockwise—the men to the North, the women to the South.

It should be noted that this outline is not complete nor is it the intention of the members of the Task Force to recommend that the Christmas celebration be implemented exactly as it was done in the past. It is necessary for the members to outline in detail the aspects of the Christmas celebration and recommend ways for it to be used today.

Easter
The Easter celebration was touched on briefly. It needs more work.

Theology
There is no clear correlation between Lakota and English religious terms for God, Father, Son, Holy Spirit. The word "god" is foreign to the Lakota way of thinking. The people use a whole range of names for "god". There is a sense in which it is too presumptuous to speak too clearly about these mysteries.

The meaning of Lakota words depends on the context. Words can have different meanings on different occasions. For instance, "Wacekiya" means to pray but it also means that one ought to address people by their proper Lakota title—aunt, uncle, etc. Lakota terms carry different meanings and one can tell the meaning by who is speaking.

1. Words for God, supreme being, Great Spirit:
    1.1. "Takuskanskan," is an ancient word for God. It translates as "a power working," or "that which causes everything to move."
    1.2. "Wakan Tanka" is the most common word for the supreme power. It would be translated as "almighty God" or "Great Spirit." The St. Joseph and St. Mary Society would use "Wakan Tanka" to refer to God almighty.
    1.3. "Tunkasila," a word which became popular to use in prayer in the 1970's, can refer to a grandfather, to the President of the United States, to a greeting of the sun as it rises, and to the supreme being. When used in the context of prayer it means the Supreme Being or the Father—this is the way it is used in the Sursum Corda book. To translate the meaning as grandfather is confusing. It should be translated as "Father" in a prayer context. It is used because it connotes greater respect.
    1.4. "Ateyapi," a word used for the "Father," can refer to the

Superintendent of the Reservation, to the President of the United States, to the Bishop. The St. Joseph and St. Mary Societies use Ateyapi to refer to God the Father. "Ate" also refers to God the Father.

1.5 The St. Joseph and St. Mary Society use "Cinca" to refer to God the Son and "Woniya Wakan" to refer to God the Holy Spirit.

2. The members of the Task Force began an analysis of the origin of the words for God.

2.1 "Wakan," Kan is an old word for vein and refers to the blood in the vein and it can also refer to nerves. Blood flowing through your veins is a mystery.

2.2 "Tunkasila," tun is a sacred term for a mysterious power that emanates from the body. It can also mean sore or the pus that comes from a sore.

Miscellaneous Items

1. Use utensils that are part of the experience of the people.
2. Use red cloth for corporals and purificators since this is the sacred color used to wrap the pipe.

A Christian Rite for Expressing Respect to One's Ancestors

Formulated by
The Ad Hoc Committee for Ancestral Liturgy

Under the commission of
The Bishop and Standing Committee
Of the
TAIWAN EPISCOPAL CHURCH
1993

Translated by
Mr. Charles B. Jones, M.A., M.T.S.
The Rev. Elizabeth Wei

Translator's Preface
This is an English translation of liturgy developed by an ad hoc committee called into being by the Bishop of the Taiwan Episcopal Church, the Right Reverend John Chi-tsung Chien, with the consent of the diocesan Standing Committee. The express purpose of this liturgy is to provide a means, within the framework of Christian worship, for Chinese Christians to express their gratitude and reverence toward their deceased ancestors. This represents a departure from the attitude taken toward the cult of the ancestors by most Christian groups in China. Up until now, the usual response has been to condemn "ancestor worship" as a form of idolatry and to forbid it among Church members. This is understandable, given that the cult of the ancestors in China contains within its worldview

and praxis elements that clearly go beyond the simple expression of sentiments of gratitude and reverence, and into the realm of religion and worship.[1]

In terms of praxis, the veneration of ancestors involves presenting them with offerings of food, paper money, and replicas of goods that they will likely need in the next world, such as houses and cars. It also involves maintaining an altar at home upon which are enshrined *p'ai'wei*, wooden tablets about eight to twelve inches (20 to 30 cm) high upon which are inscribed the names of the ancestors, sometimes accompanied by a photo. In addition, there are obligations to maintain their tombs in good repair, particularly at the festival of *Ch'ing Ming*, referred to in English as Tomb-Sweeping Day. In return for these services of maintaining the memory of the deceased and providing for their material needs, the ancestors are expected to insure the living family's prosperity, good fortune, offspring, health, and so on. There are recorded cases of family members abrogating the cult of their ancestors when these benefits have not been forthcoming.[2]

In addition to these practical aspects, there are also elements in the worldview of the ancestral cult that clearly cannot be squared with Christian doctrine. For example, the ideal Chinese funeral service lasts for forty-nine days, or seven weeks. This is based on the Chinese Buddhists belief that the "soul" of the departed hovers in a kind of limbo this period before going to the next rebirth, and its destiny can be influenced by proper religious teachings and practices during this period. To give another example, the performances of Taoist priests during a funeral are intended to reproduce for the living participants the progress of the soul as it passes through the various departments of the underworld bureaucracy. At each stage the soul must make an account of its life and receive authorization to proceed towards a good destiny.[3]

It is plain that these practices and worldviews cannot be incorporated into Christianity in the name of "cultural adaptation" without distorting it so much that it becomes unrecognizable to Christians in other parts of the world. Therefore, most Christian groups in China have simply proscribed these practices among converts.

However, outright proscription may not be the best response either, because it has historically proven a major stumbling block to evangelism and conversion. Those who simply condemn it as idolatrous and forbid its practice ignore the depth with which the average Chinese feels the obligation to his or her ancestors. This condemnation may be the result of a simple lack of empathy on the part of Western and Westernized missionaries. As I have often remarked to my Chinese fellow Christians, I, as a western observer, can argue logically for the abandonment of ancestral cult practices with some cogency and detachment. What I cannot do, in the nature of things, is know what it would feel like for a Chinese person to be faced with the decision of never again offering food or burning paper money to their ancestors. I have not been raised with stories of my ancestors turning into angry or hungry ghosts for lack of my support, and so I cannot empathize with the agony that such a decision entails.

In order to drive this point home, I propose here to offer a translation of a case study collected by the Rev. Dr. David Chee and published in the Proceedings of the Taiwan Episcopal Church's 1992 Symposium on Ancestor Worship:

> The family of Mr. Ts'ai worshipped [the god] Kuan Kung and their family ancestors at home. When they went out to temples to offer incense, then they worshipped Matsu. Mr. Ts'ai converted to Christianity while a student, and on the very day of his baptism he returned home and told his grandmother that he had become a follower of Christ. His grandmother loved him dearly, and was afraid that the gods that the family worshipped might become angry and withdraw their benefits from him, and so she told him that from then on he did not need to take part in that family's wor-

ship activities. She even made a point of setting aside a portion of food offerings before they were set on the alters of the gods so that her grandson could eat them. His mother and father were not happy [about this], but they did not say anything because of the grandmother. Thus, the days went by without incident.

However, eight years later the grandmother passed away, at which point open conflict broke out within the family over Mr. Ts'ai's failure to participate in family worship since his conversion. Evidently there had been problems all along that had been repressed for those eight years. From this point on, the rest of the family did not even consider Mr. Ts'ai to be one of them anymore, and for his part he only held himself responsible for providing financial resources. He no longer had any rights within the family, to the extent that they would not even watch his children for him when he was away. From that time to the present, even in services connected with his grandmother, he has not participated in offering incense, but has stood at the side and offered his own prayers for her. In spite of this, he and his wife have no standing or position within the family. During holidays, when his wife returns to spend time with the Ts'ai family, she receives only ridicule and scorn. His own privileges as the eldest son have now devolved upon his younger brother.

All this has not affected Mr. Ts'ai's or his own family's faith; he does not care about having any "rights" in the clan. Of course, he still prays that he may again have a harmonious relationship with his parents and siblings some day. When I asked him if things would improve were he to promise to begin offering incense again, he replied that it would be very difficult for his family to accept it. They would want him to go all the way [i.e., break with Christianity as well as resume participating in the family cultural traditions] and throw himself back into the family observances in their entirety.[4]

This is only one of innumerable case studies that could be cited to show the conflicts that may erupt when a Chinese Christian is required to abandon ancestor veneration in any form. Yet this is what the Christians churches in China have consistently required of converts.

The result has been disastrous for evangelism in the Far East. In Taiwan, it is estimated that only about five percent of the population is Christian, a number that has remained static for many years.[5] It was therefore felt within the Episcopal Church in Taiwan that some outlet for expressing gratitude and reverence for ancestors within the overall worldview of Christianity would be a better response than outright condemnation and proscription. Thus, the ad hoc committee worked for over two years to come up with the following draft liturgy, which draws on passages from such Confucian classics as the Classic on Filial Piety (Hsiao Ching) and the Book of Odes (Shih Ching) as well as the Bible for its content. It is the hope of the Taiwan Episcopal Church that having such a liturgy will not only open the door to provide a timely example of how Christianity may be "de-Westernized" for the Asian context without losing its exclusive hope in the salvific act of God in Christ in the process. The following translation is thus offered for the examination of the international missiological community.

Charles B. Jones
Taipei, June 1994

A LITURGY FOR THE HOLY EUCHARIST
AND FOR EXPRESSING RESPECT
FOR THE ANCESTORS

(CHING TSU LI WEN)

Concerning the Service

1. This liturgy has been fixed in order to fit the good customs of traditional China.

2. If this worship service is to be used at home or in some other place, it is appropriate to set up an alter.

   There should be a cross placed at the center of the altar with a candlestick on either side. It is also permissible to make offerings of fresh flowers or fruit.[6]

3. If [the participants] wish to add a photograph of the deceased, then it should be placed between the cross and the candlesticks.

4. It is permissible to hang couplet-scrolls [*tui-lien*] on either side of the alter. Below are two examples of couplets appropriate to offer:

   In the grace of Heaven eternally immersed,
   the ancestors' virtue [our] heritage for always.
   > —Mr. Ma Shou-hua

   By the Lord's grace we enjoy peace at all times,
   in abiding by the ancestors' teachings
   all generations know to strive after strength.
   > —Rev. Dr. Charles Chen

A Liturgy for Venerating the Ancestors

This liturgy for expression of respect for ancestors may be celebrated in a church or in a private home by either a priest or some other assigned person. The leader may begin the liturgy by reading one or more verses, either from the Bible or from the Chinese Classics.

Officiate:

Respect your father and mother, as I, the LORD your God, command you, so that all may go well with you and so that you may live a long time in the land that I am giving you. (Deuteronomy 5:16)[7]

or this:

The way of filial piety is to set oneself in the place [of one's ancestors], perform the ceremonies they performed, play the music they played, honor that which they honored, love that which they held dear, to serve them as if they were still alive, in their absence as if they were still present. (*The Doctrine of the Mean* [Chung Yung], trans. C.B.J.)

At this point, an appropriate hymn, song, or psalm may be sung, such as "Ancient of Days, Who Sittest Throned in Glory," "O Worship the King, All Glorious Above," *or* "The Spacious Firmament on High."

Afterwards, the officiant says:

Officiant:	The Lord be with you.
People:	And also with you.
Officiant:	Let us pray.

After a period of silence, the officiant reads the following prayer:

Prayer for the Blessing of Ancestors

Almighty and everliving God, Creator of all humankind: You called our forebears, and caused them to leave behind [for posterity] the training and virtue of conscientiously venerating ancestors. Enable us to know You better through this, that we may live long in the land that You have given us. Now, as we commemorate them, we return all thanksgiving and glory to the Lord, and may the joy of the Lord infuse all that we undertake. [In the name of] the Father, Son, and Holy Spirit, One God, Everlasting and Almighty, world without end. Amen.

After this, select for responsive reading either the Psalm or the selection *Lu Wo* from the *Book of Odes*.

I. Psalm 112:1-6.

Officiant: 1. Happy is the person who honors the Lord, who takes pleasure in obeying his commands.

People: [People of this kind are fortunate indeed][8]

Officiant: 2. The good man's children will be powerful in the land;

People: his descendents will be blessed

Officiant: 3. His family will be wealthy and rich,

People: and he will be prosperous forever.

Officiant: 4. Light shines in the darkness for good men

People: for those who are merciful, kind, and just

Officiant: 5. Happy is the person who is generous with his loans, who runs his business honestly.

People: [People of this kind are fortunate indeed.]

Officiant: 6. A good person will never fail;

People: he will always be remembered.

Officiant: Glory to the Father, and to the Son, and to the Holy Spirit;

People: As it was in the beginning, is now, and will be for ever. Amen.

II. Book of Odes, Lu Wo

Officiant:	O, my father, who begat me!
	O, my mother, who nourished me!
People:	You indulged me, you fed me!
	You held me up, you supported me,
Officiant:	You looked after me, you never left me,
	Out and in you bore me in your arms.
People:	If I would return your kindness,
	It is like great Heaven, illimitable![9]
Officiant:	Glory to the Father, and to the Son, and to the Holy Spirit;
People:	As it was in the beginning, is now, and will be for ever. Amen.

The people sit.

At this point, one or two of the following scripture lessons, or some other suitable lesson may be read. If Holy Communion is to follow, then the lessons should include the Gospel lesson.

After each reading, the congregation may sing a suitable psalm or hymn, such as "In Memory of the Virtues of our Ancestors", "Fight the Good Fight, with All Thy Might", "Breast the Wave, Christian", or "Awake, My Soul, Stretch Every Nerve".

The officiant may elect to replace the Old Testament lesson with the "Chapter on Responding to Heaven's Kindness" from the <u>Classic on Filial Piety</u>.

Old Testament: Exodus 3:14, 15.

14. God said, "I am who I am. This is what you must say to them: The one who is called I AM has sent me to you.'

15. Tell the Israelites that I, the LORD, the God of their ancestors, the God of Abraham, Isaac, and Jacob, have sent you to them. This is my name forever; this is what all future generations are to call me."

Or this

Classic on Filial Piety, Chapter on Responding to Heaven's Kindness

Show respect at the family shrine and do not neglect your relatives. Regulating the body and being circumspect in behavior constitute the [proper] fear of dishonoring the ancestors. If we pay our respects to the family shrine, then the spirits and gods will uphold us. Filial piety and the love between brothers extend to the gods; their light extends to the four seas, and there is nowhere that it does not reach. The *Odes* declare: From the west and from the east, from the south and from the north, there is no one who does not follow this.

Epistle: Ephesians 6:1-3

1. Children, it is your Christian duty to obey your parents, for this is the right thing to do.

2. "Respect your father and mother" is the first commandment that has a promise added:

3. "so that all may go well with you, and you may live a long time in the land."

Choose one of the following [Gospel] lessons:

Gospel: Matthew 5:17-19

17. "Do not think that I have come to do away with the Law of Moses and the teachings of the prophets. I have not come to do away with them, but to make their teachings come true.

18. Remember that as long as heaven and earth last, not the least point nor the smallest detail of the Law will be done away with...not until the end of all things.

19. So then, whoever disobeys even the least important of the commandments and teaches others to do the same, will be least in the Kingdom of heaven. On the other hand, whoever obeys the Law and teaches others to do the same, will be great in the Kingdom of heaven."

Or this

Gospel: John 5:25-29

25. "I am telling you the truth: the time is coming—the time has already come—when the dead will hear the voice of the Son of God, and those who hear it will come to life.

26. Just as the Father is himself the source of life, in the same way he has made his Son to be the source of life.

27. And he has given the Son the right to judge, because he is the Son of Man.

28. Do not be surprised at this; the time is coming when all the dead will hear his voice

29. and come out of their graves: those who have done good will rise and live, and those who have done evil will rise and be condemned."

Sermon or Homily

If Holy Eucharist is to be celebrated, a sermon should be preached here; otherwise, a homily may be substituted.

A Period of Silent Reflection and Remembrance

The Nicene Creed

We believe in one God, the father, the Almighty,
maker of heaven and earth, of all that is, seen and unseen.

We believe in one Lord, Jesus Christ, the only Son of God,
eternally begotten of the Father, God from God, Light from Light,
true God from true God, begotten, not made, of one Being with
the Father.
Through him all things were made.
For us and for our salvation he came down from heaven:
By the power of the Holy Spirit he became incarnate from the
Virgin Mary
and was made man.
For our sake he was crucified under Pontius Pilate;
He suffered death and was buried.
On the third day he rose again in accordance with the Scriptures;
He ascended into heaven and is seated at the right hand of the
Father.
He will come again in glory to judge the living and the dead,
and his kingdom will have no end.

We believe in the Holy Spirit, the Lord, the giver of life,
Who proceeds from the Father and the Son.
With the Father and the Son he is worshipped and glorified.
He has spoken through the Prophets.
We believe in the holy catholic and apostolic Church.
We acknowledge one baptism for the forgiveness of sins.
We look for the resurrection of the dead, and the life of the world
to come. Amen.

The Prayers of the People

The people stand or kneel.

Officiant:	The Lord be with you.
People:	And also with you.
Officiant:	Let us pray.

People and Officiant:

Our Father in heaven,
hallowed be your Name,
your kingdom come,
your will be done,
on earth as in heaven.
Give us today our daily bread
Forgive our sins, as we forgive those who sin against us.
Save us from the time of trial, and deliver us from evil.
For the kingdom, the power, and the glory are yours,
Now and forever, Amen.

Then follows this Suffrage, to be prayed responsively by Officiant and People:

V. Show us your mercy, O Lord;
R. And grant us your salvation.
V. Clothe your ministers with righteousness;
R. Let your people sing with joy.
V. Give peace, O Lord, in all the world.
R. For only in you can we live in safety.
V. Lord, keep this nation under your care;
R. And guide us in the way of justice and peace.
V. Let your way be known upon earth;
R. Your saving health among all nations.

V. Let not the needy, O Lord, be forgotten;
R. Nor the hope of the poor be taken away.
V. Create in us clean hearts, O God;
R. And sustain us with your Holy Spirit.

The Officiant then says the following Collect:

Almighty and everliving God, who are the source of life and the ground of all creation: we offer you our sincere thanks, because you have bestowed your loving care on all our ancestors and families, thus allowing life to continue without surcease. By the guidance of the Holy Spirit, You call us to recognize You as the Way, the Truth, and the Life. As long as they lived, our ancestors feared God and strove ceaselessly. We sincerely pray that you will enable us to pass this heritage on to future generations, carry on the work they began, fulfill our own missions, and return all the glory to You. We ask all these things in the name of our Lord Jesus Christ, Your Son, with the Holy Spirit, one God, eternal and almighty, world without end. Amen.

If there is to be no Holy Communion, then the priest or the bishop may bless the congregation.

The Lord bless you and keep you. May the Lord make his glory to shine upon you and give you peace, both now and forevermore. Amen.

If the Officiant is a deacon or layperson, then they may use the following prayer:

May the grace of our Lord Jesus Christ, the love of God, and the fellowship of the Holy Spirit, be with us all evermore. And may the God of hope fill us with all joy and peace in believing through the power of the Holy Spirit. Amen.

Afterwards, the officiant dismisses the people, saying:

Officiant: Go in peace to love and serve the Lord.
People: Thanks be to God.

At this time, the service concludes with the singing of "Now Thank We All Our God", "O What Their Joy and Their Glory Must Be", or some other appropriate hymn or psalm.

If Holy Communion is to follow, then the service continues with the Peace.

The Peace
Officiant: The Peace of the Lord be always with you.
People: And also with you

Then, the ministers and people may greet each other in the name of the Lord.

[Translator's note: From this point, the service continues with the Offertory and Holy Communion exactly as found on pp 361-366 of the American Book of Common Prayer, using the second of the two post-Communion prayers as found at the top of page 366. After this prayer, the service continues at the following rubric:]

After the Communion, the priest or bishop, before blessing the people, may cause the following selection from the Book of Odes *to be read responsively in either the original or modern vernacular version:*

Chiu Mu
Officiant: In the south are the trees with curved drooping
                branches;
                With the dolichos creepers clinging to them.

People:	To be rejoiced in is our Prince:- May he repose in his happiness and dignity!
Officiant:	In the south are the trees with curved drooping branches; With the dolichos creepers clinging to them.
People:	To be rejoiced in is our Prince:- May he be great in his happiness and dignity!
Officiant:	In the south are the trees with curved drooping branches; Round which the dolichos creepers twine.
People:	To be rejoiced in is our Prince:- May he be complete in his happiness and dignity![10]

END OF THE LITURGY

[1] There exists an extensive anthropological, sociological, and theological literature on the Chinese cult of the dead. David K. Jordan's *Gods, Ghosts, and Ancestors* (Berkeley: University of California Press, 1972) is especially recommended as a starting-point. Also recommended are Emily Ahern's *The Cult of the Dead in a Chinese Village* (Stanford: Stanford University Press, 1973) and Steven Harrell's "The Ancestors at Home: Domestic Worship in a Land-Poor Taiwanese Village," *In Ancestors*, ed. William H. Newell.

[2] (The Hague: Mouton, 1976), p. 373-385. Arthur Wolf reports the case of a man who destroyed his ancestral tablets and converted to Christianity because his ancestors failed to prevent the deaths of his wife and mother within a space of two years. See his "Gods, Ghosts, and Ancestors," in *Religion and Ritual in Chinese Society*,

ed. Arthur Wolf (Stanford: Stanford University Press, 1974,), P. 161.

[3] It will be noted that these two examples taken together create a self-contradictory worldview. This is not viewed as a problem by the average Chinese. The sociologist of religion Bryan Wilson has observed that, among world religions, it appears that only Christianity insists upon the "law of non-contradiction." See his *Religion in Sociological Perspective* (Oxford: Oxford University Press, 1982), p. 55-61, 101-102.

[4] Rev. David Chee, "Ts'ong Mu Hui Chiao Tu K'an 'Tsu Hsien Chi Ssu' Wen T'I" (The Question of Ancestor Worship Seen from a Pastoral Perspective"), in Taiwan Episcopal Church, Ts Hsien Chi Ssu Yet T'ao Hui (A Symposium on Ancestor Worship) Taipei: Taiwan Episcopal Church, Trinity Hall, 1992), p. 17.

[5] Hsu Chai-ch'iang, in an M.S. thesis on religion attitudes in Taiwan for Tung Hai University, provides a summary of recent surveys of religious beliefs in Taiwan. In five surveys done between 1970 and 1984, the numbers of those who identify themselves as either Protestant or Catholic ranges from 4.6% to 9.5%. This last figure is well outside the general range; the second highest number is only 6.8%. This is probably because the survey which yielded this high figure was limited to Taipei residents, and a study by Prof. Chu Hai-yuan of the Academia Sinica Ethnology Institute suggest that urban residents are more likely to be Christian (or Buddhist or atheist) than the population at large. See Hsu Chai-ch'iang, *Taiwan Tsung-chiao Hsin-yang te Jen-t'ung yu Shen-fen: I-ko Ch'u-t'an* (Self-Identification of Religious Belief and Status in Taiwan: A Preliminary Investigation) M.A. Thesis, Tung Hai University, 1991, p. 5-6; and Chu Hai-yuan, "Taiwan Ti-ch'u Min-chung Te Tsugn-chiao Hsin-yang yu Tsung-chiao T'ai-tu" ("Religious Beliefs and Attitudes of the People of Taiwan"), in *Pien-ch'ien Chung te Taiwan She-hui* (Taiwan Society in Transition), Acadamia Sinica Ethnology Institute Special Publication, no. 20, ed. Chu Hai-yuan and Yang Kuo-shu (Taipei: Acadamia Sinica, 1988), p. 249.

[6] Since the offering of foodstuffs to the dead generally denotes a belief that the dead are close at hand and in need of nourishment from the living, the presence of this rubric in a Christian liturgy requires some explanation.

What is perhaps most important here is not that food is offered, but what food is offered. Offerings to supernatural beings in Chinese folk religion vary according to what type of being it is: gods generally receive uncut slabs of meals of meat, vegetables and rice, laid out with chopsticks in a homely manner; ghosts receive smaller portions of largely unprepared food presented outside the home in order to keep them from entering. One of the significant variables in this "semantics of food" (to use Stuart Thompson's phrase) is the degree to which the food has been transformed prior to presentation. This degree of transformation provides an index to the giver's relationship to the supernatural being.

Significantly, none of the anthropological studies of this "semantics of food" consulted give any mention of fresh fruit as an offering. We may speculate that fresh fruit, which straddles the line between transformed and untransformed foods in that it can be eaten directly with little or no preparation, falls outside this semantics and thus nullifies its function as an indicator of social nearness or distance. In Buddhist temples where I have done field-work, devotees also offer fresh fruit in the course of worshiping buddhas and bohisattvas, beings who also fall outside of the god/ghost/ancestor structure.

For further reference, the reader may consult Stuart E. Thompson, "Death, Food, and Fertility," in *Death Ritual in Late Imperial and Modern China*, ed. J.L. Watson and E. Rawski (Berkeley: University of California Press, 1988), p. 71-108; and Steven Harrell, "When a Ghost Becomes a God," in *Religion and Ritual in Chinese Society*, ed. Arthur Wolf (Stanford: Stanford University Press, 1974).

[7] All Scripture citations are taken from the Good News Bible (Today's English Version), published by the British and Foreign Bible Society.

[8] Passages in brackets indicate antiphons not found in the Today's English Version of this psalm.–trans.

[9] Based on James Legge, trans. *The She King, or, the Book of Poetry*, 2nd ed. (Oxford: Oxford University Press, n.d.; reprint Taipei: Wen Shih Che, 1971), p. 351 - 352.

[10] Legge, p. 10. I have altered his translation from "princely lady" to "Prince". Legge acknowledges in his notes that Chinese commentators have differed on the interpretation of this word. I have interpreted the term *chun tzu* as "Prince" for three reasons. First, in the Confucian classics, this is the term most commonly used for the perfected scholar/government administrator. Such a person would always be male. Second, in the Christian context of this liturgy, the term is being used to refer to Christ. The dominant image is of a tree with branches that hand far down, to which clinging vines can easily attach and climb. In this way the passage reminds the Christian reader of the image of Christ as the true vine and his followers as the branches found in John 15:1-8. Third, in the vernacular rendering, the male form of the pronoun *t'a* appears, with radical nine on the left rather than radical thirty-eight, as would be common if the reference were to a female.